On the Edge of Eden

On the Edge of Eden

Tony Hammon

XULON PRESS ELITE

Xulon Press Elite
2301 Lucien Way #415
Maitland, FL 32751
407.339.4217
www.xulonpress.com

© 2020 by Tony Hammon

All rights reserved solely by the author. The author guarantees all contents are original and do not infringe upon the legal rights of any other person or work. No part of this book may be reproduced in any form without the permission of the author. The views expressed in this book are not necessarily those of the publisher.

Unless otherwise indicated, Scripture quotations taken from the Holy Bible, New International Version (NIV). Copyright © 1973, 1978, 1984, 2011 by Biblica, Inc.™. Used by permission. All rights reserved.

Printed in the United States of America.

Paperback ISBN-13: 978-1-6322-1937-4
eBook ISBN-13: 978-1-6322-1938-1

Table of Contents

Foreword..................................vii
Preface................................... ix

1. Lighting the Fire..............................1
2. Trip #1: Hotel California and Wi-What?...............19
3. Trip #2: Generous Gifts and Damalie's Dream..........74
4. Going to America!............................122
5. Trip #3: Croc Waters, a Machete, Bat Guano,
   and Minnows...............................130
6. Trip #4 Unto the Least of These...................162
7. Trip #5 Rick Strong and the Mayah.................191
8. The Trip That Almost Wasn't.....................239
9. Trip #6 Care from Head to Toe....................247
10. Trip # 7 A Village With No Name..................300
11. Trip #8 – Dropping Like Flies....................367
12. Some of Us Someday Are Going to Come to Life......431

Bibliography...............................435
Appendix #1: Statement of Faith.................439
Appendix #2: UCCS-U..........................441

To my wife, Colleen:
*Thank you for trusting God enough
to stand by my side as I run off to the next adventure.*

*To my grown children: Troy, Steve, Kathy, and Trent;
and eleven grandkids for being willing to share Dad &
Grandpa with a hungry world.*

*A special tribute to Ken and Dee Meeks (September
1923-January 2020), who singlehandedly have provided
cows that have given life-sustaining milk each day to nearly
two-thousand children.*

*A special thanks for each of my teammates who have joined in
the adventures.*

FOREWORD
by
Dr. Dino Pedrone

The Florida Association of Christian Colleges and Schools has been a leader in Christian education for years. From its founding, under the leadership of men like Al Janney and Jerry Williamson, there is a virtual list of individuals that God has led to provide a biblical education for thousands of young people. I had the privilege of being the president of the association for ten years and enjoyed rubbing shoulders with so many Christian leaders. One of those men is Tony Hammon.

In the process of those ten years, we organized the International Association of Christian Colleges and Schools; and I remember there was one man I was convinced who should be the leader of this venture. Tony Hammon is that man. Tony has been a pastor, marine biologist, educator, founder and president of a Christian school, visionary, and with a pastoral/missionary heart, has taken on the leadership of this vision. The vision was to take the association's education processes and results internationally. Tony has seen the brokenness in Uganda and identified with it, and lives are being transformed and changed.

The book you are about to read is the story of taking biblical education into the country of Uganda (and other lands as God opens doors). *On the Edge of Eden* is the story of a beautiful people in a beautiful land, who have experienced brokenness and struggle. The heartwarming stories accompanied with the educator's view from a pastoral heart will warm your soul. This story will touch your heart and probably encourage you to reach out to someone who has need.

Our Lord Jesus Christ has provided us with unconditional and perfect grace. "For you know the grace of our Lord Jesus Christ, that, though He was rich, yet for your sake He became poor, that he through His poverty might be rich" (2 Corinthians 9:6). Through Tony and IACCS efforts, Uganda is experiencing the blessed grace of God.

Thank you, Tony, for your obedience to God and your unparalleled leadership in providing for these people you have such a love for. You remind us of the words of the Psalmist, "The sacrifices of God are a broken spirit: a broken and contrite heart thou wilt not despise" (Psalm 51:17). Through the sacrifice of your labor, IACCS is making a huge difference in the country of Uganda.

Preface

As you read my book, you will be traveling on three separate journeys. The first will be a spiritual adventure of God's unending, ever-growing shaping of my life and the lives of others who have joined me on the adventure. My prayer would be that God will speak to you at various times as you travel with me, and that spiritual growth will result.

The second will be a growing, ever-learning annual trek into Uganda, beginning in 2011 (with a couple of side trips to Haiti along the way). These trips will be interrupted with several sidebars that will be teaching moments that deal with side issues important to the journey. If you feel yourself getting bogged down in the details of the story, lightly read through the daily journey and concentrate on the sidebar lessons that are woven into the story.

The third journey is one of coming face-to-face with the call to action when we see and understand the reality and crisis of global poverty, injustice, hunger, and disease that people around the planet face each and every day. It is my prayer that God will ignite what I will explain as a "Popeye Moment" in each of our lives.

Hopefully, you will learn how you can be a part of the solution instead of ignoring the problem, which, in essence, makes it worse. You will see things that we as Western missionaries or volunteers can do that will do more harm than good, and ultimately enable, frustrate, and create resentment. It is one thing to have indigenous groups get angry toward us, but if it creates resistance towards the Lord, it is unacceptable.

The final thing that I hope you will gain is a deeper understanding of the essential role Christian education plays in shaping the hearts and minds of the next generation and why that is so important; that you will be absolutely convinced that Jesus Christ truly is the hope of the world.

Chapter 1
Lighting the Fire

"Imagine yourself as a living house. God comes in to rebuild that house. At first, perhaps, you can understand what He is doing. He is getting the drains right and stopping the leaks in the roof and so on; you knew that those jobs needed doing and so you are not surprised. But presently He starts knocking the house about in a way that hurts abominably and does not seem to make any sense. What on earth is He up to? The explanation is that He is building quite a different house from the one you thought of – throwing out a new wing here, putting on an extra floor there, running up towers, making courtyards. You thought you were being made into a decent little cottage: but He is building a palace. He intends to come and live in it Himself."

– C. S. Lewis, "Mere Christianity" (1952)

"Don't screw this up!" Those words offered by a friend (actually the man whose foreword you just read) rang in my ears as I thought about the commitment that my "yes" response to this invitation could possibly involve. The call was to accept the presidency of the International Association of Christian College and

Schools. The door was wide open to make IACCS anything the Lord would design it to be.

I had been in education all of my adult life.

In fact, before I was an adult!

In my senior year of high school, I had been a teacher's aide. Much of my time was assigned to working with "special needs" children. In the sixties, it was not uncommon for all children that did not fit in a traditional classroom to be placed in a "special education class." I remember the challenge of working with children with severe mental deficiencies, physical handicaps, and behavioral problems all in the same room at the same time.

But I loved it! At the end of the year, it was the custom of the school to have an awards assembly, recognizing various achievements of the high school seniors. I was sitting next to my friend and football quarterback, Dale Crawshaw. There was a moment in the assembly when a sorority of elderly retired teachers made their way to the stage. I looked up and thought, "Wow, I don't know any of these ladies. They must be at least 102!"

As they began to give out their award, they talked about teaching as a calling and began to describe a student who they said, "Had great promise as a future teacher." They spoke of his accomplishments in working with students and the things that teachers had reported about his interaction with students. I remember thinking, "Wow, I wonder who that is?" And then they said, "Today, we are honored to give the award for 'The Most Promising Teacher' to Tony Hammon." I was stunned! I elbowed Dale and said, "Boy, do they have the wrong guy! I hope I never see another classroom!"

But, in spite of that comment, the next year, I enrolled in community college (because of my wife-to-be and baseball).

But somehow, I also found myself working in a program sponsored by a government grant, called the 89-10 program, as a teacher's aide. I was assigned to the same school I had just graduated from, and with many of the children I had worked with the previous year. This time, I moved from class to class, giving the teachers a break.

Most of the time, the teachers would leave me with teaching assignments to complete. Those months in the classroom proved to be some of the most valuable and confidence-building learning experiences of my life. I couldn't have ever imagined how important they would be.

As valuable as that experience was by itself, the learning curve was about to skyrocket upward. We were well into the school year when I walked into the office, and the principal slid a stack of books across the counter and said, "Congratulations, you are the new sixth-grade teacher. Don't kill any of them (meaning the students), and don't let them kill you!" I guess he could tell I was stunned and full of a bunch of questions, so he continued to explain, "The teachers are on strike, so you have them (the class) until it's all over."

So, off to the portables I went. Eighteen years old, scared, but confident and excited to take this challenge on (I seemed to hear the voices of those elderly, retired teachers saying, "And the most promising teacher award goes to...").

I walked through the door, and after all of the students had arrived, I announced, "Guess what, guys. I'm your new sixth-grade teacher." There was some pretty wild cheering for a few minutes.

I recently learned that this was the first teacher strike in the United States. It was statewide, and ran for three weeks, beginning on Feb 18, 1968. Recalling the strike, Assistant Superintendent (later to become the superintendent for decades) A.J. "Bookie" Henriquez is quoted as saying, "We were bringing in anyone that had any blood flowing — warm bodies."[1]

I had no idea I had been a part of educational history, or that I met all of Bookie's criteria as a teacher. But those three weeks lit a fire and launched me on a lifetime call to education.

Colleen and I graduated from the University of Miami with degrees in education and returned to that same school where it all began in 1967 to do our internship. We quickly took on the role as regular faculty members and were teaching classes very soon after arriving. After finishing our internship, we served as substitute teachers for the remainder of the year and were married over Easter Break, so we would not miss any teaching opportunities. During that year, I had learned that there was no marine science program offered. We were in the Florida Keys, surrounded by ocean, and there was no marine science program!

How could that be?

I went to the principal and said, "We must have marine science in our schools!" His reply was, "We don't have any curriculum."

I had anticipated that response and had put together a full curriculum.

I plopped a large, very thick notebook on his desk and said, "We do now."

His next response was, "I don't know that we have any students that want it." I had anticipated that response as well, so I said, "Well, here is a list of eighty students who have signed up for it for next year if we will offer it."

His final response was a last attempt to dodge having to put a new program in place, "We don't have the money."

I was ready for that as well and said, "I will raise the money to put the program together. You come up with the money for my salary, and I'll do the rest. Besides, you desperately need my wife as a business teacher, and we are a package deal."

He smiled, shook my hand, and said, "I guess you both have jobs."

The next year Colleen and I were both excited about entering our first year as full-time teachers. We were assigned to be senior sponsors and carried full teaching loads. I became the head baseball coach, and Colleen was the yearbook editor. I say all that to say we were fully engaged in the life of the school and our students, and we loved it, and we loved our kids!

As I mentioned earlier, we were married on March 25, 1972. We were still in our honeymoon stage both in marriage and in teaching that first year.

But, almost exactly nine months into our marriage, something occurred that would prove to be life and career-changing. The way I always tell the story is to say Colleen, and I had been married nine months and gave birth to a bubbly, vibrant sixteen-year-old cheerleader. A young girl that was in Colleen's homeroom had just lost her mom, broken up with a long-time boyfriend, and stepfather had just been arrested. In other words, the girl's life was a wreck; she was hurting and pretty much had to fend for herself. Colleen asked if we could invite her to our house for the weekend to just try to encourage her, feed her, and give her some attention.

Linda came to our home for the weekend and was surprisingly joyful and balanced in the midst of all she was going through (I would soon find out why). On Monday morning, the principal of the school, who also happened to have been my mentor, and baseball and football coach in high school, called me into his office. He said, "You know, Leftie (his name for me), Linda is not 18 yet, and she is going to have to leave school if she doesn't have a legal guardian." He then made one of his signature moves, when he was ready for you to see things his way – he rocked back in his old wooden desk chair, folded his hands behind his head and smiled.

I said, "Coach, are you asking us to make a home for Linda?" He said, "Can't think of a better couple to do it."

I thought a minute, and said, "Well, let me go check with Colleen."

I walked down to her room, homeroom was just about to begin, so we only had seconds to talk, but she said, "Sure, I guess so!" We then asked Linda, and she eagerly accepted the invitation. We took care of the paperwork and became her legal guardians.

Linda was full of life. She was involved in everything, school, sports, cheerleading, homecoming court, theater... There wasn't much she wasn't doing. But there was one thing that might have been a "deal-breaker" had I known it from the beginning. She was a committed Christian and was deeply involved in her church. I, on the other hand, was a biology teacher, who hated any thought or conversation about God. Linda would say things about church or Jesus, and my blood would boil, especially when she would talk about Jesus. I wrote about this in more detail in my first book, *Bone of My Bone*, so I won't go into detail here.

Suffice it to say there was an enormous internal and external spiritual battle going on.

To add to this, several of my marine biology students were Christian kids and were asking God-related questions in class.

One week they came to me and said, "The pastor at Island Community Church was going to speak on science and Scripture. Would you please go and hear him?" After a considerable push from the students, I blurted, "Alright! I will go hear what that ignorant bumpkin has to say if you will leave me alone."

Keeping that promise was life changing. I went, and the pastor presented a compelling, evidence-packed message about the compatibility of science and the Bible.

At a point in his message, he placed his Bible on the corner of the pulpit and said something along these lines, "The Bible claims to be the Word of God. If it is His Word, it should be without error or contradiction; and indeed, there should be no lies about who Jesus is. I challenge you to put it to the test. If you can disprove the Bible, I will stop preaching."

After the service, I approached him and said, "You're on. I accept your challenge. You better look for another job in two weeks."

I now look back at the arrogance of my response to him and think, "How foolish!" But I was launched on a quest. I read, listened, and researched everything I could get my hands on about the reliability of the Bible.

Two weeks went by, then two months, six months, a year, and finally, I went back to the pastor and said, "I give up." I found, and am still discovering, far more evidence for the Bible and the existence of God than I had ever imagined.

The pastor smiled and said, "And?"

I responded, "And, I would be a fool not to believe what it says about Jesus. The Bible is unwaveringly clear that He came with one purpose – to be our Savior; to pay the penalty for our sins.

I understand that it is a gift from God, and it would be crazy not to accept that forgiveness."

That was 1973. There was no way I could have ever known what that decision was going to do in redirecting the course of my life.

I love teaching. I particularly love teaching biology, and I most certainly love teaching marine science. But one day, as I was teaching a marine science class, a passage of Scripture came to mind. They were the very words of Jesus, *"What good is it for someone to gain the whole world, yet forfeit their soul? Or what can anyone give in exchange for their soul?"* (Mark 8:36,37) I looked out at the class full of bright young men and women and thought these thoughts, "I can produce the best marine biologists and scientists in the world, but what good is that if they forfeit their soul?"

From that thought, another fire was ignited.

It was a Popeye moment.

Do you remember what a Popeye moment was?

In many of the Popeye cartoons, remember what Popeye would often say before he popped open his can of spinach and knocked Bruno to the moon? He would see the offense and mutter, "I can't stands it! I just can't stands it no more!!" He would chug down a can of spinach and rescue Olive from the clutches of the villain.

That's what I mean when I say this was a Popeye moment for me. I could no longer just train students in biology without introducing them to the Author and Creator of biology. I began to try to figure out how to do both – produce well-trained students in marine science and do everything that I could to be sure that they understood the love of God.

The solution for how to do both became obvious within days. The same pastor that had challenged me to disprove the Bible and investigate the claims of Christ approached me and asked if I had any interest in helping start a Christian School. At first, I said with a scoff, "No, I am a biology teacher and coach, not a school administrator!" But then the Holy Spirit nudged me and said, "Remember that Popeye moment? That was me. That was my prodding. Here is the way to do both."

So, in 1974 we started a Christian school. I was the school principal from 1974 through 1988 (with a leave to get a master's degree in school administration), and from 1989-2018, the superintendent of a Christian school.

I had sensed a calling to Christian education in a broader sense from the beginning. In the early eighties, I was asked to join the Board of Directors of the Florida Association of Christian Colleges and School, the Florida state arm of the American Association of Christian Colleges and Schools (at that time).

I was honored to join this board and have served every year since.

Because I had been serving on the FACCS board, we are back to the invitation to accept the presidency of IACCS.

Three events occurred in rapid succession that I believe were God moments that drove this decision.

Here is how I described the first event in *Bone of My Bone, The Journey Continues*. I have had the honor of serving on the Board of Directors of the Florida Association of Christian Colleges and Schools for several decades. I've served under four presidents (Drs. A.C. Janney, Dan Burrell, Dino Pedrone, and Pastor Marc Mortenson), all great men who have taught me much. I have been honored to serve simply as a board member and have never sought nor desired to be an officer. But in 2011, my role with FACCS took a dramatic turn. As a board, we had been discussing the possibilities of reaching out internationally to see if there was any way that we could serve and establish Christian schools in other lands.

Dr. Pedrone was the Association's president at that time but had just accepted the presidency of Davis College in Johnson City, New York. Davis College is one of the oldest Christian colleges in the East. Not long before Dr. Pedrone left for his new assignment, he called and said that he wanted to nominate me to be the president of our newly formed International Association of Christian Colleges and Schools (IACCS). I told him I would prayerfully consider it, but that I felt woefully inadequate for the task. He assured me that my educational experience was what was needed to get IACCS off the ground.

I was still praying and thinking about the position when I attended a leadership event that I have made part of my summer training for the past 20 years. It is the most exceptional two days of leadership training that can be found anywhere. It's called the Global Leadership Summit (GLS) and has provided leadership training to millions around the globe. At the 2011 GLS, founding pastor of Willow Creek Community Church, Bill Hybels, was speaking about tough callings. He was using the Old Testament story of Jeremiah. Here is a paraphrase of how Bill told the story:

Very early in his life, Jeremiah got a tough calling. He responded to God's call and was probably excited to see what God was going to do. But nothing ever went right. Jeremiah felt like nothing he tried would ever succeed. He even had a bout of cursing God, but then he regrouped and decided to go forward with God's plan. But round two doesn't go any better.

As a prophet of God, he is called to deliver some tough messages to the people God sends him to. In an effort to shut him up, they toss him into a deep, mud-filled cistern. Imagine standing waist-deep in the damp, rat-infested, smelly pit, and thinking, this is how it is all going to end for me. I am going to starve to death in this mud pit, and no one will ever find me! But someone had sympathy on him and rescued him. So once again, he continued to preach. He preached for years, but the people never listened. Then one day, the enemy comes riding into town and attacks the people of God and carries everyone—including Jeremiah—into captivity back to the enemy's land. Sometime after that, Jeremiah goes off by himself and sits down by a river and writes a book, a lament. It is included in the Bible; we call it the Book of Lamentations. In this book, he tells us how wrong everything has gone. But near the end of the book, he has a moment of clarity and says:

So, I say, "My splendor is gone and all that I had hoped from the LORD." I remember my affliction and my wandering, the bitterness and the gall. I well remember them, and my soul is downcast within me. Yet this I call to mind and therefore I have hope: Because of the LORD's great love we are not consumed, for his compassions never fail. They are new every morning; great is your faithfulness. I say to myself, "The LORD is my portion; therefore, I will wait for him." The LORD is good to those whose hope is in him, to the one who seeks him; it is good to wait quietly for the salvation of the LORD. It is good for a man to bear the yoke while he is young. (Lam. 3:18-27)

Keep in mind, I had just been asked to pray about the presidency of IACCS, God was working on my heart, and He used Bill to drop this next message bomb on me!

So, at the end, Jeremiah says, "It's been hard, but at the end of the day, if I had it to do all over again, I would. Because great is Your faithfulness."

Then Bill slowed his cadence a bit and said, "I am not worthy of having my name mentioned in the same sentence with Jeremiah... part of what's been a blast about leading Willow Creek is that for the most part, it has gone up and to the right...I got an easy calling, really. I got to lead a church in a suburban area in one of the most affluent cities in the United States...I have had very little true hardship in carrying out what God has asked me to do."

He then said, "Here is the heart of what I want to talk to you about. If you watch one episode of the evening news (only takes one these days.), you know our world is broken, and it is getting worse. And the fixes that are going to be required for many of the ills of our society are not going to be easy assignments. They are not going to be short term. They are not going to have compensation packages for the leaders who are addressing these problems. The fixes are going to take decades or lifetimes, not short-term services. And all throughout history, and in today's environment, God is looking for some strong-shouldered leaders who will say, 'You know, if there is a tough assignment anywhere in this world, to be attacked, I'm available. I don't have to have all of this earthly success packages affixed to it. I'll take a tough calling! I will sign up for anything, God, if you ask me to.'"

Bill's eyes got a bit misty as he went on to say, "It takes more courage than first meets the eye." He then recounted serving on the selection committee for World Vision as they searched for their next president. He told about interviewing all these high-profile candidates, all making substantial six-figure-plus-salaries and telling them that their job description would include flying to some of the most challenging, under-resourced regions around the globe (and fly coach, nonetheless). Then there would be the coming home to try to raise millions of dollars, in a tough economy, to help solve some of these tough fixes, oh, and by the way, at half the salary or less than you now earn.

Not surprisingly, they got a lot of, "Thanks, but no thanks" responses. But Bill described how Richard Sterns lit up at the offer. He didn't accept immediately, but after going home and praying and spending some sleepless nights, he took the position as the president of World Vision and has held this position since June of 1998, and has quadrupled the reach and effectiveness of World Vision. He became President Emeritus in 2018 and still serves World Vision with passion.

When Bill asked him what the toughest part about the job was, he replied, "Having your heart exposed to misery again and again and again."

Then Bill talked about Amanda Lindhout, a 30-year-old Canadian journalist who heard about all the horrible things going on in Somalia. She informs the paper she works for that she wants to go report on what is going on. Amanda travels to Somalia to report on the situation and, not long after she arrives, she is kidnapped, held hostage and abused for 15 months, beaten and starved, and treated in ways that should embarrass the world. Family and friends finally raised the ransom money for her, and she was released. Afterward, she returned to Canada and began the healing process. Then, God spoke to her and said, "Go back. Go back, not as a journalist, but as one to serve the children of Somalia." That's courage for a tough calling.

Then Bill began to challenge each of us at the Summit. He said: "I stand in awe of leaders who get tough assignments. Some of you at the Summit have rocking businesses, and God isn't necessarily asking you to leave them, but God has been whispering to you, 'In addition to your business, there is a little cause in your community that needs leadership, that is not well-led.' He has called you to apply some of your leadership skills to make a difference. Have you listened?"

Jeremiah was once asked by God to go buy a jar. This was at the point in Jeremiah's life where he is already quite disillusioned. So, Jeremiah says to God, "What do you want me to do with this jar?" God says, "Well, go buy it, and I'll tell you on the way." So, Jeremiah dutifully goes and buys the jar. And on the way, God says, "Here is what I want you to do with the pot. After you buy it, I want you to gather as many people around as possible. And then, I want you to tell them one more time that if they don't humble themselves—if they don't stop mistreating the poor, the orphans, and the windows—that I'm going to smash their country. And as you are telling them that, I want you to smash the vase for effect—so they have a little picture of what the deal is." Jeremiah is no idiot. He says, "Now wait. If I smash this jar and tell them that you are going to smash them, they are going to smash me!" And God says, "Yes, that's probably how it's going to go down." So, Jeremiah takes a deep breath, and...at this point, Bill throws down a large clay pot he has been carrying around during this entire conversation. The pot smashes into a thousand pieces all over the floor. And it goes down just like Jeremiah thought. They grab him and beat him to within an inch of his life. Jeremiah moans, "That didn't turn out so well."

Then Bill picked up a piece of the broken clay pot and said, "When you came into this session today, everybody received a little chunk of pottery. Take it out if you would. We are going to end this session by asking you to take this small piece of clay and if you're serious about the things of God, about the condition of our world, take a pen and write something on this piece of clay. This is between you and God. You might put today's date on it and say, 'On this date, I said, 'God I'm available for a tough calling if you have one for me. I'm available. I'm open God. I'm ready God.'"

After that challenge, and with the strong challenge of IACCS looming before me, what choice did I have?! So, I wrote these words and numbers on my piece of clay:

IACCS
8-12-2011

As I looked at my broken piece of clay, I said, "Lord, I am not much, but I am Yours. If You choose to use this broken piece of clay, I am Yours. Use me as You see fit."

I agreed to let the board vote. I was elected President, and Dr. Howard Mills, from Nassau, Bahamas, was elected Vice-President. I had no idea where this journey was going to lead. Dr. Pedrone and I met for one last time before he left for his new position at Davis College. He had a few parting words for me— "Don't screw this up!" Thanks, Dino!

On a personal side note – As some of you reading this will probably know, Bill ended his pastorate at Willow Creek under the shadow of some strong allegations. An independent review board of unbiased Christian leaders was called to investigate these reports. They determined that some of the allegations were "credible." That is tragic, and I do not in any way wish to diminish or disrespect those who were harmed in any way by these actions.

In spite of this, I have to say that I still consider Bill a friend, and he has had a significant impact on my ministry and on me personally. I am reminded that Scripture says, *"We all stumble in many ways. Anyone who is never at fault in what they say is perfect, able to keep their whole body in check.* (James 3:2). It is a solemn reminder that we must guard our hearts, walk as the Bible calls it circumspectly, and have a healthy system of accountability in place. I have learned over the years that I have plenty to work on just taking care of me and that I have no place standing in judgment over others. Dear God, keep my heart pure!

Lord, I'm broken clay. Use me as you see fit.

This was followed by two other events that launched my IACCS adventures.

The first of the two events came from reading a life-changing book, *A Hole in Our Gospel,* by Richard Stearns, the man I just mentioned.

As President of World Vision, Richard has had first-hand experience with the tremendous needs throughout the world.

Here is a brief excerpt that sums up the issue of the "Hole."

Speaking of Matthew 25:31-46 He writes, *"Surely this is another one of those passages that would be easy to cut from our Bibles. We would much rather believe that the only things needed for our salvation are saying the right words and believing the right things—not living lives that are characterized by Christ's concern for the poor. Why is this passage so sobering for us to read in the twenty-first century? Might it be that it hits us very close to home? Let me take some liberties and paraphrase these verses for today's reader:*

For I was hungry, while you had all you needed. I was thirsty, but you drank bottled water. I was a stranger, and you wanted me deported. I needed clothes, but you needed more clothes. I was sick, and you pointed out the behaviors that led to my sickness. I was in prison, and you said I was getting what I deserved. (RESV—Richard E. Stearns Version)

If we are honest, our response to the poor might sometimes be better described by this irreverent version. Whatever the case, Christ's words in this passage cannot be dismissed out of hand. We have to face their implications no matter how disquieting.

God has clear expectations for those who choose to follow him."[2]

As Richard struggled with his decision about accepting the presidency of World Vision, he was forced to deal with two compelling questions.

They were the same two questions that were about to reshape my world.

- "What if there are children who will suffer somehow because I failed to obey God?"
- "What if my cowardice costs even one child somewhere in the world his or her life?"[3]

Instead of feeling inadequate for the job or offering excuses about how I already had plenty on my plate pastoring a church, superintending a school, serving on boards....I had to stare squarely at the truth in those two questions. Every few months, I am drawn back to those questions and am forced to answer them once again.

The final event occurred when I attended a local ministerial association meeting. (True confession – I miss far too many of these meetings because I get busy, distracted, or simply forget.) A Southern Baptist pastor from our area brought a guest.

The guest introduced himself as Pastor Timothy Kakooza. He proceeded to tell me that he was a bishop from Uganda, and without knowing anything of my wrestling match with the IACCS decision, began to describe the plight of the orphans in Uganda. I shared an IACCS brochure with him, he studied it more intently than I had expected, and in a few moments, said, "We need this."

I said, "Well, if I can ever help, just give me a call." Truthfully, I thought that would be the end of it, but in a few weeks, I received a call from Timothy inviting me to come and help the orphanages and schools in Uganda. I agreed and then realized that I didn't have a clue about what to do to help.

I prayed like crazy, began to do lots of homework (like looking at a map to be sure I knew where Uganda even was), and work on a game plan for the trip. Honestly, I simply took this to the Lord, asking Him for wisdom and direction. Plans began to be made for a journey—shots, visas, malaria meds, water purification systems, insect netting, etc.

Looking back on this process and my apprehension is quite humorous now. Will I be sleeping in a jungle in a hut with dirt floors? Will snakes and insects slither across my body while I sleep? What would I eat? WOULD I BE EATEN? Would there be charging rhinos, hungry lions, elephants, gorillas, or giraffes? Would I be abducted and held for ransom? Would anyone pay the ransom? Would I bring home some dreaded diseases? How would we travel (I imagined a dugout canoe or on the back of an elephant)? Would it be an arid desert with starving children everywhere? How would I communicate with the people? I began to practice my best Tarzan yell (the neighbors kept calling the police thinking something was wrong!)

So, as a clueless Mzungu (Ugandan for a white traveler), I boarded a British Airways jet bound for Uganda on September 23, 2011.

Chapter 2
Trip #1: Hotel California and Wi-What?

"And that is precisely what Christianity is about. This world is a great sculptor's shop. We are the statues and there is a rumour going round the shop that some of us are some day going to come to life." - C.S. Lewis, "Mere Christianity" (1952)

Most of the fears and preconceived images were misguided. They disappeared within moments of arriving at Entebbe Airport—at least most of them! Sitting on the northern edge of Lake Victoria is this perplexing land of Uganda. It is a fertile, beautiful land, filled with lovely people. But it is also a land with more than its share of problems. According to the Uganda Population Clock, as of 2017, the population of Uganda is 42.9 million! The median age of the people of Uganda is 15.7 years. The U.N. estimates there to be a total of 2.7 million orphans living in Uganda. I believe this is a conservative estimate because of the difficulty of even knowing how many unnamed, uncared for orphans actually exist.

Aids, malaria, genocide, and a host of other causes have left Uganda a nation of children, a shocking number of who are orphans. Malaria, diarrhea, HIV, and pneumonia account for over 70% of the deaths of children under five years of age.

Another major issue that is still a haunting problem in Uganda is the influence of village witch doctors. The witch doctors, telling those they influenced not to listen to Westerners, have contributed significantly to the spread of AIDS and other diseases. For several years, they convinced many people of their villages that the AIDS medications, treatments, and the methods of prevention prescribed by Western doctors were the cause of AIDS. So, many of the people listened to the witch doctors and AIDS ravaged an entire generation.

Another horror taking place at the hands of the witch doctors (most Americans can't even imagine this happening) is the abduction of young children. Many of them are dragged into the jungle, mutilated, their private parts cut off, and left to die. According to Missionary Katherine Hines, the going price for a child's head is $300.[4]

The belief is that this mutilation will bring prosperity or luck to their village. These witch doctors will often travel to Kampala, the nation's capital, and snatch vulnerable children. Usually, their take comes from the thousands of unnamed street children who call these streets and streets of other city centers their home. Reports vary on the exact count of children living on the streets of Kampala, but the number exceeds 10,000.

Additionally, these children undergo abuse from those who should be caring for and protecting them. It is common for some (certainly not all) policemen to beat the children with canes and strike them with their fists, or kick at them. They treat them as "chokora" (scavengers—like stray street dogs).

Trip #1: Hotel California and Wi-What?

Treating them as *chokora*

But with all that said, Uganda is officially a Christian nation. That does not mean everyone has a clear profession of faith. However, Christianity has clearly influenced and continues to impact the Ugandan culture. AIDS is on the decline. Those practicing Christianity are committed to monogamy and to having only as many children as they can care for. It is the norm to meet a Christian man who will shake your hand and state with great pride and vigor, "My name is (and state their full Ugandan name), and I am the husband of but one wife." It is a way of saying, "I am proudly living out my faith."

The President of Uganda, Yoweri Museveni (pronounced Mu-seven), and his wife, Janet Museveni, have made significant strides in human rights reform. Her Excellency, Janet Museveni, led the nation in several initiatives in recent years to assist in providing programs for the aid and protection of orphans. Their leadership has also provided one of the most effective national responses to HIV/AIDS in Africa.

On this first visit to Uganda, the plane banked over the massive Source of the Nile River, Lake Victoria, as we prepared to set down at Entebbe. As the plane landed, I became acutely aware of how different Entebbe's airport is to almost any airport in the world. If you have seen the movie, *The Last King of Scotland* (though it is not a movie I would necessarily recommend), you would immediately realize that you're standing in the movie set. Much of the film took place at this airport.

There is still a significant U.N. presence in Uganda, evident from the large number of their planes parked around the perimeter of the runway.

As passengers deplaned, we exited via stairs (no jet way until 2016). You are instantly struck with the smells, humidity, and temperature that are uniquely Ugandan. I have come to love these because they are so, well, Ugandan! The people of Uganda are even more unique. There is friendliness unlike anywhere else I have ever visited. Almost everyone has a smile and is eager to help—even while clearing Customs.

Having cleared Customs and gotten my bags, I walked into the main ticketing area to look for a familiar face. There was no familiar face to be seen, and I began to wonder if I would recognize Pastor Timothy when I saw him. I waited for what seemed like hours looking for Timothy. I had no phone number, no way to contact him, no way to call home. I walked to an information desk and asked the girl behind the counter, "Do you have Wi-Fi?" She politely smiled and said, "Wi–what?"

I thought, "Well, I guess we're not in Kansas anymore, Toto."

Fear began to set in. Okay, Lord, what's the deal? Did you send me all this way just to have me climb back on a plane and fly home? What lessons are you trying to teach me? I was seriously contemplating checking with the ticket agent to see when the next flight back to Miami might be leaving. But before I had to make that drastic call, I suddenly saw the familiar face I had been looking for.

Timothy gave me a warm greeting, apologized for being late (he had a flat tire coming through the jungle). Making it to the airport at all had taken a significant effort. There is no AAA in Uganda!

We loaded my bags in his Toyota SUV and started the long drive back toward his village.

Timothy decided I needed to eat, so he pulled into a small Ugandan restaurant that served some food that he thought would fit the palate of a mzungu. I clearly was not quite ready to experience authentic Ugandan cuisine.

He had brought his daughter, Jireh, along for the long trip. Traveling through the jungle, fighting the traffic of Kampala, and the drive to Entebbe can be long and tedious. What I didn't know was that he had also brought her along to help keep me awake so that I would acclimate to the time change. After settling in for a bite, Timothy said, "I will be back in a little while," and disappeared into the streets of Kampala. Jireh's assignment? Keep me awake, no matter how heavy my eyelids became.

After two hours of very sleepy conversation, Timothy returned, and we resumed our journey.

I have now learned to sleep as much as possible on the plane because when you arrive in Uganda, there is so much work to be done that you sleep very little.

We drove on through Kampala and pulled into a little gated compound in Mukono. This was going to be my home for the next week. It was called a resort and conference center but forget anything you might have in mind from an American perspective.

Since I had no communication with my family for three days, I was feeling an urgency to let them know that I had arrived safely. I asked the receptionist at the hotel if they had Wi-Fi because I needed to contact my family in America. She said they did not have Wi-Fi. I had noticed two young guys sitting in the lobby when I entered but had not really paid much attention to them. One of them said, "We will take you to a place where there is Wi-Fi." Maybe it was total exhaustion or desperation to communicate with my family. Whatever it was, I got in a car with two guys I had never met, and we started driving across town. As we pulled away, I thought, this could be a terrible idea!

Within seconds, the young driver introduced himself, and pulled out a business card with a scantily clad Ugandan girl on it and said, "I also run a discotheque." I wondered what the other part of the "also run" meant... but didn't ask. I smiled and said, "Man, you don't want to be showing me this! I'm a preacher!" That didn't seem to faze him, and he went on telling me about his disco. In a few minutes, we reached a gated facility that was clearly a more high-end resort. We went in, and I was able to connect to Wi-Fi and communicate with my family for the first time since arriving in Uganda.

When I finished talking with everyone back home, my new friend said, "Let me show you around the resort. This is where my disco is some of the time." As we started walking, I learned something else that is very different from our American culture. He reached over and took my hand and walked me around the grounds, hand-in-hand. As uncomfortable as that seemed at the time, I have learned that it is prevalent in Ugandan culture and is an expression of friendship. We will learn more about this new friend shortly.

When I arrived back at the place I was staying, I was escorted through a central lounge area with old chairs, couches, and a T.V.

Trip #1: Hotel California and Wi-What?

The room was filled with several Asian men who were sitting, staring at nothing. They appeared totally unaware of my presence. My first thought, "Oh, great! I'm staying in an opium den!" I never did find out whether that was the case or not. I was taken down a narrow, very dark hallway to what looked every bit like a prison cell! There were bars on the windows, metal door with a little metal flap that you reached through to padlock your room once inside. The good news was there was a bed (covered with mosquito netting!) and not a grass mat on the floor.

Thankfully, there was a bathroom with a flush toilet and even toilet paper. (I learned early on that is not the norm in Uganda—enough said!) There was a shower, of sorts, directly above the toilet. I thought great, a hot shower, and some sleep! I turned the showerhead on...no water. I thought that maybe there was an adjustment on the showerhead up by the ceiling. I grabbed it, turned it, and snap. I was now holding a broken showerhead in my hand and looking at broken PVC pipe, but still no water. I threw on a pair of shorts and ran past the "opium den" and across the courtyard. I noticed several people staring intently at me. I instantly realized that white legs sticking out of a pair of shorts is not a common site in Uganda. I haven't worn shorts since!

I told them what had happened to the shower, so they put me in another room. This time there was no toilet seat on the toilet. I thought, "Well, that must be the way they use these things in Uganda." Still no water! I gave up, put on my headset, and went to sleep listening to Hotel California (which seemed very appropriate for the moment). I got up in the middle of the night, and to my pleasant surprise, there was water! Nothing like a 3 a.m. shower, and then back to bed. Thank you, Lord, for water. And it was even warm. I later learned that warm water is not always the case. In fact, a good part of your time in Uganda, you are doing everything possible to ensure that you are getting or staying clean. You always use bottled water, and when you brush your teeth or shower, you do everything in your power not to drink any of it.

While we are talking about water, I am reminded of a sad, shocking sight not long after arriving in Kampala. We stopped to buy a case of bottled water for my room. The shopping area we choose had a large concrete wall surrounding it, with an armed guard standing outside. Timothy said this was like the Ugandan Wal-Mart. I thought, "Bet they don't have much theft!" As we were pulling into the parking area, I saw a sight that will forever be burned into my memory. Placed or propped up against the wall was a man who had nothing from his waist down. Nothing! He had been dropped there by others, and his entire existence consisted of sitting, begging, and hoping for pity. I asked Timothy if he knew what had happened. He said he was not sure, but it was probably from a land mine from Idi Amin's day. I asked what hope and what help this man might have? Timothy's response was, "None." As we drove away, I began to realize that this was just a glimpse of the magnitude of the problems Uganda was facing.

When I woke up that first morning, I decided to explore. I unlocked my "cell door," walked out the narrow hallway, passed the empty opium den, and out into the sun-drenched courtyard. I thought how strange, here I am on the other side of the world; the sun is still shining, there is still oxygen to breathe, and even the temperature seems the same as when I left home. It was reassuring. As I walked around the grounds, I made a new friend who appeared to be a groundskeeper. He was quick to tell me that he was a Christian and had made that decision within the last year. It was such a joy to see his excitement and enthusiasm for letting others know about his newfound faith in Christ. He told me how The Lord's Resistance Army and Joseph Kony had abducted him. He showed me two bullet holes (one in his side and the other in his leg) where he had been shot as he escaped their terror and fled into the northern Uganda jungle, where he hid for three weeks. He then made his way through the forest and on to Kampala, where he lived in a cardboard box on the streets. Eventually, he found work in the hotel. He was sending most of his earnings back to care for his mother, still trapped in northern Uganda, having been abandoned by his father. I thought, Lord, this trip is going to be more than I could have ever imagined. The sun may still be in the sky, and the temperature may be the same, but my world will never be the same! This was my first trip to Uganda, and I could never have imagined what I would experience.

I had a small breakfast, Timothy picked me up to go teach a group of Christian leaders in Katosi and to spend time in prayer with a group of men and women. I thought I knew what prayer looked like–I was so wrong. I saw a sense of faith and urgency as I have never seen before. They laid hands on me and prayed for God's power and strength for what we were about to attempt for the nation of Uganda. As we finished, one elderly woman approached me and asked if I would pray for her. She said she was a street evangelist in Kampala and her prayer was that she "would finish strong." That was 2011, and her words still ring in my ears. Oh, Lord, that I may "finish strong!"

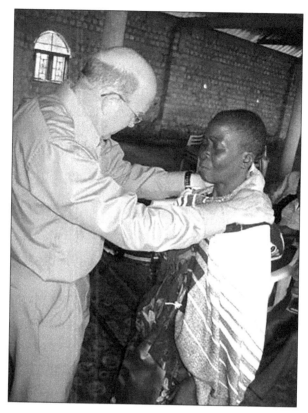

Pray that I may finish strong.

After the prayer meeting, I was spent and thought, "Wow, what a day! Now for some dinner and early bed (Jet lag was really hitting me hard)." Not a chance. On the way back toward Mukono, Timothy said we were going to go do a radio show. He wanted me to talk about several things. He wanted us to discuss the importance of Christian education and the association we were about to launch. But he also really wanted to drive home the importance of staying in school, and of having only the number of children you were able to care for. I have repeated this message over and over again on my trips to Uganda.

We arrived at the station. It looked like any radio station you might see in America. Just before we were to begin the broadcast,

I asked, "By the way, how many people are being reached by this broadcast tonight?" Timothy's response left me almost speechless. He said, "Between six and eight million."

"What? How can that be?" I asked.

He replied, "No T.V. People listen to the radio in the villages and towns all over Uganda." So, in addition to talking about the things Timothy had asked me to talk about, I spent a great deal of time presenting the Gospel as clearly as I possibly could.

A radio broadcast, but was anyone listening?

As we left, I thought, "Could that have been true? Did I get to share Christ with six to eight million people? Maybe Timothy just made that number up." So, the Lord had a way of showing me. I returned to my room and was settling in for the night when I heard a knock at my door. I peeked out the window into the hall. There was the man who had given me the ride to call Colleen the day before. I thought, "How in the world did he find my room or know where I was staying?"

He said, "Pastor Tonny?" (They always say and spell Tony with an extra "n"). I opened the door and let him in, wondering all the while if I was about to be robbed. He said, "I listened to your radio show. I want to promise you that I will keep my children in school. It is their only hope for a better life. And I want you to know that I am going to church tomorrow."

I gave him a copy of my first book, *Bone of My Bone*, and signed it for him. You would have thought that I had given him a great treasure. He left shortly, and I never got to see him again. I thought, "Well, I don't know if six or eight million people heard the show, but I know one did, and it made a difference."

"I listened to your radio show. I promise you I will keep my children in school!"

When you visit the churches and orphanages, you feel in many ways like you stepped back in time 2,000 years to when the first churches were being formed as described in Acts 2. While many of the churches in Uganda are called Pentecostal, they aren't at all what you think of when you think of an American Pentecostal church. Instead, think of what the first churches must have looked like right after the Day of Pentecost. People loving and sharing and caring like the church was designed to be. Oh, that the churches of America could become Acts 2 churches! I will explain this more in a moment.

Sunday morning came before I wanted it to. I was still on Florida time, and a 7:00AM wake up was 2:00AM on my biological clock. I was supposed to preach at the church in Katosi and wondered if I would even be able to communicate with the people of the church. Driving from Mukono to Katosi was an adventure in itself in 2011.

The roads were all red clay and had been thoroughly washed out in many areas. All the plants along the route are covered in a rust-red coating from the dust in the air. Most of the vehicles have taken severe beatings on these roads, have holes in their floorboards, and their air conditioning system is so clogged with clay that they won't work. You get a full workout rolling the windows up and down to keep the dirt out as approaching vehicles pass. As soon as the cloud of dust settles, your windows come down because the temp inside gets so hot. Arriving in Katosi, the roads get even worse, in fact, they become impassable in certain spots. We came to a large boulder just off the side of the way and Timothy took a sharp left past it. We started driving up a very steep hill, but eventually, the road was so rutted and the grade so steep that we had to stop and walk the rest of the way. I wondered whether anyone would be at this church since it required mountain climbing skills just to get there! At the top of the road, I could see a large building – open windows, rough clay brick, dirt floor, under a metal roof. As we approached, I could hear voices, but could not tell what was going on. We arrived at the base of the building, there was a rough wooden ramp leading up into the building. I climbed the slope and stood at the doorway, marveling at the sight in front of me.

There were dozens of people walking about the building, arms outstretched, lifting their voices to God in prayer. They were speaking in Lugandan, the dominant native tongue of that region of Uganda.

I didn't need to speak their language to understand what was taking place. They were bathing the church service, the people, and the message that was to come in fervent prayer. I was no longer sleepy and was energized to see what God was going to do.

I have learned that church names and denominational ties don't seem to mean very much in Uganda. I have been in several different denominational Ugandan (not American Missionary) churches. I would have difficulty telling one from the other.

The worship is vibrant, full of life. There was a choir/worship team dance group that sang and worshiped with joy and sincerity that would be hard to match anywhere else in the world.

There was a young man there with his family that I would later learn was one of the elders of the church. He was a tall, lanky man by Ugandan standards. His joy for the Lord was reflected in everything he did – from his smile, his words, and especially in his dance. Emma couldn't just stand and sing. When the music started, Emma started to move. I believe he was double-jointed in every joint in his body. He was like a rubber man. My first reaction was, "Woo, this guy's a little too far off the reservation for my comfort zone!" But over the years, I have grown to appreciate Emma, his family, and his love for God. Each year as we are getting ready to leave, Emma comes to us with gifts and items for us to buy. They are intended for us to "take back to America to remind us of our family in Uganda."

Many times, there has been a gas generator humming just outside an open window with an extension cord running inside to power everything, from musical instruments and microphones to single light bulbs dangling from a string looped over a wood beam. Timothy's church is called Katosi Community Church. It is called a Pentecostal church, but as I just mentioned, it is not at all what we think of in America when we think of Pentecostal churches. In Uganda, as best I can tell, Pentecostal takes on the meaning of "we are a church like the church right after the Day of Pentecost." What do I mean by the-church-right-after-the-Day-of-Pentecost? Take a look at Acts 2:40-47: *With many other words, he warned them; and he pleaded with them, "Save yourselves from this corrupt generation." Those who accepted his message were baptized, and about three thousand were added to their number that day.*

They devoted themselves to the apostles' teaching and to fellowship, to the breaking of bread and to prayer. Everyone was filled with awe at the many wonders and signs performed by the apostles. All the believers were together and had everything in common. They sold property and possessions to give to anyone who had need. Every day they continued to meet together in the temple courts. They broke bread in their homes and ate together with glad and sincere hearts, praising God, and enjoying the favor of all the people. And the Lord added to their number daily those who were being saved.

I watched as people who had nothing, love God and each other in ways that I have rarely seen in American churches. At the end of the service this first Sunday, I saw people come forward and put what little money they had into large wicker baskets; all so that a man could have enough money to travel back to northern Uganda to care for his critically ill mother. These weren't token gifts given out of plenty, but sacrificial gifts given out of poverty.

Some may have been giving all they had, but they provided with a sense of joy, love, and urgency.

My job this Sunday was to bring a message that would honor our God, challenge the people, and help them understand the importance of my purpose in Uganda. Most of the people of Uganda speak English, but it would be difficult for them to understand my American English. So, I had to learn their cadence and the rhythm of speaking, with a translator speaking every sentence behind me, hoping that he was saying the same thing I was.

The message I brought on this first trip to Uganda was one that I prayed would convey what God was about to do. I began by stating a phrase that I have repeated many times to the Christian community in Uganda: "Because of Jesus Christ and your faith in Him, you are the hope of Uganda! The future of Uganda rests in your hands. Without Christ, there is little hope for the world. The children you are training today will be the leaders of tomorrow." Then I launched into the message. The essence of the sermon was taken from 2 Kings 3:13-20.

The backdrop behind this passage is this: Ahab and Jezebel are both dead. Joram, Ahab's son, is now the king of Israel during the time when the kingdom was divided. The king of Moab rebels against him, and in fear, recruits King Jehoshaphat of Judah and the king of Edom to help him. With their three combined armies, this was a fearsome trio who should easily take the Moabites. But there was an almost immediate problem—they ran out of water for both the men and the livestock. How could they fight when they were in danger of dying of thirst? Desperation does something that we often see in Scripture, Joram looked for some kind of help from the gods. He didn't care which god, but he was looking for divine intervention.

King Jehoshaphat had a servant who reminded him of the prophet Elisha. The kings and their armies head out to find the prophet. So, let's pick the text up from here:

2 Kings 3:13-20

Elisha said to the king of Israel, "Why do you want to involve me? Go to the prophets of your father and the prophets of your mother."

"No," the king of Israel answered, "because it was the Lord who called us three kings together to deliver us into the hands of Moab."

Elisha said, "As surely as the Lord Almighty lives, whom I serve if I did not have respect for the presence of Jehoshaphat king of Judah, I would not pay any attention to you. But now bring me a harpist."

While the harpist was playing, the hand of the Lord came on Elisha, and he said, "This is what the Lord says: I will fill this valley with pools of water. For this is what the Lord says: You will see neither wind nor rain, yet this valley will be filled with water, and you, your cattle and your other animals will drink. This is an easy thing in the eyes of the Lord; he will also deliver Moab into your hands. You will overthrow every fortified city and every major town. You will cut down every good tree, stop up all the springs, and ruin every good field with stones."

The next morning, about the time for offering the sacrifice, there it was—water flowing from the direction of Edom! And the land was filled with water.

Then I said, "Here is something I want us all to understand – Elisha (speaking for God) didn't say, 'Dig a ditch.' He said, 'Make this valley full of ditches.' Not one ditch, not two, but fill the valley with ditches." I went on to explain that when God calls us to something, He doesn't want us to enter in half-heartedly. He wants a total commitment so that we can truly see the power and presence of God manifest in our lives and in our endeavors. When we do this, His power will be undeniable.

We don't get to say, "Okay, Lord. I'll dig a ditch, but don't ask me to dig an entire valley full of ditches."

Or, "What's the point? I don't see any sign of water!" Nor do we get to say, "I have a few minutes of spare time and some pocket change, but don't ask me to commit wholeheartedly to you." I also stated that they must have all really pitched in because the ditches were completed in one night. What happened next? The next morning God filled the ditches.

Then I made my point: I am here because I am convinced that God has called me to this. I am digging ditches, and I'm trusting God to fill them with water. I then challenged the people of the church to be faithful in digging the ditches, trusting God to do the filling. I said, "I'm not sure what this is all going to look like, but I know that it has been bathed in powerful, believing, sincere faith." I ended the message by giving a clear explanation of God's plan of salvation and an invitation to accept His forgiveness.

After the service, person after person came to greet me and thank me for loving the people of Uganda (I have since learned that is an often-repeated statement of gratitude). It was especially difficult to get used to the way the women of the church would greet. They would kneel in front of you, bow their head, and extend their right hand. I kept saying, "Please, no. Please stand. I am only a man. You don't have to do that!" But it is part of their culture and is a way of paying honor (as some of the ladies of the church have gotten used to me over the years, they sense that I am uncomfortable with this and so are merciful to me and won't bow).

From there, we headed to Timothy and Janepher's home for my first real Ugandan lunch. On the way down the steep hill leading back to his house, we drove very slowly through the main street of Katosi. It was a dirt road filled with people. It is always filled with people! There are open-air shops selling everything, slabs of beef (flies included, and the price goes down as the hours of the day go on without a sale), tilapia, vegetables and fruits, shoes, cell phones, backpacks, clothes, and of course Coca-Cola. Timothy stopped abruptly and called a man on a bicycle over. On the back of the bike were two large, green, warty-looking fruits as large as a watermelon. After some negotiating from Janepher, she handed the man some money, and he handed one of the fruits back to me. I was amazed at its weight and wondered what I had just been given. Timothy, anticipating my question, said, "Jackfruit."

Negotiating the price for jackfruit

We arrived at their home – it was a very comfortable home that could have been in many suburbs of America with a couple of exceptions, there was no kitchen as we think of kitchens, and there was no bathroom as we think of bathrooms. In Uganda, most homes have a cooking room (or outdoor area) where an open fire and boiling pots of food are prepared. There is often no refrigeration, so perishable foods are made daily. The bathrooms are typically away from the house. They are much like American outhouses, except that there is no toilet, no toilet paper, and no sink! American visitors are usually taken to bathrooms with a place to sit and toilet paper, USUALLY! I am no longer considered a visitor!

After several minutes of casual, get-to-know-one-another-better conversations, lunch was served. A special meal, as this one was, included a stew with beef or fish, rice, beans, chapati (a flatbread), pineapple (the best in the world!), mango, posho, and matoke. I later learned that these items, minus the stew, make up a large part of the meals in Uganda. The jackfruit was served as sort of a dessert. You eat the meat off of large, oblong seeds found inside. It is very sweet and takes some getting used to.

I was entirely spent and running on very little sleep, so we took the very bumpy ride back to Mukono. I arrived in my room, locked the metal prison-like door, and got ready for a good hot shower – nope, no water! So, I crawled under the sheets, tucked my mosquito netting around my bed, thinking about this amazing land and the beautiful people that I had experienced over the last two days.

My world had been rocked, and the real work with the orphanages and forming the Uganda Association of Christian Colleges and Schools (later officially named the Union of Christian Colleges and Schools – Uganda) had not even begun yet.

Monday morning, after a light Ugandan breakfast, Timothy picked me up, and we began one of the most exciting days I have ever experienced. We traveled from orphanage to orphanage, visiting dozens of orphanages with thousands of precious children. I can't begin to describe what was happening to my heart and soul. I saw children who had never had a pair of shoes on their feet, eating food out of plastic buckets. Some of the children had been born with AIDS and others were suffering from malaria. But I also saw something grand. Despite all of this, there was still a sense of joy, gratitude, and love that I have never experienced anywhere else in the world. Often, before we would even arrive in a village, there would be children alongside the road, cheering and running alongside the car. It seemed like they thought the President of the United States was coming for a visit. I would get out of the car and be surrounded by dozens (sometimes hundreds) of children, all hugging, touching, just wanting someone to love them. One of the heartbreaks you experience very early on is the small tug on your pant leg, and when you look down, you are looking into this sweet little face that says, "Take me with you. I want to go to America." Oh, to be able to do that! To put them all on a plane and lift them out of their poverty! But then you soon realize that might be the worst thing you could do for them. To remove them from their culture ultimately could be a horrible mistake for them and for the future of Uganda.

At each stop, I would bring the same simple, but important message. It always began with me telling about the love of Jesus. Then the challenge: "Stay in school; you are the hope of Uganda; practice abstinence; live for Jesus...."

One of our first visits was to an orphanage and school deep in the jungle, not far from the shore of Lake Victoria. Several things make this orphanage/school stand out in my memory. It is called Chosen Generation. To get to Chosen Generation, you drive down a dirt road that is more a footpath than a road. When you can drive no further, you stop and walk through thick jungle. As we were walking through the dense understory, I asked Timothy if there were any critters to be concerned about. He said very calmly, but without a hint of a smile, "Yes." I was far less calm and asked, "What?!" Again, a calm reply, "Black Mamba." I was very cautious about where I stepped from then on. After walking what seemed like miles (it was probably only a few hundred yards), we made a sharp right turn and began to climb a steep hill through still a very dense jungle. Suddenly, the slope flattened out, and there was a large clearing filled with children and a few buildings scattered about. As I walked around the flat area, I saw a ball made of banana leaves tightly wrapped with vine. That was their soccer ball. I kicked it around with a few of the children for a few minutes, and we were best buds. That moment also led to planting the desire to bring as many soccer balls and other sports equipment with me each year. I assumed the buildings were makeshift barns for livestock, but I was guided to one of the buildings to observe a group of children sitting in small handmade, rough-hewn, wooden desks. These weren't barns, they were classrooms!

Classrooms and a school kitchen

The next stop was the school's food service area. The photos above capture about all there is that needs to be said! Open fire, open pots of rice, beans, posho, matoke, and minnows (if fortunate enough to have any meat). Imagine the task of trying to feed all of the children in Ugandan orphanages! This particular school/orphanage was different from most of the others. The children were not in school uniforms, primarily because they were too impoverished. This requires a little further explanation. Most schools require school uniforms, and it is somewhat of a social status thing. It shows that your children are attending school and striving to get an education. The uniforms cost almost nothing (under $10.00 US), but when you are living on a dollar a day, it is an enormous fee. The families, if they have families, don't even make that! Why not? Because they make jungle brew that keeps them in a stupor all day, every day. One of the primary goals of Chosen Generation is to break this cycle of addiction and poverty. The children will all stand to demonstrate their commitment to this cause, and in unison, repeat, "We are the children of a Chosen Generation, called by God to bring change to this village." Their goal is to break the chains of cultural slavery that has such a death-grip on their community. These chains run deep, and they are generational.

We are children of a CHOSEN GENERATION, called to bring change to this village.

As I walked from one part of the school to another section of the same ministry, we had to walk through a region that had several huts and shelters. As we literally walked through one of the structures, people were sitting around staring at us but looking at nothing. The host leading us said somewhat casually, "That's the village witch doctor," as we walked past a huge woman sitting on a stool. She looked our way but gave no acknowledgment of our presence. I was more than happy to keep moving but thought I would have never guessed that she was a witch doctor!

That was and still is an important realization. The witch doctors don't always look like witch doctors, and evil doesn't always look mean and nasty. That's true whether in Uganda or the USA.

Witch doctor? I don't know, but I was happy to move on.

Chosen Generation is an exceptional example of education taking place under extremely adverse conditions. One of my favorite moments was observing an excellent teacher, teaching outdoors, with a homemade blackboard tied to a tree. As she gave instruction, she held the board steady with one hand and wrote with a piece of chalk with the other. I marveled as she taught some somewhat complex geometry to what we would call middle-school students. They were sitting on wooden benches, holding writing tablets in their laps, or writing on a handmade table. She was exquisitely dressed, looking more like she was going on a dinner date than teaching outdoors in the middle of the jungle.

Good teaching can take place under adverse conditions.

It was nearing time for this first, eye-opening visit to come to an end. We still had dozens of orphanages and schools to visit. Before we left, we were escorted to the school office to sign their guest book. I have since learned that this is an honor and usual practice for guests to sign their book. This office was the most unique one visited on any of my trips. It was outside, under the shade of mango trees. I asked, "What happens when it rains?" Their reply came with a shrug and typical Ugandan smile, "We get wet."

The next stop was Katosi Community School, the school and orphanage started and administered by Timothy. Timothy Kakooza has a fantastic story of his own.
Timothy was born into a Muslim family.
Timothy had to drop out of school and went to live with his mother in one of the poorest slums of Kampala called Katwe. If you want to get a feel for this place, watch the Disney movie *The Queen of Katwe*. He, his mom, and other family members lived in an eight-foot by eight-foot room. His mother sold cooked food along the side of the road to support her family. In a determined effort to help his mother, Timothy began to go to the market, buy pineapples, slice them, and sell them on the streets of Kampala.
As he was selling pineapple, he was exposed to street evangelists and their message of the need to receive Jesus as Savior.
They would shout their message at the top of their lungs, but as a young Muslim boy, their message made no sense to Timothy. "I had a hardened heart," are his own words. But God has a way of softening hearts. One Wednesday, after selling their pineapples, Timothy and a friend decided to walk around the slum where they were living. As they went by a building, they could hear people joyfully singing. Timothy and his friend were peeking through an open window when they were spotted by a pastor. He invited the boys in, and they sat down. Timothy says, "I can't even remember what the pastor was saying that day, but the one thing I remember is that after he had finished speaking, he came and gave us a big hug and said, 'Thank you for coming.' And he gave us the

invitation to come to church on Sunday. We went back home; personally, I was touched by that big heart of that man."

Saturday and Sunday were crucial days for street pineapple salesmen. Saturday was a day when they could sell a lot of pineapples, and Sunday was the day that they could buy pineapple at a reduced price because the market was trying to sell off old stock to make room for fresh pineapple. To give up selling pineapple on Sunday would mean a loss of much-needed income. Still, Timothy reminded his friend that they had promised the pastor that they would come to church. His friend said, "I was kidding! I'm not going to church. I have to make money!" Timothy said, "But we promised him. After a lengthy discussion, we parted ways. He went to the market, and I went to church. That morning a guest pastor was speaking on the second coming of Christ. He talked about how those who had received Christ would be taken up to meet Him, and those who had rejected Him would be left behind.

At the end of the service, the pastor gave an invitation. He said, "I felt like the pastor was speaking directly to me, and I raised my hand to receive Christ. That is the day I became a Christian. I stayed in that church for eleven years. I was mentored. I was discipled. I was loved. I was cared for. I grew up in my Christian life. I started to minister." After eleven years of serving in various capacities in the church, the pastor asked a group to travel to the fishing village of Katosi to do a church plant. About ten people received Christ that day, and the pastor asked if any of the young men who had traveled with him from Kampala would be willing to stay behind and pastor this new church that had just been birthed. They all said, "No, we can't give up life in the city to come live in this small village." But after several months, the pastor called Timothy into his office and said he felt like he was the one the Lord wanted to pastor the church in Katosi. Timothy and Janepher did move to Katosi full time.

At the time they made the move, it was a dark season in Ugandan history because so many children had parents dying of AIDS. It wasn't long before they had 25-30 orphaned children living in their small home.

From those days, God has blessed and allowed them to build a dynamic church, school (Katosi Community School), several outlying childcare facilities, and a clinic. The orphanages and schools minister to a total of over a thousand children.

(I will probably say this more than once in this writing, but I can't even imagine what it must be like to figure out how to feed that many children daily!)

Katosi Community School was so very different from Chosen Generation. Each school was doing what should and could be done with the resources they had.

Chosen Generation, one of the poorest of poor, had excellent teachers, eager to teach and learn, and to love the children in front of them.

Katosi had many more teachers with the same heart for their children, but with more significant buildings (some even concrete) and a clear ongoing developmental plan. It was a joy to see many of the younger teachers sitting around a table under a large shade tree working together to sharpen their teaching skills. These teachers were building a culture of learning that was evident among many of the students. I saw some excellent teaching under adverse and unusual conditions, like the 5-year old kindergarten class with one teacher and two aides and nearly a hundred students. I am not saying this is ideal, but it sure beats the alternative of the children without the care and education they are receiving.

Another teacher I had the honor of watching teach was teaching, and teaching well, the concept of photosynthesis to her students while holding her baby in her arms. She never missed a beat as a teacher or as a caring mother.

Teaching photosynthesis and being a mom at the same time

I also marveled at the artistic skills of some of the older children. Almost every orphanage had a choir that I think could hold their own with most formally trained groups in America. The children also love to recite readings and perform dramas for their visitors. There is a refreshing quality that I see in these artists. There was a shyness of spirit, humility, but an eagerness to show their work at the same time.

I marveled at the artistic skills of some of the older children.

I didn't realize it, but there were still several more orphanages that Timothy had scheduled us to see between what was left of this first day and the next. We visited a dozen or so ministries, most with names I can remember and each with their own unique personalities; places like Goshen Land, a vibrant orphanage high on a hill overlooking the city. The children of Goshen Land were waiting along the side of the hill. As we approached, they began to sing, play musical instruments, and recite Scripture and other things they had memorized for this visit. It was a healthy, beautiful place for the children to be safely nurtured.

We made a quick stop at an orphanage where the needs seemed even more significant than the other places we were visiting. This was the darkest place we visited. Hopelessness seemed to be on the faces of the children and the teachers. This was the type of organization that desperately needed IACCS and the Ugandan Association.

Then there was the orphanage where a young pastor had grown up as an orphan, gone to university, and returned to pastor and run the program.

When we arrived, there were several young children sitting on a walkway eating meager servings of beans and rice with their fingers (no silverware). The pastor told me that they had given them their names after they had been brought to the orphanage because they had no names before that. As we were touring the facility, I noticed a room with beds but no insect netting. I asked, "Is this room secure enough that you don't need netting over the beds?" He said, "No, when you have to choose between netting and food, food wins!"

He then pointed back to the children and said this would be all their food for the day.

He pointed to one of the children and told me that he was not doing well because he had been born with AIDS. Sadly, within the year after I had visited with the child, he passed away from complications due to his weakened immune system.

Trip #1: Hotel California and Wi-What?

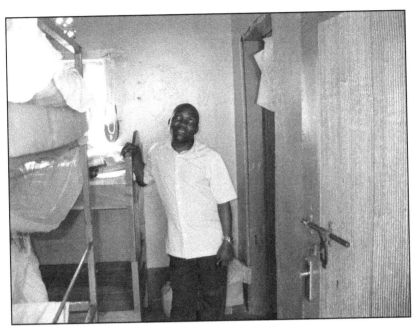

This was my bed, my home, now I am the pastor.

AIDS claims the innocent.

Each of these stops and visits took longer than we anticipated. They always had their children sing or recite or put on a drama. The dramas almost always dealt with subjects that no child of their age should have to deal with – issues like an adult pastor who took in an orphan, abused and raped her and left her pregnant, or the quartet of girls who in a whiny voice ask,

> *"Parents, Parents, Parents, why are you mistreating us?*
> *Why leaving us on the streets?*
> *Leaving us without food, clothing and shelter!*
> *Fathers, Fathers, Fathers, Why so stupid? Leaving us in households where there is such violence, where they are ready to kill.*
> *Government, Government, Government, why so quiet?*
> *This is our life. We are a neglected generation.*

Not all of the performances were as dark and foreboding as these. But the dramas that were burned a hole in my heart!

Our next stop proved to be an important and encouraging stop. Victors' Junior Christian School Day and Boarding was a large ministry with many orphans and boarding students. The classroom buildings were all concrete and were better equipped and relatively modern, compared to most of the other ministries we had visited. I visited his facility and was impressed with his initiative and forward thinking. He had installed a lake on the campus where he was raising lungfish for food. The lake was teeming with large eatable lungfish (when was the last time you ate a lungfish?). There was also a separate building being used to grind and store grain and produce other food sources. There was also a well-thought-out, yet still Ugandan kitchen.

In our conversation, he said that one of their biggest challenges was that they could not get enough adequately trained teachers and nurses.

I asked, "What do you do with your building at night?" "What do you mean?" he questioned.

"Do you have electricity at night for your classrooms?" "Most of the time."

Then I issued this challenge, "I commission you to start a training center in the evenings for teachers and nurses."

In the photo below, you see the following actual conversation taking place. If you look closely at this photo, you can probably see the light bulb going off above the pastor's head. A simple planting of an idea prompted by God has created a training center that is now up and running and has trained several teachers and nurses.

I left that ministry thinking to myself, "What authority do you have commissioning this man to take on such a task?" But it had come on so suddenly, unexpectedly even, that I had to think it was orchestrated by God. I am so grateful that God used this man to catch the vision and take the necessary steps to make it a success. Each year that I return I ask if they are providing training in this facility for teachers and nurses and his answer is always the same. Yes, and then he gives me a total of those that have been trained. The following photo is of that commissioning vision conversation.

Casting the vision for a training center for teachers and nurses

The next day was filled with stops, visiting schools and orphanages of all shapes and sizes; each unique in their own way.

One of the things that caught me off guard over and over was the living conditions of many of dormitories in the orphanages. To say they were poor would be an understatement. The rooms were packed wall-to-wall with children. Those fortunate enough to have them had metal bunk beds with foam mattresses. If there were no bunk beds, there were just mattresses lying on the bare concrete floor. If there were no mattresses, there was only a piece of foam. If there was no foam, there was just a mat. Some had sheets or blankets; some did not. Many of the orphans had a small storage locker that contained all of their personal belongings. They were positioned at the head of their bed. If available, there was insect netting; usually full of large enough holes that most insects could fly straight through. One of the essential treasures that each of these children had was a bucket, dish, bowl, or cup. These were a necessity when meals were served. The tough part was to look at these children, no shoes, only one or two changes of clothes, and very little else, and realize that as deplorable as these conditions are, each child's life would be so much worse if they did not have this place to care for them. With that said, however, I must add that one of the most wicked things that can occur is that in some instances, some of the proprietors have purposely left the children in conditions that could be improved. By leaving them destitute, they can raise more money – the more pitiful the child looks, the more money can be raised! That is the dark side that can occur in Ugandan orphanages. I am constantly trying to discern whether this is occurring and asking God never to allow this to happen in the ministries we are helping.

All they have!

Let's get back to our visits. One of the ministries that left a positive lasting impression was Lugazi Community Day and Boarding School. This is probably the largest of the schools visited. There were well over a thousand children of all ages in a sea of bright blue uniforms. I was asked to speak to the children and teachers, so they began to press in closer and closer. I was concerned that the little ones were going to be trampled. They pushed in closer and closer until there was no more room to push. Many just wanted to touch the skin of a mzungu. I looked out across this sea of blue and began to speak, having to yell at the top of my lungs because there was no sound system. My message was simple: "You matter to God, He loves you and has a plan for your future, make your life count for Him, stay in school, you are the hope of Uganda." As I addressed the students, I was moved to tears as I caught just a glimpse of the difference Christian education was making in the lives of these young people.

As I addressed the students, I was moved to tears as I caught just a glimpse of the difference Christian education was making in the lives of these young people.

At that moment, I think God gave me a sharper and clearer vision of what could be accomplished if we allowed God to direct us as we formed the new Christian School Association through IACCS. I was introduced to Bernard Bogere, the proprietor of the school.

Bernard had been raised by American missionaries. They were part of the Christian Missionary Alliance Church and had served as missionaries in Uganda for several years. As do many of the missionaries, they took Bernard in as their son. When Idi Amin drove all Christian missionaries out of Uganda, they were forced to leave, and Bernard, as a young teenager, was thrown into prison. When Amin was overthrown, he was released. He then started the Lugazi Community Day & Boarding Primary School. By the time of our meeting, Bernard already had a well-respected voice in Uganda and was an ideal man to be one of the men paving the way for this association to form. He had a clear vision for what could be done through the unification that UCCSU would provide.

Because of his time with his missionary parents, he also had the enormous advantage of knowing the way Americans think and act. Timothy was also very familiar with Americans, so the two of them were vital to bridging the gap between Ugandan and American cultures.

When we finished at Lugazi School, I was assuming we were going to head back to Mukono to get some dinner and some much-needed rest. I had grown quite comfortable with Hotel California! Fatigue will do that for you. But Timothy said, "We have one more stop. There is a school where the students have been waiting for us to arrive all day." It was 5:30 or 6:00 in the evening when we pulled up at the school. I expected the place to be empty by now, but to my surprise, there on the lawn were a couple hundred high school students. They were dressed in sharp yellow shirts and green pants, waiting eagerly to greet us and to hear words of encouragement. I couldn't help but think about how inattentive most American teenagers would be if they had been waiting for hours, and two old guys showed up to offer some WORDS. But these teens were thoughtful and listened intently to the message. At the request of the leadership, I spoke on many of the things I had been speaking on at the other schools – stay in school. God has a purpose for you. Live for Christ. Because you know God's truth and obey it, you are the hope of Uganda. But these were teenagers, and they needed more. I was asked to encourage them to have only one husband/wife, to not have sex outside of marriage. Having multiple wives or husbands was a common practice outside the Christian community, as was sex outside of marriage. AIDS had made this message especially urgent for this generation to hear. Many Ugandans had not believed the truth about AIDS. The witch doctors had convinced them that it was a curse and that it was western medicine that was causing AIDS. Tragically AIDS is on the rise again in Uganda after headway had been made in the past to eradicate it. Continuing to educate this next generation is critical if victory is to be gained in defeating this disease.

The message to these high schoolers had a heightened sense of urgency.

As we pulled away, the sun was almost gone. We drove back to Mukono where we grabbed a quick dinner, and I headed back to my room to finish up last-minute details for the big day that was ahead of us. The next day was to be the kickoff organizational meeting to see if a new Christian school association would be formed for Uganda.

The key mission on this first trip was two-fold: to visit orphanages/schools for several days to encourage them. But there was also something vitally important for me to learn. I had to begin to get a feel for the needs and the culture of the orphans of Uganda. I soon learned that the word "orphan" does not mean the same thing it means in America. An orphan in Uganda may have a parent or parents, or other relatives. But those relatives simply can't care for them. Don't get me wrong, there are plenty of orphans with no parents because disease or calamity has destroyed the family. These facilities are very large by American standards. The smallest of the orphanages will have several dozen children and the largest ones will have several hundred to a thousand. One of the reasons is that Uganda's public educational system is required to educate only two children from each family. The problem is that most families have four to six children. Were it not for the private sector (primarily churches and other NGO's), these children would go uncared for, often left homeless, with a future of unthinkable neglect and abuse.

A second and primary purpose of this trip was to encourage each orphanage/school to attend an organizational meeting to help launch a Christian school association. Our goal was to build an association that would accomplish several vital things. Here are just a few of them:

- It would give them a unified voice and allow them to work together to improve the quality of all programs.
- It would make each ministry more aware of the other, reduce competition, and contribute to a cooperative spirit between them.
- It would eventually provide a vehicle for accreditation, teacher training, and certification.
- It would provide for annual Christian educators conventions.
- It would provide for people of like faith to find support and strength.
- It would provide a venue for academic and athletic competitions and demonstrations.

I planned to take the By-Laws, Statement of Faith and other documents used for FACCS/IACCS and convert them to a format that would be suitable for Uganda.

I was astounded on the first day of the organizational meeting. As I walked into the room, it was filled with over two hundred representatives from schools and orphanages. Some people had traveled from throughout Uganda, Rwanda, and Kenya. One man had made his way from Northern Uganda (at least a day's travel). He had ridden on the back of a boda boda, had gotten in a crash, then hitched another ride all the way to Kampala. He had no idea where he would stay or how he would get home, but felt like this meeting was too important to miss.

At the end of two days of organizational meetings, I watched this man walk off into the streets as the sun was setting. I asked Timothy what the man was going to do. Timothy simply said, "Go home." I asked, "On a boda boda?" He said, "Probably." I thought about the determination of this man and for that matter, all those attending these meetings. What would happen for the cause of Christ in America if we had that same level of resolve?

When we arrived at the organizational meeting, a very distinguished, well-spoken gentleman was already speaking to the crowd. As I got close enough to the building to recognize him, I realized that it was Bernard, the man who had been raised by American missionaries. I thought, what a perfect man this was to be making these introductory remarks. It never ceases to amaze me how God can use our past to make us the leaders He intends us to be. Timothy and Bernard, very different men, being used by God in very different ways, both accomplishing great things for the Kingdom.

The organizational meeting forming the Union of Christian Colleges and Schools–Uganda

Pastor Timothy spoke and then introduced me. I got up, and God gave the words necessary to challenge and affirm these men and women. We handed out the paperwork, a Statement of Faith, By-Laws, and an Application. People immediately began to fill them out for submission. Next, I sat back and watched as God birthed the Uganda Christian Colleges and Schools Union. I marveled as they elected their officers and immediately began to plan their future.

TRIP #1: HOTEL CALIFORNIA AND WI-WHAT?

I sat back and watched God work.

The Uganda Christian Colleges and Schools Union was founded with over 150 schools, with over 68,000 students, from 11 districts, joining that first day. This indeed was the work of God. He directed the words and the process in bigger and better ways than I could have imagined.

After the meeting, we returned to my motel, where we looked over the schools that had signed up and talked about future plans. With this part of the mission accomplished, Timothy had to leave to travel to another conference. I was left under the care of Janepher, one of her friends, and a driver. It was a tough assignment: Go visit Jinja and the Source of the Nile the next day before I boarded a plane to return home. The meeting ended, I planned to skip dinner but went in to get something to drink, and the waitresses brought me a plate of chips (home fries) and some unidentifiable meat (I think it was very well cooked pork.) This was a little dining area associated with the motel. As I was reading, a young Ugandan lady, who was obviously bright and very well educated, plopped down at my table and introduced herself as Sue. She was there at the resort, leading a medical conference. As we talked, she volunteered that she was a born-again Christian. She then proceeded to give me a very strong caution to be careful because so many pastors in Uganda take advantage of Americans. I received this as a cautionary gift from God.

She got up from the table and walked away, and I never saw her again. I thought to myself, "Was she an angel sent to temper me with some caution?"

Thursday was the last full day of the trip. I couldn't sleep because I kept thinking about the events of the incredible, God-directed day before as the newly formed Christian school association took shape. The sun was starting to peek over the horizon, so I decided to take my camera and go do a little exploring. I wasn't sure how I would be received but was up for the adventure. I walked out to the main highway and there was already heavy traffic both on the road and on foot. I fell in line with the crowd walking along the edge of the road. I would occasionally get a glance or hear someone say "mzungu," but never felt threatened or uncomfortable. As I walked, I stopped to get my daily Mountain Dew, which is more like lemonade in Uganda (I speculate that is because it is made with cane sugar). I enjoyed striking up a conversation with several of the people in this little roadside stand. I started to walk away with my bottle of Mountain Dew in hand, but the store owner stopped to let me know that I had to pay for the bottle. I had not seen a redeemable bottle in the States in many years. I stayed by the stand, enjoyed the conversations, and left when my drink was finished. Once again, I walked away, marveling at the kindness and friendliness of the people of Uganda. I walked back to the hotel to get ready to travel to see the Source of the Nile.

Several years ago, I had been fascinated by a BBC mini-series entitled *In Search of the Nile*. It was the story of David Livingstone's search for the Nile and his life of surrender as a missionary. The actual lake was first reported as being discovered by a European British explorer John Hanning Speke. He and Richard Francis Burton had been exploring Central Africa. He named the lake for the Queen of the United Kingdom.

I was very excited to see this place that held so much history and intrigue. I had also read of Gandhi's attraction to the Nile and particularly to this place. His ashes were spread here as one of his final requests. The town of Jinja is unlike any of the other cities I visited. It had more upscale hotels and obviously had taken advantage of consistent international tourist traffic.

The beauty of the Nile is a stark contrast to the poverty that you see among the people of Uganda. It makes you realize what a rich, fertile land Uganda is. The soil is a lush red, nutrient-rich mix that can grow almost anything. I remember thinking, "This is almost Eden!" But the poverty and abuse reminded me that it was far from Eden. The Nile looks like it literally bubbles up out of Lake Victoria right in front of a small island, several hundred yards away from an observation area.

The Source of the Nile

There are native dancers and music groups scattered around the area, performing in hopes of getting a few shillings from the tourists who stop to watch. Like most places around the world where tourists gather and are eager to spend money, there are vendors anxious to take your money. They are selling everything, from handmade jewelry, native music instruments, banana-leaf soccer balls, to wooden carved figures.

There are vendors offering boat rides and others running white water kayak adventures. At the top of the hill overlooking the Nile, there is a park with picnic tables scattered under the canopy of towering jungle trees. There I finally see the first wild animals I had seen since arriving in Uganda. There were several wild monkeys in the trees and scurrying around the picnic tables. They reminded me of raccoons that hang around American campgrounds.

One of the things that caught my attention was a large sign right at the entrance of the park. It was a sign with a message that I was very familiar with – It was a ROTARY sign with the 4-Way Test. It reminded me of how grateful I am to be a Rotarian.

The work that had been accomplished by Rotary has profoundly benefited virtually every nation on the planet. The eradication of polio stands alone as one of the most significant contributions of this organization.

Rotary's presence is felt in every nation.

As we headed back from Jinja to Mukono, I was blessed to be able to hear Janepher and her friend singing. They joyfully sang one Ugandan worship song after the other. As we rode along, I again marveled at the beauty of the land – dense jungle, fields of tea, an occasional rice paddy, mango, banana trees, and pineapple.

When I got back from our trip, there were several more ministry opportunities that I had not anticipated. The hotel staff told me that the young man that had first taken me to contact Colleen, and then had listened to the radio program and that I had given a copy of my book to had come by to say goodbye. I was touched that he had made such an effort and hope that our paths will cross on future trips. As I walked out of the office, two young men that I had met earlier greeted me. They asked if they could show me their Bibles and the notes they had taken and their Bible curriculum. They went on to tell me that they were enrolled in a Bible college in Kampala. They wanted to know if I had any advice for them as young Christians trying to determine God's will for their future. I am sure they would have been happy to have me give them money to help with their schooling, but at this point, I had spent everything I could contribute. So, I gave them the "silver and gold have I none" talk, and said what I did have to offer was advice. The advice was the same as I had given dozens of times during my time in Uganda: stay in school, study hard, stay faithful, and start a church when you finish school.

I then had to return back to my room, figure out what I wanted to return to America with and what I was going to leave behind. I packed the essentials and grabbed a bag of other things that I took to the hotel staff. One of the things most memorable was that one of the waitresses had a child who was ill. Before leaving for this trip, I had purchased a "Developing Country Medical Kit." Additionally, my secretary had packed me with every imaginable over-the-counter drug that I might need in all of Africa. I was able to leave much of the necessary medical supplies for the child.

I returned to my room and set my alarm for a very early wake-up.

It was a long, slow ride to Entebbe Airport, and I needed to be there at least two hours early. In anticipation of all of this, I set my alarm for 3:00 AM. It was a short night. I got up, and fortunately, the shower was working. I was supposed to be picked up in my room, but no one came, so I thought to save time I better drag my luggage to the front of the hotel. It was pitch black outside, I thought I knew my way around the hotel grounds, but I had forgotten a four-foot ledge drop off. Dragging a suitcase and wearing a backpack, I stepped into a dark free-fall. I landed flat on my front side on the asphalt driveway below. I laid there a few seconds, and didn't feel any significant pain, blood, or any protruding broken bones. I got up slowly and realized that I was a little hasty on the no-blood assessment. I could feel blood running down my leg and found a hole in the knee of the pants I had to fly home in. Fortunately, I had saved a few bandages and some antibiotic. So, there in the darkness of the early morning, I shucked my torn pants, bandaged my knee, and dug out from my bag the best pair of least dirty pants to wear home. I thought, "This could be a very long flight home!"

I stood in the parking area in front of the hotel, waiting for my ride, but still, no one came. I was now starting to worry. I knew it was going to be close, to make it to the airport, even by Ugandan standards. I was about to have a security guard I had been talking to, call someone to get me to the airport when my ride finally arrived. No explanation, no sense of urgency, but we made it to the airport with moments to spare. Janepher had accompanied the driver to bid me farewell. On my ride to the airport, I thought about all the things I had learned. I thought about the children I had seen and fallen in love with. I reflected on the work that had been accomplished. I had a heightened sense of urgency for Christian education around the globe. As I got out of the car, I found saying goodbye more difficult than I had expected.

I reached in my pocket, took out all the remaining money I had, gave it to Janepher, and said, "Take this, it is all the money I have left. The children need this more than I will." I handed over all the Ugandan currency I had left. It was a substantial amount of money, but I didn't even want to count it! I only had one stop in London and didn't think I would need any money before arriving back in Miami, except for just enough to get a much-craved hamburger when I landed in London. It is incredible how good something as simple as a hamburger can be when you have been eating "mystery foods" for several days!

That was the beginning of an amazing spiritual adventure. I have returned to Uganda each year since. Each trip has had more than its share of rich spiritual opportunities that will be described in the chapters to come.

Each journey has also led to a sharper view of the culture of the orphanages, the essential role they play, and the cautions that need to be observed. I am sadly now more aware of the abuse that some orphans experience. At times, it comes from those who are supposed to be the ones that love and care for them; from authorities, from teachers, other students, and relatives. As mentioned earlier, there are times that you see deplorable living conditions and lack of hope in some of the facilities. It is often driven by the daunting task of continually providing food for so many children and the lack of adequate funding. As a result there is significant malnutrition and diseases associated with poor nutrition. But the alternative is so awful! There would be little hope for their future, left to the streets. Witch doctors still prey on these un-named orphans, dragging them into the jungle and mutilate them because they think it brings prosperity or luck to their villages. Albino children or children with special needs are often discarded, left to die, or are actually killed because they are different.

This is why the church is so important in caring for these children.

This is why the pure, loving Gospel of Jesus Christ must be presented at every opportunity and lived out in the lives of the precious children.

One last surprise and cultural adventure occurred just before we got ready to taxi away. A flight attendant, in a very proper British accent, came on the microphone and said, "Ladies and gentlemen in a few moments we will be walking up and down the aisles spraying a sanitizing agent that will disinfect you. Please close your eyes, keep your mouth closed, and don't breathe as we come by your seat." I am not sure that is precisely what she said. What I was hearing in my head was this: "You have been to Africa. You are all filthy and infected with disease. We have to care for you on this flight, so we are going to kill anything that might cause us to get sick or die! But don't be alarmed." The spraying didn't kill me, and hopefully, I didn't bring any disease into Great Britain when we landed. My son did quarantine me from seeing my grandkids for a few days when I returned home – just in case!

As my plane lifted off the runway, I looked out at the beauty of Lake Victoria. It was abundantly clear that I had created memories that would be cherished for a lifetime. I knew that I was just beginning to find out how they had forever changed my life. Most of all, I reflected on the incredible work that God had done and wondered what the next chapters of IACCS would bring. I thought about how little I knew before the trip and how much I had learned in such a short time. But I had a sense that there was so much more to learn. I looked forward to what I would be taught in the future about this place, the people, and God's working.

CHAPTER 3
TRIP #2: GENEROUS GIFTS AND DAMALIE'S DREAM

Nothing that you have not given away will ever be really yours. - C.S. Lewis, "Mere Christianity" (1952)

When I returned to the United States, I couldn't stop talking about Uganda, the people, and what God had done in my short time there. I had hundreds of photos and videos that I had taken, so it was pretty easy to put together an effective media presentation. I was speaking about Uganda and IACCS everywhere – schools, churches, Rotary Clubs, civic groups, and conferences. Truth is, I would talk to anyone that would listen. People began to ask how they could help, and then people began to ask how they could go with me.

In the meantime, Timothy planned to come to America and asked if I could arrange a place for him to stay and some speaking opportunities. We arranged for him and Janepher to stay at a beautiful oceanfront resort in Islamorada.

We wanted them to have the trip of their lives. I had great fun exposing Timothy to some foods that I knew he would probably never have eaten in Uganda. We went to a local restaurant, and I ordered a round of alligator as an appetizer. Timothy couldn't believe it and ate about half a bite. I am sure he couldn't separate the alligator on the menu from crocs in the Nile. At another meal, I ordered some calamari (squid for you landlubbers). After a while, it came to be that the only thing I could get Timothy to order from any menu was chicken. I continually tease him, "I go to Uganda and eat anything you put in front of me, and you come to America and will only eat chicken! There is something wrong with that!"

The trip turned out to be more than we could have ever expected, and it started with a simple gift from a child.

Here is how it came about. One morning I was showing Timothy around the school at our church. He would greet each class and talk about the children of Uganda. As we left a third-grade classroom, one of the third graders came running down the hall after us with a twenty-dollar bill in his hand.

He handed it to Timothy and said, "Today is my birthday, my parents gave me this as a present. I want you to have it." It was one of the few times that I have seen Timothy's eyes tear up. He thanked the young man who turned and went back to his class, and we proceeded to the other classes.

That Sunday, the student and his mom and dad were in church as Timothy presented his ministry and its needs. After the service, they asked if we could join them at their home. When we arrived, they said they wanted to help with his orphanage and the people of the village. They then proceeded to demonstrate enormous generosity. They gave enough money to build an entire concrete educational building, stock a medical clinic, buy a personal computer, and iPad for Timothy. They also paid for a water system that supplied not only the orphanage, but also the village with clean water.

Sidebar: Timothy tells a chilling story of how before the water system was installed that two orphans had gone to Lake Victoria to draw water. As they gathered the water, they were attacked and eaten by crocs. The chilling thing about the story was how matter-of-factly he told the story. Death in Uganda is such a common thing. In fact, most of the time you drive down a main road and look out the window, you see wooden, handmade furniture, intricately carved beds, couches, chairs, and tables. But in some districts, right there amid the furniture, you see handmade wooden coffins being sold like furniture. Death is just too frequent for these people!

In August 2012, I had the honor of traveling back to Uganda with the father and the young son who had given that original gift.

I was a bit nervous taking a young child to Uganda with me, but he was very determined, and his mom and dad were both in agreement that it would be a good experience for him. This family has been very generous, and this trip was no exception.

The father booked our flights in business class. The comfort of traveling business class for a trip that takes so long was a real pleasure.

But I had a reality check when I looked up the cost. My trips will be economy class as long as I'm buying the ticket! I did not feel that having the father and son staying at "Hotel California" was a good idea. I booked our rooms at the Collene Resort. The same resort I had visited to make contact with Colleen on the first trip. This was the resort where the Disco Man had taken me. It was the best resort I had seen in Mukono. It is where heads-of-state and dignitaries stay while in this region of Uganda. I thought it would be a safe place for us to lodge if it was affordable. I was shocked when I got the quote for the rooms 170,500 Ugandan shillings! Then I did the conversion–$45.64 US dollars. Needless to say, I booked our rooms.

We arrived on Friday morning, August 24, 2012. Timothy and his team gave us a warm greeting at the airport. I noticed that Timothy's energy level (always high!) didn't seem to be quite as perky as usual. I asked if he was okay. He told me that he had malaria but went on as if that was an everyday event.

We settled in at the Collene Resort, and then off we went for a very full day of activities. The first order of business was to travel the dusty, bumpy road from Mukono to Katosi. In these first trips, the roads were barely passable in some places, so it took nearly an hour to make the approximately 20-mile ride. No ride at Disney would give you more thrills than this one!

Our first stop in Katosi was at Winners Children's Home and School, to get our first glimpse of the new building, the water system, and the clinic.

The first look at the educational building that they had named Wilsie House (more about that later) and the water system was impressive. It was clear that these projects had been worked on right up to the time of our arrival.

In fact, in some areas, the water stations that had been built still had wet concrete.

Timothy took us to each of the additions and expressed great gratitude at each stop. After our private tour, we headed to our next event.

Timothy had also set up a grand Children's Day celebration.

It was interesting as we pulled up to a large gated compound, we could hear children singing and cheering. The gate opened, and as we pulled in, children came running to the van. The cheers continued for several minutes. We were greeted by several adults and then swarmed by children.

They especially wanted to get next to and talk to an American child. The questions were coming rapid-fire, and he handled himself like a seasoned pro. At one point, I looked over at him, and he was sitting on a chair and was surrounded on all sides by children of all ages. One older girl seemed to be their spokesperson. She was asking questions that seemed to be the questions the entire group wanted to know: Can you dance? What kind of music do you like?

Can you rap? I was amazed at how much like American kids these kids on the other side of the world were. They had obviously had at least a Hollywood version exposure to what American culture was like.

Timothy informed us that as guests, the three of us were going to serve lunch to all the children. We were escorted to a small room with large pots full of rice, beans, and a stew-like mix of vegetables and fish from Lake Victoria. The children lined up in what looked like a never-ending line. Each of us was given a large serving ladle. As the children stood in front of us, they would hold out their plate, and we each would scoop a serving of whichever food item we had been designated to serve. I ended up in front of the fish stew pot, and things were going well, until I scooped a big serving of stew up and the spoon was so heavy that I could barely pull it out of the pot. I looked down, and there was a giant fish head staring back at me. I mean GIANT – gills, mouth open, teeth showing, eyeballs bulging fish head! I dropped it back in the pot and told my traveling companion that I thought it was his turn to serve fish stew!

After we finished serving the children, we were escorted to a large guest table. We were served fish stew as the children sat in front of us. These children were remarkable. They were so eager to show what they had learned and to present what they had prepared.

Their faces radiated a joy that can't be described. In the midst of extreme poverty, these children have found joy. It is a joy not found in stuff, but the joy of being alive and cared for. It is a joy found in dependence on one another. One little girl especially got my attention. She was very tiny, probably much smaller than her age, and her face was severely scarred. She had somewhat of a permanent sardonic smile. She made eye contact with me with a

Trip #2: Generous Gifts and Damalie's Dream

look that showed great sorrow and a hollowness that wasn't seen in the other children. Her look said, "Is there nothing you can do to help?"

We were never able to communicate verbally, but it was the moment that I began to make plans to bring medical personnel with me whenever I had the chance. As I watched the other children interact with this little girl, I noticed something else about them. They were very purposeful about looking after each other. They seemed to be protective of her and made sure she had food and that no one took advantage of her. I asked Timothy what had happened to her. He said it was a sad story. As an infant, she had fallen into an open cooking fire and had nearly burned to death.

After that, she was neglected and abandoned by her family. That is how she ended up under the care of Winners Home.

(Side note–I have looked for this child on subsequent trips when I have had a doctor with me but have not seen the child since this day at the celebration.)

As we ate, they presented various songs, reading, and dramas, and Timothy explained all that was going to take place over the next few days. I've learned, though, that that can change at any moment and usually does. I've also learned that when you think the day is over and you are going to call it an evening, there will often be a few more tasks in Timothy's plan. This day was no exception. As we were getting ready to climb back in our van for our next adventure, I noticed a young teenage girl acting a bit sneaky. She was not doing anything wrong, but I saw that she was working her way closer and closer to the dad traveling with me. More out of curiosity than anything else, I kept an eye on what might be taking place.

She pulled my friend down so she could whisper to him. She was attempting to get his information in a way that was not acceptable in Ugandan culture. At best, it would have most certainly meant a continual appeal for money, and at worst, an uninvited house guest showing up at your front door one day. One of the most challenging things to deal with emotionally is that you regularly feel a little one tugging on your pant leg. As you look down, there is this sweet face looking back at you, saying, "Please take me with you."

In the case of this young woman, it was not the case, and Timothy spotted her. His bark was sharper than most of the times I've heard him speak to one of the orphans. It was an indication that she was attempting to do something completely unacceptable in their culture. She ran away, knowing that she had crossed a dangerous line.

As time goes on, you began to get a feel for these kinds of appeals. It comes from children and adults alike. You can almost sense it as they approach you. You see it in their body language; you see it in their eyes. They tend to sort of slither or shuffle toward you, speak in low, secretive tones, and tend to look down or away rather than make direct eye contact. I must confess I have fallen victim to these appeals more than once and will surely do so in the future.

All in all, the Children's Day was beautiful and was a full day in itself, but before we headed back to Mukono, I wanted the father and son to get a chance to see the waterfront and the fishing industry associated with it. Since we live in a fishing community ourselves, I thought it would be interesting for them to see and experience this part of the culture. Katosi is a fishing village dependent on Lake Victoria and its health. The interesting thing is that the largest fish in the lake is the Nile perch. It is not native to the lake; it is an invasive species and is creating a problematic environmental imbalance. When you think of perch, forget the North American version. When you think of Nile perch, think giant tarpon, or bass on steroids or goliath grouper! They can grow to over 400 pounds! A 400-pound fish consumes a lot of other little fish, and that's a big problem.

Hoisting a huge Nile perch onto the scales at the fish market

One of the most important catches is the "silver fish" in English, *mukene*, in Lugandan (sounds cooler in Lugandan!); the mukene sold to humans are spread on a table or a cloth to dry. Those sold for animals are spread out on the ground. These get mixed in with beans and rice and are a major source of protein for people and animals.

Tilapia is also found in abundance in the lake and is probably the more sustainable fish for the future as necessary conservation steps are taken to preserve the long-term future of the lake. But conservation and fisheries science are not very high on the radar of people just trying to stay alive day-to-day.

The day that I took the photo of the enormous Nile perch, I heard a man shouting in a billowing, demanding voice, "No! No!" He was looking directly at me and obviously wanted no pictures taken of whatever was taking place at the market. I have often wondered what was going on that he didn't want to be photographed. As I teach the teachers and administrators in the conferences each year, I try to slip in as many conservation and good fisheries examples as I can. More than anything else, that is because of my marine science background. I recognize how vital conservation is to the survival of the lake. If I can convince the teachers of the importance of preserving the lake, (and therefore the Nile), they can teach the children, and the children can lead the change needed for the future of the lake. I asked Timothy one time if they had any fishing regulations that governed the catch. He looked at me like I was speaking a completely foreign language to him. I said, "You know like catch limits, or season limits, or size limits, or fishing technique regulations – mesh net size, size of the nets?" I was caught off guard by his response, "I am not sure the people would allow that." Interestingly, Timothy's brother is now the Minister of Tourism, Antiquities, and Wildlife. We have had several interesting conversations that I hope will eventually make a difference.

Here are some numbers to help us understand the importance of this. More than thirty million people in Tanzania, Kenya, and Uganda rely on the lake for its natural resources. Lake Victoria is the largest lake in Africa and the chief reservoir of the Nile. Its area is 26,828 square miles. It is the second-largest freshwater lake in the world, exceeded only by Lake Superior. The fishery industry represents a major source of revenue for the nations that surround the lake. They are a substantial source of employment for 3 million people who are directly involved in fishing. There is also considerable support for the subsidiary fisheries industry, fish processing, fish trade, boat building, net making, fishing equipment, fisheries research, etc.

The annual fish catch from Lake Victoria is about 750,000 metric tons, generating more than $400 million US dollars; almost 500 billion Uganda shillings per year. More than half of that ($250 million) comes from exporting fish and fish products out of this region of Africa.

As we stood at the water's edge, I noticed more boats and people milling around, climbing on boats, or getting out of boats as they beached.

I asked Timothy why there were so many people. He told me that they were people living on the islands coming to shore to go to town to buy supplies.

That was my first introduction to the Lake Victoria islands and the people who live on them.

Island people coming ashore to buy supplies.

Some of the boats are over-loaded with 15 or 20 people.

There are more than three thousand islands on the lake. One is a floating island that literally floats around on the lake with a full population of fishermen living on it. Another island, Migingo, is about the size of half a football (soccer) pitch (field). To no surprise, its inhabitants are fishermen. It is estimated to be the third most populated place on Planet Earth. This tiny island is home to at least 131 inhabitants, with some estimates ranging much higher.

Tiny Migingo Island with a large population

Now, back to our trip. As we headed back toward the Collene, Timothy said, "I think we should go do another radio show." So, off we went, past the Collene, through Mukono, into the incredibly busy streets of Kampala, back toward the radio station I had visited on trip #1. Some of the sights and sounds of this massive city are difficult to view. Crippled, mutilated bodies left over from Idi Amin's terror or the LRA (that you will read about later) are seen begging nearly everywhere. There are times that there are so many people pressing in on the streets that traffic can't move. You have to roll your windows up so that someone won't reach in and snatch a camera or phone or purse.

At one point, while the traffic was moving well and our windows were rolled down, we began to smell one of the most horrific smells I have ever encountered. I started looking around, unsure of what I would see that could create such a scent. As we drove through a roundabout, I looked over and spotted the cause. There was an open truck loaded, no, overloaded, with huge carcasses of some kind. At first, I was horrified because I saw what appeared to be protruding tusks from a truckload of flesh and hide pile. I thought, "Oh, no! Those are elephant or Rhino tusks! Are these poachers smuggling ivory in the middle of Kampala in broad daylight?" It turned out that they were the remains of several giant ox that had been butchered. I am not sure where the remains were going, but I will never forget that smell!

Kampala is the capital of Uganda and is by far the most populated city. No matter the time of the day or night, there are thousands of people on the streets. It isn't very easy to get accurate numbers. However, it is estimated that there are between 1.75 and 2.4 million people that call Kampala home. That's about 8,400 people per square mile.

The sheer density of the population creates problems that we never seem to have to face in America. Each year that I go to

Uganda, and the more I study, the more complex I realize the problems really are. Before we continue our journey to the radio station, let me share some facts and recommend an important book to you that will help you get a better view of this. I believe that many Americans come to Uganda and have on rose-colored glasses. I certainly know I did and still do, to some degree.

But here are some of the hard facts from UNICEF and my own observations that may help us take those glasses off or at least lighten the hue:

- Only one in five primary school teachers are competent in English and math. Yet English is the official language.
- 60% of teachers are not in school teaching.
- Only 16% of secondary-aged children are in school.
- More than half of the children 5-7 years of age are working.
- On average, schools have only one latrine per 70 pupils.
- Two-thirds of schools have no hand washing facilities.
- 58% of 15–19-year-old young women have experienced physical or sexual violence.
- The median age in Uganda is 15.7 years of age. More than 50% of the population is below the age of 14.
- More than 50% of the population live on less than $1.00 per day. The per capita income averages $240.
- Child abduction and mutilation still occur far too often.
- "Night commuters" is the name given to children who must sneak out of their mud huts just as nightfall is descending on them. They then cautiously walk in groups to a more densely populated town or city. Why? Because armed men come into their homes and snatch them. Some of these children are never seen again.[5]

Look at this quote from Paul Raffaele in Smithsonian Magazine:

Around the time of my trip to northern Uganda this past November, some 21,000 night commuters trudged each twilight into Gulu, and another 20,000, aid workers said, flocked into the town of Kitgum, about 60 miles away. The children, typically bedding down on woven mats they'd brought with them, packed themselves into tents, schools, hospitals and other public buildings serving as makeshift sanctuaries that were funded by foreign governments and charities and guarded by Ugandan Army soldiers.

The children were hiding from the Lord's Resistance Army (LRA), a murderous cult that has been fighting the Ugandan government and terrorizing civilians for nearly two decades. Led by Joseph Kony, a self-styled Christian prophet believed to be in his 40s, the LRA has captured and enslaved more than 20,000 children, most under age 13, U.N. officials say. Kony and his foot soldiers have raped many of the girls—Kony has said he is trying to create a "pure" tribal nation—and brutally forced the boys to serve as guerrilla soldiers. Aid workers have documented cases in which the LRA forced abducted children to ax or batter their own parents to death. The LRA has also killed or tortured children caught trying to escape.[6]

Further, into the article, Raffaele relates this chilling account:

The Children of War Rehabilitation Center, a facility run by World Vision, an international Christian charity, was hidden behind high shuttered gates and walls studded with broken glass. Inside, one-story buildings and tents filled the small compound. At the time of my visit, 458 children were awaiting relocation. Some kicked a soccer ball, some skipped rope, others passed the time performing traditional dances. I saw about 20 children who were missing a leg and hobbling on crutches. One could tell the most recent arrivals by their shadowy silences, bowed heads, haunted stares, and bone-thin bodies disfigured by sores. Some had been captured or rescued only days earlier when Ugandan Army helicopter gunships attacked the rebel unit holding them. Jacqueline Akongo, a counselor at the center, said the most deeply scarred children are those whom Kony had ordered, under penalty of death, to kill other children. But virtually all the children are traumatized. "The others who don't kill by themselves see people being killed, and that disturbs their mind so much," Akongo told me.[6]

The book mentioned earlier that helped me get a more in-depth view of some of the struggles in Uganda is, *The Garden of the Lost and Abandoned, The Extraordinary Story of One Ordinary Woman and the Children She Saves,* by Jessica Yu, published by Houghton Mifflin Harcourt Publishing in 2019. I try to get all of those who travel with me to read this book. It is the true story of Gladys Kalibbala, a newspaper reporter for New Vision newspapers in Kampala who has given herself for decades now to rescuing lost and abandoned children.

We arrived at the radio station late because the traffic had been so backed up in Kampala. I am not sure how it all works in Uganda, but the radio producers didn't seem to miss a beat. They had us seated with headsets on and microphones in our faces. Timothy acted as a host and greeted us and asked each of us a series of questions designed to encourage children to stay in school.

The father that had accompanied me handled himself like a seasoned pro, saying all the things the Ugandan listeners needed to hear. Timothy talked about the benefits and advantages of becoming a member of IACCS/UCCSU and the teacher training I was going to do later in the week. I got to speak and talked about the importance of Christian education for the future of the nation of Uganda. I then used that to give the Gospel and the new life that can be found in Christ. I also tried to encourage the teachers, especially those teaching out in remote villages with no equipment, and sometimes no walls, in over-crowded conditions. I told them that they were doing remarkable jobs. They were making an immeasurable difference in the lives of the children under their care, and American teachers could learn some valuable lessons from them. The radio show ended, and as we were walking out, I once again asked Timothy about the number of listeners. He gave the same answer, "Six to eight million." I often do this double ask, to make sure Timothy's numbers are accurate from year to year. It is challenging to get accurate statistics in Uganda, so numbers are often rough guesses.

We finally returned to the Collene, grabbed a late dinner with Timothy, and talked about the events of the next day. This was going to be a very big day. This would be a day of celebration as we dedicated all of these projects.

Saturday morning came quickly. We were picked up by a driver and started the bumpy, dusty ride to Katosi. When we arrived, we pulled through the front gate of Winners Home, where there were several brightly colored tents and banners spread all across the grounds. People were lined up, cheering and singing and welcoming us. I would guess there were over a thousand people there to celebrate this day of dedication. The first part of the celebration was for the water system. The system consisted of a deep water well, with water pumped to the surface with a large electric pump. There was a concrete room built around the pump system, and on top of the room sat a large holding tank. From the pump room ran underground pipes that came up to watering stations throughout the compound. There were also pipes running through the fence into the community to provide water for the people of Katosi. Remember, this came about because Timothy told the chilling tale of two orphans being killed by crocodiles while gathering water from the lake.

The water system providing water for Winners Home and the village.

Trip #2: Generous Gifts and Damalie's Dream

After the dedication of the water system, we moved down the steep hill that is part of the landscape inside the compound of Winners Home. As you stop at the top of the rise and look out toward the beauty of Lake Victoria, it is easy to forget that you are standing inside a facility that cares for nearly a thousand children; children that would have little or no hope were it not for the vision of the Kakooza's and the staff at Winners. When we got to the bottom of the hill, the celebration amped up even more. The drums, the singing, the ever-present sound of the high shrill cheer that seems to come from Ugandan women when they want to express extreme joy or praise. I think it is some unique combination of the rolling of the tongue near the speed of light and vibrating on the roof of the mouth – just a guess.

This part of the celebration was the dedication of the beautiful education building. It is one of the finest buildings in any of the school/orphanages we have visited. The blessing was that it was paid for through the generosity of this father and son team and their mother. We gathered on the concrete porch that ran the length of a row of classrooms.

There was a ribbon tied to the pillars and a brass dedication plaque with the name Wilsie House, mounted to the wall. There is a wonderful/sad/humorous story behind the naming of this building. Wilsie House was named after the mother of the wife of the family that had given so generously. Hopefully, I am remembering all of the details of the story correctly.

Apparently, the grandfather was somewhat of a drinker and would go on extended binges. He would be gone from the home for extended periods, then come home, his wife would be with child, and off he would go again. Each time the wife would ask her husband what she wanted to name the baby. On this occasion, the grandfather came home, had been drinking, and when the wife handed the new baby to him and asked, "What do you want to call our new daughter?" I guess he had run out of names or that he couldn't think clearly through the fog, so he looked at the baby and said, "We'll see." His wife, in perhaps a spiteful mood, named their new baby, Wilsie! Now every time I go to Uganda and look at the beautiful building erected in her honor, I break into a smile and thank God for this great gift and the other gifts that this family has provided.

There were dignitaries from all over Uganda and from a variety of professions gathered for this day of dedication. There were representatives from the education department, government cabinet members, bishops, pastors, school administrators, teachers, and children; oh were there ever children! The children were so excited, running, dancing, singing all in celebration of the new school building. It seems that when one person gets blessed in Uganda, everyone gets blessed.

The Wilsie House, a truly magnificent addition

As with most Ugandan celebrations, they go on for several hours. Usually, the thing that ends the party is the setting sun and people wanting to travel home before dark. As this celebration went on, there is an unfortunate twist in the story that clouded things a bit. The ceremony had settled into a series of Ugandan celebrations that the father/son team nor I were particularly a part of. I suggested that we escape for a few minutes and go check out the clinic to see what work had been completed there. We walked up the hill, past the classrooms, and dormitories through the front gate and water tanks to the clinic. The clinic is directly across a dirt road from the school. As I approached the clinic, I became concerned.

The clinic was actually in much worse shape than it had been the year before.

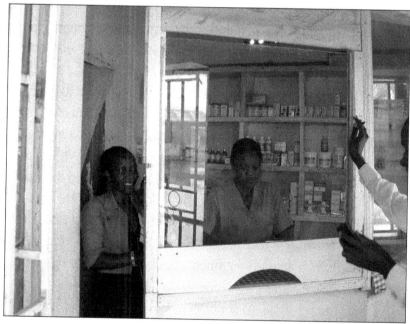

TRIP #2: GENEROUS GIFTS AND DAMALIE'S DREAM

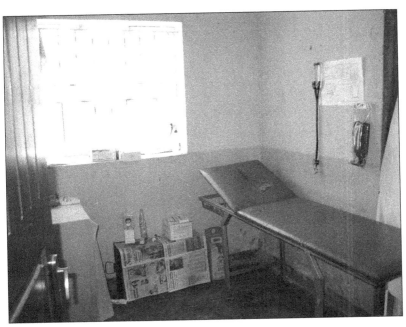

The Clinic. Some years good, other years not so good

I did not say anything but knew that the dad that had given so much was noticing the lack of use and condition of the facility. I thought, "Well, they just must not have had time to complete the project."

As we were walking down an exterior hallway, we were startled by a large bunch of bats that came swooping out of a hole in the ceiling. I wondered if there would be any conversation about this later. There was, but I will explain when we get to that part of the story.

It had been a long day, and I was not looking forward to the long, hot, dusty ride back to Mukono. About the time I was thinking about the journey, Timothy approached me and asked if we minded riding back to the Collene with his brother. This was the same brother who was the Minister of Tourism, Wildlife, and Antiquities for the nation of Uganda. He was important enough in the Ugandan government that he went nowhere without an armed guard. I thought it was an opportunity to talk with him about fish conservation issues on the lake. I also wanted to lobby for the protection of their jungles. The sugar cane growers were trying to convince the government to allow them to cut huge sections out of the jungle to produce more sugar. As one who has watched firsthand the destruction of the natural environment of South Florida, I could speak with some authority on not allowing that to happen. I told him about how the Florida Everglades and the Florida Bay were in real peril.

I explained how food chains were being destroyed and how the economy and infrastructure of all of South Florida were so dependent on the health of these two major ecosystems. Nearly every year since, we have had continuing conversations about this. I marveled at how only God could orchestrate such a meeting. When his car arrived to pick us up, it was like icing on the cake. His car was a brand-new Toyota Land Cruiser, with AC! It was a very comfortable, enjoyable, productive ride.

The next morning was Sunday, and I wondered how my traveling companions were going to do with this enthusiastic, very non-American church service. When we arrived, I realized that this was more than the usual service I had experienced the year before. The women always dressed in beautiful Uganda dresses known as *busuuti* or more formal dresses known as *gomesi*. The men wear suits, and for more formal celebrations they typically wear a long white robe known as a kanzu, with a sports jacket usually blue or black. When you see men dressed in this traditional wear you know that you are in a big event.

This Sunday morning, we were in for a very, very big celebration based on the dress of the crowd. As we walked up the steep hill toward the church, you could hear singing and praying coming out of the church, filling the surrounding area. As we approached the building, I noted that it had a layer of plaster, a fresh coat of paint, and the old wooden ramp leading up to the entrance had been replaced with concrete stairs. These changes will lead to an issue that we will discuss late in the chapter, but for now, let the celebration begin! We walk into singing and cheering. As I looked around the large sanctuary, I saw many familiar faces from the year before. But the room was also packed with people I didn't recognize. I soon learned that many of the unfamiliar faces were bishops and pastors from around the region and members of their congregations. There was another group that represented dignitaries from around the Southern Ugandan districts. Like the day before, this was a special day of dedication. The service was a lengthy one, because a number of the guests spoke, including all three of us as guest Mzungus. It seemed that half of Southern Uganda knew about the gifts that this generous family had given and wanted to express their gratitude.

Each time that I have gone to Uganda, I have been asked to speak at the Sunday morning service. There was no exception, even though there were several other speakers scheduled to talk. Before it was my turn to speak, one of the elderly bishops got up, and beginning in Genesis, did a preaching tour of the entire Bible. Rarely have I heard a better proclaiming of God's faithfulness and goodness to His people. I was blown away by this man's knowledge of Scripture and his ability to recall such rapid-fire vivid detail of so much of the Bible. I was in awe, and then it was my turn to speak.

Suddenly I felt inadequate to even stand at the pulpit after the bishop's eloquent oratory. But as I was getting up, I received a Holy Spirit nudge to remind me of who I was serving, who I was to speak for and to allow Him to lead. In other words, get your eyes off yourself and focus on God! These are the exact words I delivered that morning:

You are my heroes. You inspire me every day of my life. In the Book of Acts, when the first churches were forming, I believe they looked much like your churches here in Uganda. The Acts 2 Church is the hope of the world! You are the hope of Uganda! When the local church is doing what it is supposed to do, there is nothing better!

If that sounds a lot like what I said the first year, it is. It is because I believe that about Ugandan churches so strongly.

Take the biblically-functioning church out of Uganda (or any other part of the world for that matter), and I can't imagine what a mess it would be.

After talking about the Acts 2 Church, I shifted to the Old Testament. I spoke about the rebuilding of the wall around Jerusalem by Nehemiah. I used the passage Nehemiah 4:2-6:

> *Now when Sanballat heard that we were building the wall, he was angry and greatly enraged, and he jeered at the Jews. And he said in the presence of his brothers and of the army of Samaria, "What are these feeble Jews doing? Will they restore it for themselves? Will they sacrifice? Will they finish up in a day? Will they revive the stones out of the heaps of rubbish, and burned ones at that?" Tobiah the Ammonite was beside him, and he said, "Yes, what they are building—if a fox goes up on it he will break down their stone wall!" Hear, O our God, for we are despised. Turn back their taunt on their own heads and give them up to be plundered in a land where they are captives. Do not cover their guilt, and let not their sin be blotted out from your sight, for they have provoked you to anger in the presence of the builders.*

So we built the wall. And all the wall was joined together to half its height, **for the people had a mind to work.**

The last phrase was the point of emphasis, **for the people had a mind to work.** I talked about how IACCS and the UCCSU could impact Uganda if the people have a mind to work. I tried to paint a picture of what the future of Uganda could look like if the church and these associations continue to train more and more boys and girls for Christ. As they become adults, the training they have received and the principles of integrity they put in place would quite literally change the nation of Uganda.

Knowing that there were probably several individuals who did not regularly attend church, I closed the message by carefully explaining the Gospel. And then asked for a response to the invitation to receive Christ as personal Savior. I am never sure whether it is just Ugandan politeness or if they didn't understand what I was asking when hands all over the room shoot up. Or, maybe they truly understood how much God loved them and accepted His forgiveness for the first time.

The service ended, and we moved just outside the main door. There was a concrete landing and then the stairs. There were no guardrails, and there were so many people so tightly jammed in in this little space that I was concerned someone was going to fall to their death (or at least serious injury)! The drop-off from the platform was at least seven or eight feet, and then if someone fell, they would probably tumble down the hill. It didn't seem to concern anyone else; and we uncovered a plaque dedicating the church, and then several of the dignitaries prayed. I noticed at this dedication that the dad that had given so much did not seem overly impressed by this ceremony. I could almost read his mind: "Let's see, church newly plastered and painted, stairs completed, clinic run-down and in disrepair...I bet my money went to fix up the church at the expense of the clinic!" He is a gracious and polite man, so he didn't say anything at that time, however. I didn't say anything either, but I did file it away in my mind as a concern and wondered if a discussion might take place later on.

The next morning, we were up early and ready to go visit schools and orphanages. I had really been looking forward to this day because I hoped the father and son would experience what had so touched my heart the year before.

They had seen the pictures and heard me talk about Chosen Generation and so I was excited that this was going to be our first stop. The road/path had gotten no better since the first trip. We drove in as far as we could drive, and I said, "Okay, we just have to hike another ten miles through the jungle!" Father and son said in unison, "What!" I smiled and said, "No, it's just up the hill." It made that climb seem so much shorter, and I didn't bother mentioning anything about Black Mambas.

When we got to the top of the hill, it was silent. No sound of children in classes, no children running up to greet us. Instead of them lined up in rows in a classroom, there was a stack of wooden benches and desk piled under a tree!

The place was empty, only a child or two running about. I asked Timothy, "Timothy, what's going on? Where are the children?" It was then that I began to learn what the meaning of the word "orphan" means in Uganda as compared to the United States. Timothy explained that they were generally in school for three months and off a month. I was confused. I asked, "If there are orphans, how can they be off a month with no place to stay, no food, no one to care for them?" I pictured children fending for themselves and living in the jungle. Timothy explained that many "orphans" actually had a family – aunts and uncles, grandparents, older siblings, and some even had a parent. But for a variety of reasons, they could not care for the child.

They had to come to the orphanage, or they could very well be abandoned. The one month off allowed the orphanages to make necessary repairs, or gather supplies, raise funds, and have a little breathing room to survive. Since then, I've learned that the meaning of family is very different in Uganda. It is prevalent to have your own children, but if you take other children in, they are often called your children as well. A person that is called "mother" or "father" may be an aunt or uncle, or not related at all

(for example, I have a Ugandan pastor who calls me his father and refers to himself as my son. He is probably 50 years old, but he insists on referring to us in this way. You will read more about this "son" in later chapters).

I noticed that the dad who was with me seemed a bit skeptical, and I think he wondered, even though not too seriously if this was all some kind of scam. I tried to reassure him that the school really was full of children last year.

The good news was that in the days that followed we did go to regions where there were plenty of children in the schools.

I love these days because we travel from orphanage/school to orphanage/school (the reason I keep using "orphanage/school" is that some of the orphanages have schools, and some do not. Most of the schools that we visit have some orphans). As we travel through the jungle, past homes and small villages, the sights and sounds are endless. There were two stops in particular that left lasting impressions in all of us. The first one took us deep into the jungle. There have been a few times that we have gotten so far off the beaten path that it has left an uneasy feeling. Will we see lions? Or Kony's Army? Or unfriendly witch doctors? Or...This was one of those times. Your mind starts playing weird tricks on you. Actually, I think it is fear planted by the Evil One. You began to question whether you can trust the people who have brought you into the jungle, and dozens of other lies.

We had to walk some distance along a dirt trail until we arrived at a makeshift structure. It was not a building, but more of a shelter made of poles tied together with vine rope and pieces of plastic covering the roof and sides.

Timothy explained that this orphanage was run by a woman whose husband had died. She had absolutely nothing but was doing everything she could to care for these children. As we were speaking, a sweet, elderly woman approached. As she stood in front of Timothy, she bowed in a humbling posture that I spoke of earlier. Timothy did something that I have seen him do over and over. He reached in his pocket, pulled out a wad of money, and handed it to her to help her with her needs. The photo below shows the gratitude and humility of this sweet lady. Just imagine what this lady's life must be like living in a remote part of the jungle as a widow, caring for a group of orphans as they are brought to her. When I start to think that life or ministry is tough, I often think about this dear lady.

TRIP #2: GENEROUS GIFTS AND DAMALIE'S DREAM

Uganda widow kneeling in a way Ugandans show honor. Running an orphanage in the jungle by herself.

A second stop that left an impression on all of us was at an orphanage for abandoned babies. It was Sangaalo Babies Home. The young lady who looked like a teenager (but was not), was Damalie Nahyuha Kimuli.

When Damalie was 9-years old, she began to take care of her siblings. She had to leave school to provide care for them. She talked about how she had been angry at having to leave school, but swore that one day she would have a home where babies were loved and cared for. Looking back, she says, "It was the hand of God directing me to my calling." She told how she got a job in a children's home, worked there for 9 years, and was mentored and trained by the lady running the center. She said, "My desire is to obey God. I prayed and asked Him to give me the name. And He did." Sangaalo Babies Home because the name Sangaalo means "joy." She took us to an area where some of her helpers were sitting, caring for several babies. She pointed to one that I will never forget. As she told the story about this child, we all stood with tears running down our faces.

She said, "That one (nodding toward a tiny child in red and white baby clothes), her mother tried to kill her by drowning her in a tub. But the baby wouldn't die. So, she then took the baby and put her on the street to die. The police found her and brought her to me to care for. She was born HIV-positive, so the mother did not want her." Damalie went on to tell us that she currently cared for 15 abandoned babies.

You could hear the joy in her voice and see it in her countenance.

She also said one of the most impactful things that has benefited nearly a hundred different orphanages that care for infants.

She talked about how she was proud of the fact that the home was self-sustaining. She spoke of the things they grew in their garden and the chickens and eggs they were raising. She said they were able to sell the surplus to get money for the orphans. I asked, "What would help you be more self-sustaining? What are your biggest needs? "Her answer was simple, but it launched an entire side ministry that I have had the honor of assisting in. Without a moment of hesitation, she replied, "Milk for the babies." I asked, "How could you best do that?" She confidently replied, "With a cow." "You could feed and maintain a cow?" I asked. She smiled and said, "Oh, yes." I repeated the question to make sure I hadn't misunderstood, "A cow?!" You can you care for a cow? What would you do with a cow?" (I wanted to make sure that it was not just going to become a steak dinner) She explained that the milk would be one of the most life-sustaining foods that the babies could receive. I was thrilled that she was thinking beyond the immediate (eating the cow) to the long-term benefits of having the cow. On a later trip, I would learn how much a single cow could

Trip #2: Generous Gifts and Damalie's Dream

provide. I will share it now and probably again in a later chapter because the impact is so significant.

Here is the math several of the Ugandan caregivers explained to me.

A healthy cow produces about 10 liters of milk in the morning and 7 liters of milk in the evening. The milk is cut three to one with a mix of water, rice, and sugar, and each baby gets one-half a liter a day. Unless my math is faulty (17 liters X 4 = 68 liters. If each baby gets ½ liter, 68 X 2 = 136 babies receiving life-sustaining nourishment), a single cow is providing food for over 100 babies a day!

I didn't know these numbers at the time that Damalie told me about needing a cow, but I still thought it was a great idea.

I told her that when I got back to America, I would see if there was any way to get a cow for her.

I asked Timothy how much he thought we could get a good milk cow for. He said, "About a $1,000 if we have to transport it" (I have since learned how to get that price down).

It was in those moments that the "Cow Project," as we now call it, was birthed. We didn't know that was happening until we got back to the States, and friend and now fellow Ugandan traveler Peter Reynolds offered to give a $1000 gift for the first cow. There will be much more about Pete in a later chapter.

Damalie Nahyuha Kimuli and her babies

A somber side note before we leave Damalie and her babies. The little one who had been born HIV-positive and her mother had tried to kill, passed away within the year following our visit. I asked Damalie what had happened, and she said that the baby had been through too much and her immune system was so low that she could not get strong enough to live.

This is another of the harsh realities of life and death in Uganda.

Diseases that would be serious in developed countries, but rarely fatal, are far too often the cause of death in developing and 3rd world countries. Look at the following numbers and let them sink in. In Uganda for children under five years of age these are some of the statistics:

Neonatal deaths account for 21%; nearly 20% die from malaria; 14% from diarrhea; 11% from pneumonia; and 4% dying from HIV/AIDS, the same as the number of children in this age category that die from injuries. Undernutrition contributes to more than one-third of all deaths. To help add to the understanding of the numbers, look at these figures:

In 2015, nearly 1,700,000 babies were born in Uganda. That's about 4,600 births everyday. Approximately 81 babies die each day before reaching the first month of life, and 96 stillbirths occur each day. Staggering numbers aren't they? This should serve as a call for every church in developed countries to step it up if we are to respond biblically to the call to "Love our neighbor as ourselves" (Matthew 22:39). Or, what if the Church in America really acted and looked like the Acts 2 Church we've been talking about? It might be the difference between just playing church and really being the Church! To help put this in perspective, think of it this way, which is more important, buying that latest piece of sound or lighting equipment, or providing resources that fall into the 911 category?

It was hard to leave Damalie and her babies, but we still had several more places to visit. We loaded back in the van. It had already been a long day, and remember, I mentioned at the beginning of the chapter that Timothy had malaria. He was struggling to have the energy necessary to keep the pace he was trying to keep. As I looked over at Timothy and the young man who had started all this with his gift back in Islamorada, they were both leaning on each other, sound asleep. I thought what a wonderful sight that was and how comfortable he was with this new friend from Uganda.

We got back to the Collene and were ready for a good night's sleep. My room was on the side of the hotel that was very quiet, but I found out very early the next morning that my father/son co-travelers had not had such a restful night.

Their room was just a few feet away from the main road going through Mukono. In addition to the endless gridlock of traffic, the people of Uganda can stay up all night. Apparently, there was a night club/bar that had speakers out on the street, directly under their room. After complaining to the front desk multiple times through the night, it became evident that there was absolutely nothing that the Collene could do. Apparently, there are absolutely no noise ordinances in Uganda; another reminder that we weren't in the USA.

With morning upon us, and a full schedule of activities, we grabbed our Ugandan breakfast. We had a second reminder that we weren't in America, at least not on American time! Ugandan time is very, very flexible. Events begin when the crowd shows up (and people usually keep showing up throughout the event). When you are given a time in the morning for departure, I have learned that your ride may arrive anytime except the designated time. I usually plan anywhere from thirty minutes to two hours later.

When Timothy arrived, he told us that we were going to visit a vocational center in the heart of town. He explained that the people who were being trained were women rescued off the streets of Mukono and Kampala. He described how they were being given the life skills that would allow them to have successful, safe jobs. I was very anxious to see such a place because it went along with the idea of helping people be self-sufficient and self-sustaining, as Damalie had talked about. We drove through busy streets with street vendors selling everything imaginable, from chicken-on-a-stick to soccer balls, shoes, and clothing of all types. I always have to chuckle at all the mannequins they hang clothes on. They are all white and look like they dropped out of a 1950's department store. I am sure there must be someone in some other country that has bought every old, worn-out mannequin from someplace where old mannequins are stashed away to die, and shipped them to Uganda.

After driving several miles, we parked the car along the road. Cars and boda boda zipped by so close that it was dangerous, even to open the door. You have to be very careful because all transportation is the opposite of what your intuition tells you to do. You tend always to look the wrong way and are in danger of getting run over! I usually only cross the road with a group of people (I figure if it works for fish to school up for safety, it will probably work for crossing the road. So far so good).

We walked across the street and made our way to a pole structure covered with green and yellow tarps right on the side of the road. There was a makeshift wooden A-frame sign that read, *You are Welcome to Shammah Vocational Institution*; named after one of the names of God given in the Hebrew Old Testament, Jehovah Shammah, meaning "the Lord is there."

On the Edge of Eden

Shammah Vocational Training Center

These ladies were being taught to be seamstresses and beauticians; both widely needed services in the busy cultural and population centers.

Many of the sewing machines were old Singer sewing machines with foot pedals to drive them.

They were exactly like the ones my grandmother used to use in the 1940s and '50s. In subsequent years, I have seen many of the training centers established and believe that they are giving many young ladies new skills for a better life.

An organization that I have come to respect in recent years is a microloan organization known as KIVA (KIVA.org). On their website, they state the following: *We envision a financially inclusive world where all people hold the power to improve their lives.* These are microloans that allow you to loan as little or as much as you care. You can select from a list of people all around the world who are trying to do just that, to improve their lives. I have never had a loan not repaid. I have always used the money to reinvest in an investment to another individual. It is certainly worth checking out their website. It is an easy way to make a real difference while still at home, and with a few dollars you can benefit generations to come.

From the vocational center, we went on to visit several more schools and orphanages on the way toward Jinja and the Source of the Nile. Timothy had told me about two schools in Jinja that he wanted us to visit.

As mentioned in the previous chapter, Jinja is a more affluent city than many in Uganda, and has been influenced by a steady tourist trade. As we pulled up to the front gate of this school, it was clear that they had benefited from being more resourced than many of the organizations we had visited. The facilities of this school, called Dayspring School, were all constructed of concrete or brick and were freshly painted. The students were on break, but the teachers were gathered in different locations working on curriculum and lesson plans. I was very encouraged, and for the first time since coming to Uganda, felt like this school was ready to begin the rigors of going through IACCS accreditation.

The impressive Dayspring School

It was very evident that many of the staff and administration had received substantial formal educational training.

I would have enjoyed staying at Dayspring for several more hours, but we still had one more school to visit before we went to the Nile.

Timothy explained that this next program was an early education facility and that I would be impressed with their administrator.

Within the first five minutes of entering the school office, looking at the walls covered with handmade educational posters, and talking with the school administrator, it was clear that this lady knew early education and education theory better than most. This was a first-class program, just as Dayspring was, but geared for preschoolers. Any parent should be delighted to have their child attend. This is definitely another school that is close to being ready for accreditation.

An impressive early education expert serving in a remote part of the world.

As we visited the various schools and orphanages, something was becoming very clear. There was a huge need for basic teacher education in almost every village and district of Uganda. It was a validation of what my friend had told me on my last visit, and the motivation for providing his training center for teachers and nurses.

It was also becoming evident to me that we need to conduct educators conferences, Teaching Education 101, in as many districts as possible. The harsh reality was that teachers in remote areas had no access to formal educational training. They were doing the best they could in sort of self-taught environments.

If they did have formal training, they were usually hired away by schools in more substantial towns because they could earn larger salaries. This was setting the stage for what we were about to launch the next day. For the next two days, my traveling companions and I were going to go in different directions. The father and son were going to do some guided siteseeing. I was going to be conducting two days of Teaching Education 101 to a large gathering of teachers and administrators that had come together in Mukono. This would be the first ever UCCSU Christian Educators Conference.

The first day when I walked into the conference, I was greeted with a warm welcome and spotted several people I had met the year before or this year. I was astonished at the number. I would guess there were over 200 educators on this first day. In addition to all of the teachers and administrators, a film crew and news reporters were waiting to do an interview about this new association and the conference.

After interviewing me for several minutes, they made a statement that I have now heard several times while visiting Uganda, "You are changing the course of the nation of Uganda." I pray that is true. As I began to teach, there were a couple of undeniable things.

First, the teachers were very eager to learn. I had given them study sheets, and they took prolific notes. The second thing was that I had not overestimated the need for Education 101. We covered several key topics, such as curriculum development, building a scope and sequence, lesson plan formation, test and measurements, classroom management, and many more areas essential for an effective school. For many, this was the first exposure to formal training in education.

One of the challenges I face every time I speak in Uganda is preparing too much. Because a translator is restating everything I say, I have to learn to prepare half as much to say, and I have to really focus on how to say things succinctly. It has also become evident that American colloquiums, heroes, and illustrations won't work. I was trying to make a point that failure was not fatal, and I was going to use Walt Disney and Thomas Edison to make the point. As I started telling Walt Disney's story, I could tell from the blank stares that I was not connecting. They had no idea who Walt Disney was. There was a child in the room in a Mickey Mouse shirt. He saved the day; when I pointed to Mickey Mouse, they knew who he was. As for Edison, I had to point to a light bulb and explain his whole story. Fortunately, Edison was a cousin of Grandma Hammon, so I was pretty familiar with his story. I could get them to understand that he failed many times before he finally found the correct combinations in many of his inventions.

I once mentioned Michael Jordan – blank looks again. They did know Muhammad Ali and were very aware of Barack Obama. There were schools in very remote regions that had President Obama's picture posted with famous Africans.

If they had trouble recognizing the people I was using for illustration, can you imagine how colloquiums like, "where the rubber meets the road" came across?

There have been some pretty humorous moments when I forget that I am in Uganda and try to present American illustrations.

On the way to this conference, Timothy made two important stops for me personally. The first was to see a girl that I had known indirectly for several years. I had known Sharon from her picture that had been hanging on our refrigerator. We had been sponsoring her since 2011. Each year I try to see her and bring some small gifts (fast forward – Sharon has now graduated, no longer lives at Winners, and has started her adult life).

Meeting with Sharon and sharing some gifts and love.

This is probably a good place to take another sidebar to talk about sponsoring children in Uganda. The truth is, some organizations do a much better job actually attaching your gift to an individual child, but many of the orphanages are not nearly that well organized. In reality, when you sponsor a child in many of these ministries, you are merely making it possible for them to provide food or care for one more child. In other words, it is not going to a specific child, but to support a non-specified child. Are there ever abuses or misuse of dollars with this method? Probably, and that is why it is crucial to gain as much firsthand information about the ministry or organization as possible. There are several excellent and trusted international organizations that can be used if that is a concern to those giving. Here are just a few that I have used personally:

Samaritan's Purse–https://www.samaritanspurse.org
Compassion International–https://www.compassion.com
World Vision–https://www.worldvision.org
International Justice Mission–https://www.ijm.org

I have used each of these organizations and have found them to be very trustworthy.

Now, back to our travels. The second stop was to see the new UCCSU/IACCS office. It was good to see that the leadership was taking the advancement of the UCCSU seriously. I had pushed to have an office in the nation's capital to establish a presence and credibility.

Timothy proudly shows of the main office of the UCCSU

I taught for two days of the conference, with Pastor Timothy and Bernard adding to my content and making applications to Ugandan culture where I couldn't. It was very evident that UCCSU was gaining traction in Uganda and that it had the potential to do what the reporter had said – to change the course of the nation of Uganda.

The first UCCSU Christian Educators' Conference

During the two days while I was teaching, the father and son had the opportunity to see Kampala, do some shopping, and visit some other sites. The last day, they joined me for a few hours at the conference. Timothy used the opportunity to share with everyone at the convention how this young boy's birthday gift had been multiplied several times over to benefit the people of Uganda.

However, there were a couple of costly mistakes that I think were made on this trip. The first was the fact that the church had undergone so much remodeling, and the clinic was in such bad condition. It did not go unnoticed by the father traveling with me. He expressed his concerns about whether some of the money his family had given had been used in a way that had not been agreed to. I asked Timothy directly, and he assured me that the money had come from other sources and that the funds for the clinic was being used for some materials that had been ordered but had not come in yet.

This is one of those times that you have to accept the word of the person and then trust God to be the judge of all that took place. The dad had also commented that the concrete on the water stations was still wet. Meaning that he suspected that these projects had been completed in haste because we were coming. These issues planted a seed of skepticism in the mind of these very generous donors, and I believe it prevented further gifts from being given by them. The experience and learning from this have caused me to be as careful as I possibly can with the money we spend in Uganda. I try to send team members to always witness the purchases and ask for receipts on all purchases.

The other mistake that was made that I have made sure not to repeat in subsequent trips was that we went in the summer, and there were far fewer children in the orphanages. People traveling from America want to have firsthand ministry with as many children as possible.

One more comment about the clinic. It is still a work in progress (each year I have gone back, I have seen the clinic in various forms, and it is a work that needs continual attention). One of my greatest concerns for these outlying villages is that there is very little medical help with an adequate response distance and even fewer medical supplies. One of Pastor Timothy's many dreams is to get an ambulance for the village of Katosi, but that will only be the beginning of meeting the medical needs. On this second trip, my hope was to one day be able to bring a doctor or doctors and a medical team along on my trips to heighten their awareness of the medical needs, not just rural Africa, but all third world countries (as you will read in later chapters, that desire has come to fruition. A medical doctor and/or volunteers have joined our team the last three trips to work in the clinic alongside a young Ugandan doctor who visits the village regularly.)

As trip number two was coming to an end, I spent some time reflecting on all that had been accomplished on just this one trip.

- The completion of an entire educational building.
- A water system supplying not only an orphanage, but a whole village with life-giving water.
- The never-to-be-forgotten sweet inspiration from Damalie, which launched the Cow Project.
- The launch of the UCCSU Annual Christian Educators' Convention.
- The establishment of a UCCSU office.
- The radio broadcast reaching so many.
- The lengthy conversations with Timothy's brother, the Minister of Tourism, Wildlife, and Antiquities.
- Perhaps above all, to see the impact a trip like this can have on the life of a third-grade American child.

As we boarded the plane, I thanked the Lord for the gift of meeting and spending time with the precious children at each of the orphanages, and for the teachers who looked after them. I was grateful for this family, their gift and the impact it will have for the future of Uganda. It had been a truly successful and memorable trip.

CHAPTER 4
GOING TO AMERICA!

There are far, far better things ahead that anything we leave behind. - C.S. Lewis, "Collected Letters of C. S. Lewis" (2006)

On almost every IACCS trip, there is someone or several someones from the country I am visiting, who will be quick to tell me that they want to come to America. But on the 2012 trip, Timothy and several of the administrators talked seriously about coming to America to attend our annual FACCS Christian Educators' Convention held in October.

Initially, I thought it would probably be Timothy and Bernard who would attend, but the numbers kept growing. The final count was seven delegates. Many of the delegates had traveled to the US before and knew the routine well enough to get by. But that was not the case with all of them.

I worked with the leadership of UCCSU and told them that we would cover the cost of their rooms and meals for the days of the convention and wave all convention fees. We also planned to set up a booth and a display where the convention attendees could come and visit and get information on the ministries in Uganda. There was a scheduled time at the final general assembly where we would interview several of our Ugandan guests.

When the delegates finally all arrived to Orlando, there was one delegate missing. I asked what happened to the other delegate. They informed me that when the person had arrived in New York, there was something wrong and that the Customs agents would not allow them to enter the country. They had no idea what had happened to their fellow traveler. I immediately began to call everyone I could, from the State Department to our State Representative, but they had no information. Eventually, I found out that it seemed that the person might have been trying to manipulate the circumstances to remain in the United States. To the best of my knowledge, this person has never returned to Uganda. I have been told that they somehow managed to stay in Great Britain. I have asked about their whereabouts and have received no solid answer other than they are not in Uganda. At the date of this writing, this is still a mystery.

We finally got all of our guests (minus one) settled into their motel rooms.

Taking them all out to eat at one of the restaurants close by on International Drive was quite an experience. They stared at the menu for a long time, just amazed at all of the food choices, but none that looked like any part of their typical Uganda food items, except chicken.

When they ordered, they really ordered! I felt my credit card screaming for mercy, but I also enjoyed seeing the joy they had in their American feasts.

After their meal, we walked over to the Orange County Convention Center to give them their first view of this massive structure.

They were speechless, and I wondered what must have been going through their minds. Were they excited about the potential they could see for their Uganda Association? Were they intimidated because they felt it was so far out of reach for their association that they could see no way to achieve comparable results? It was going to be one of my most significant challenges–to keep casting vision and giving them hope for the future of UCCSU.

After showing them around the exhibit area, which is massive in its own right, I took them to their booth to help them set up for the next two days of the conference. The FACCS/IACCS Christian Educators' Convention is one of the largest in the nation. The exhibitors are displaying just about anything an educator could dream for, from the major Christian curriculum publishers to school buses. Just visiting the vendors would serve as an excellent opportunity for our Ugandan educators to catch a vision for products they could produce or emulate in Africa. From the first visit, I have been encouraging the Ugandan ministries to not look to the United States for school supplies, but to produce them within their ministries. I have told the story over and over about one of the leading Christian textbook and curriculum producers in America starting out from the vision of the wife of the founder of a large Christian school ministry. She began by producing a series of preschool phonics-based readers. A leading textbook and curriculum company developed over the years from that simple start. They now provide top quality materials for Christian education all over the world. I have encouraged the Ugandans that they can do the same.

The reason for this encouragement is multifaceted.

Even the Christian schools in Uganda are required to use the government-produced and issued curriculum, and administer the government-required exams. Any textbook or curriculum that they would produce would have to be designed to supplement the materials they are currently using. A second issue is that the cost of supplying Christian textbooks and curriculum would be cost-prohibitive. The cost of a set of textbooks for an individual student would be more than a family's entire yearly salary (I am continuing to talk with major Christian book and curriculum producers to try to get them to work with me to develop a plan to get materials to third world or developing countries at an affordable price). Another major obstacle is that shipping costs are actually more than the value of the textbooks. For Uganda, the problem is compounded by the fact that it is completely landlocked.

Everything has to be shipped by air, rail, or truck. The products must pass through several nations. Some of those nations are notorious for preventing goods from getting to where they are supposed to go.

So, the stakes for these Ugandan guests were perhaps higher than they could imagine. If they could catch a vision for what they or their ministries could produce in their homeland, they could indeed become self-sustaining.

It didn't take long for our guests to settle in and begin to make friends with hundreds of Christian educators. One of the goals of the Ugandan leaders was to do what they called "twinning" with American Christian schools. It took me some time to wrap around precisely what they mean by that term. Basically, what they wanted was for American schools to adopt a Ugandan school.

It took me quite a bit of time to explain that many American Christian schools did not have the resources to truly "twin" with their schools. I suggested that adopting a classroom, teacher, or a group of students would probably be more effective. This has not gone as well as we would like. I believe the reason for this goes back in part to the issue I explained earlier. Teachers in US Christian schools think of supporting an individual child with a name and face associated with their gift. But that is not that easy for Uganda schools, where the technology for accurate record keeping is less available, and where merely getting a wire transfer to go through is a significant challenge. When you are trying to feed and educate several hundred or even a thousand children each day, it is tough to have the time to do record keeping to the level required to attach individual dollars to individual children. As stated earlier, the safest way to ensure that money goes to the correct sources and is being used as you intended it, is to give to a well-known, reputable NGO working in Uganda. Another way is to give to a ministry that you know and trust, or give to one of the several US-based charitable organizations. I listed several of them in the last chapter. One safeguard, especially for American-based groups, is to be sure that the charitable organization is to make sure that they are part of the ECFA (Evangelical Council for Financial Accountability). The organizations I listed in the previous chapter are members of ECFA and are very dependable.

Helping our Ugandan friends understand how important financial accountability is to American donors has been a challenge. I have often illustrated it this way: imagine that you give a seven-year-old child living right next door to a candy store a hundred dollars and tell them that they can't buy any candy with their new money. The temptation would just be too high for many children! Or think of it this way, remember my young pastor friend who grew up in the orphanage he now manages?

His comment when asked about insect netting for the room was, "When you have to choose between food or insect netting, food wins!" Now, imagine you had given him $500 for netting. His children are starving, and the greater need was to buy food to keep them alive. What does he do? In the perfect world, he would contact you, ask permission to redirect your funds, and then do whatever you said. But in the real world, it might take two to three days to communicate this message effectively, and in the meantime, children are starving. So, what does he do?

That is the authentic dilemma these ministries face all the time. It does not excuse misuse of funds, nor does it justify abusing a gift or giver.

With all this in mind, I had a sense that our Ugandan guests would probably be disappointed in the amount of financial support they would get from delegates at the convention. It seems like they are gaining an increased understanding that the primary purpose of IACCS is not to be an endless "money train" for American dollars. IACCS is attempting to train, help organize, and strengthen these Christian ministries, rather than merely providing a steady stream of financial support (there aren't enough dollars in all the world to address these needs continuously). Actually, mathematically, there would be, if every Christian tithed to their local churches and the Church answered the call to serve Jerusalem, Judea, and the outermost parts of the world (Acts 1:8). But that would not be the best thing for the people or church of Uganda or the future of the nation. It is our goal to provide organizational support and training that will educate and equip the schools and orphanages to become more self-sustaining.

The purpose of them coming to the convention, from our perspective, was to give them a vision for what could be done.

It was interesting and at times, amusing, to watch the interaction between convention delegates and our Ugandan guests as they made themselves comfortable in and around their booth on the exhibit floor. They thought nothing of sitting on the floor, carrying on conversations with each other and delegates who stopped by for a visit. If they were eating a snack and someone came by, they were quick to ask them to share in the bite with them. No silverware, no problem, just use your fingers–that's the Ugandan way. I have now heard that phrase many times when I question why something is done a certain way in Uganda. I have also learned that when they get to know you and don't give you silverware (or plastic ware) to eat with, it is a way of saying you are one of us now, you don't need eating utensils, fingers will do fine.

They also didn't realize that exhibitors were to remain in their designated booth area, so we had considerable Ugandan sprawl going on as they spilled over into the exhibit booth next to them and into the aisle.

It was interesting though, because neither fellow exhibitors nor delegates seemed to mind. It was almost as if they found it appealing and part of this new culture they were observing.

It was also interesting to see how they settled into their motel accommodations. It seemed that they almost preferred packing into a couple of rooms rather than each having their own room. Some of them also seemed to prefer to make a mat on the floor rather than sleeping on the bed.

On the last day of the convention, we had a final general assembly with all of the delegates gathered together for one last charge before we returned to our schools. At that gathering, I spoke about IACCS, the UCCSU, and then introduced our Ugandan delegation to the audience. Both Timothy and Bernard talked to the audience. They did an excellent job painting a picture of life in these Ugandan schools and the great need that they faced.

A love offering was taken, and the proceeds were designated to the UCCSU.

The convention ended, and the delegation was off for their return trip to Uganda. They had a great experience interacting with teachers and administrators and attending excellent workshops. They left with renewed vision and excitement about the potential for their own ministries on the African continent.

It was a wonderful experience for the delegation, but an expensive venture for IACCS. When everything was counted up, it cost us in the neighborhood of $10,000.

I knew that there would be others that would want to come and experience the convention again, but I have been very reluctant to encourage that. When I think of how far $10,000 will go toward meeting the real and urgent needs in the orphanages, it isn't very easy to justify the expense to host a team in America.

CHAPTER 5

TRIP #3: CROC WATERS, A MACHETE, BAT GUANO, AND MINNOWS

The task of the modern educator is not to cut down jungles, but to irrigate deserts. - C. S. Lewis, "The Abolition of Man"

Most Wednesday mornings for about the last 20 years has started with a men's breakfast. A group of men gather at a restaurant to read Scripture, pray, challenge each other, and generally shoot the breeze. They are mainly from the church I pastored, with a few others from a mix of churches, and a few unchurched guys, as well. There are some real characters in this group, each with a unique story. One of the primary characters is a guy named Peter Reynolds.

Pete is from the UK and has had quite an honorable past as part of the Royal Guard at Buckingham Palace and part of British Special Forces. He has told delightful stories about conversations with the Queen and Princess Diana. Pete can do just about anything and has done just about everything! One of those things is that as part of his training, he had been a paratrooper. He loved it so much that he became a skydiving instructor. I asked him recently how many jumps he had made. Without hesitation, he replied, "13,700+." But the most important thing about Peter is that several years ago, he made a decision to receive Christ as his personal Savior (Jumping out of an airplane 13,700+ times might do that to you!)

As was usual, when I returned from an IACCS Trip, the men wanted to hear all about it. I was telling them about trip 2 and showing them pictures of all that had taken place. I showed them the video clip of Damalie telling her story and talking about being self-sustaining. I looked over at Peter, and tears had welled up in his eyes as he listened to her, and I told about what she had said about needing a cow. He said, "I'll buy a cow. How much?"

I said, "A thousand dollars."

He said, "No problem, let's get her a cow."

So began the Ugandan Cow Ministry. One "self-sustaining" young woman who refuses just to let the babies die, and a man who had a simple vision for what he could do to make a difference, launched a side ministry to IACCS that has benefited thousands of babies.

From the Damalie cow, the project has grown each year. The second year, a Rotary Club member and retired banker friend of mine said he wanted to give some money for the cows. He initially said he wanted to give $5,000, but when I was handed the check a few weeks later, it was for $10,000! He said, "I just felt like I should add a little to it."

People began to give money for the work in Uganda. I had never asked for money, but it started to come in. People grew increasingly excited about what was happening in Uganda. There had been little consideration of the necessity of a return trip.

A workout buddy and member of our church with a wealth of missions experience in third world and developing countries indicated that he would like to go with me on the next trip to Uganda. In addition to his missions experience, he also brought another plus to his arsenal of useful tools for helping in Uganda. He was trained as a medical technician and could, at the very least, be of help in organizing the clinic.

We began to talk and plan, and before long, we had selected the dates July 17-25, 2014, for the next trip to Uganda. The one thing I made sure of was that children were going to be in school and at the orphanages.

No matter when you leave the airport in the United States, it is going to take the better part of two days traveling before you finally arrive in Entebbe, Uganda. I had learned a hard lesson on trip #1 about not getting enough sleep on the plane. I planned to sleep as much as possible on all flights on this trip. David agreed with that plan, but he went a step further.

Have you ever known someone that prayed, even simple, sometimes seemingly trite prayers but really believe they are going to get answered? David is one of those guys! He said, "I'm going to pray that I have an entire row to myself, so I can stretch out and really sleep." Being a man of strong faith, I said, "Don't hold your breath, buddy!" He just smiled but said no more. I am sure you can guess where this story is going. We boarded the plane, I settled into my aisle seat (which I always try to get on long flights), and David took the seat directly behind me. This leg of the trip was from Miami to London, usually a fairly full flight. All the seats around me were taken, but not David's row. After we took off and the seatbelt sign was turned off, I stood up and turned to see how David was doing. He was cozily tucked in under a blanket, a pillow under his head, and stretched out across an entire row of seats, already sawing logs. I think he slept until we began our approach to Heathrow. As we were deplaning, I said, "Next time I'm praying, and you get the full row of people." He, more or less, said, "Go for it."

Trip #3: Croc Waters, a Machete, Bat Guano, and Minnows

We had departed Miami at about 9:00 PM and arrived in Heathrow at 10:15 AM. It is important to remember that on both legs of the flight going over, you are losing time.

So, we left on Thursday night, and it was now Friday morning in London. We had about a two-and-a-half-hour layover and boarded the next plane to Entebbe 12:30 PM. This leg of the trip can be tough. You are anticipating your arrival and the excitement of the week ahead, but again you have to fight for sleep. This flight is about an eight-and-a-half-hour trip, and you are losing time all the way. I boarded the plane and uttered a quick prayer, "Lord, if you love me as much as you love David, you will give me a whole row to sleep in like you did David."

I sat down in my aisle seat and waited to see the seats empty like the parting of the Red Sea, but that didn't happen.

In fact, every square inch of available seating around me was filled to overflowing. But David? I looked back to where he was – empty row and a big smile!

But as it turned out, the Lord had other plans in mind for me. We had just settled in when a very distinguished, well-spoken Ugandan lady struck up a conversation with me. She was from a region of Uganda known for their cattle and was a cattle rancher herself.

She gave me a wealth of information about Ugandan cattle, the cattle business in her district, and some vital tips on how to get the best price for the best cows. I marveled at how the Lord had put us on the same plane, in seats right next to each other, as we were about to go buy our first cattle. As for David? He slept well. What I didn't know at the time while talking with this lady was the depth of culture and the deep generational roots associated with cattle in certain regions of Uganda. In her book, *My Life's Journey*, Janet Kataaha Museveni, First Lady of Uganda, writes of growing up in the district of Ntungamo, in southwestern Uganda. The land was called Irenga. She describes it this way: *It is a beautiful land with hills and valleys, streams and rivers that water the valleys. It is always green, and the temperature is cool throughout the year.*[7]

In describing the people of her region known as Bahima, a pastoralist group of people who have raised Ankole long horn cows for many generations, she says: *We were very connected to nature and enjoyed a simple, yet rich lifestyle. As far as the Bahima are concerned, rearing cattle is more than merely an economic activity; it is part of who they are. Cattle are not merely a symbol of wealth; rather, they are regarded as treasured members of the family. Cows are prized and given praise names by their owners; they sing songs about them and praise their beauty and strength. The Bahima depended on cows for everything, from food, was primarily milk in its different forms, to bride price for a wife.*[8]

What I had not realized at the beginning of the side ministry of purchasing cows was that God was leading us into doing something that had profound cultural roots to many people of Uganda. It helped me understand the level of joy and celebration that we see every time we get the honor of giving a cow to an orphanage.

Back to our flight, when we landed in Entebbe, it was already 11:00 PM and we still had at least two hours of clearing Customs. In addition to that, Timothy had informed me that I would not be staying in Mukono this year but would be actually staying in Katosi.

The ride from Entebbe to Katosi is another two hours at least. And remember, this was through some of the bumpiest roads imaginable. I was more than a little nervous about where we were going to stay in Katosi because I had seen nothing that looked like a motel or guesthouse there. It was after 3:00 AM when we pulled up to a gated compound, and the driver honked the horn for the gate to be opened. As the gate opened, I thought, though in a sleep-deprived brain, "This place looks familiar."

Timothy got us settled in our rooms and said we could get some rest until morning. I said, "Timothy, it already is morning!" He just replied, "Rest."

When we got up in the morning, I realized why this place looked familiar the night before.

This is where the Children's Day had been held last year. This is where we had served fish head stew, and the place where hundreds of children had been scurrying about. I didn't know it at the time, but this place would be my home-away-from-home for several years to come.

An unexpected oasis

Staying at Hotel Cross City is a far cry from the accommodations I had imagined before my first trip. I had envisioned a dirt floor, mud hut, thatched roof, and deadly critters. None of that was the case, but a room in Uganda still has some things to get used to.

First, there is no AC. It is not necessary, because even though Katosi is directly on the equator, it is also over 3000 feet above sea level. The evening, which is about the only time you are in your room, is delightful, with low humidity. It is not a good idea to open the windows, because there are enough flying critters around to appear as uninvited guests. All beds have insect netting, but honestly, there are more insects in South Florida than I have experienced in Uganda. The bathroom definitely takes some getting used to because the shower is just a little hose attached to the wall with a small showerhead on it. There is a drain next to the toilet for the shower to drain. The drainpipe under the sink flows onto the floor and into the drain on the floor. You have to really schedule your events in the bathroom. The shower should be the last thing you do; otherwise, you are standing in a pool of water. You soon learn to work around these things and are incredibly grateful to have a shower and a flush toilet...with a seat. Most of the rooms have a plastic table with one or two plastic chairs. There is no closet, so your room becomes one giant closet. You don't need an alarm because you are awakened by Islamic prayer chants as the sun is coming up. Timothy says they are community announcements, but if they are, they are done in the singsong tone of Islamic prayer.

That first night was a very short one because Timothy had scheduled a Saturday Christian Education Convention in Buwenge, in Busoga Region.

Each year that I traveled to Uganda, there seemed to be a disconnect between the schedule that Timothy would line up and the day we arrived. If we left Miami on Thursday, Timothy would have an extra day scheduled in (an extra day that doesn't actually exist). I finally realized that it is because we lose a half-day traveling for the US to Uganda.

So, when we arrived in Uganda late Friday, we had already missed a day of activities he had planned. He had a full Conference scheduled for the next morning. We had four hours of sleep after two full days of travel. Figuring this out has been an enormous help because now I try to build in a full or at least half-day before we have to really hit a hard schedule.

Even though it had been a short night, adrenaline kicked in (along with slugging down a 5-Hour Energy drink), and I walked into a packed room of Christian educators and pastors. I was excited to have the opportunity to speak once again to them. This year, the first thing I wanted to do was talk to them as a pastor, not just as an educator. So, for the first session, I chose the title, *From a Pastor's Heart*, to set the tone for the conference.

Here, in essence, is what I had to say to this group. The bullet points represent the main areas I covered:

- You've got to smell like sheep. Using the passage from John 10:7-13:

Therefore, Jesus said again, "I tell you the truth, I am the gate for the sheep. All who ever came before me were thieves and robbers, but the sheep did not listen to them. I am the gate; whoever enters through me will be saved. He will come in and go out and find pasture. The thief comes only to steal and kill and destroy; I have come that they may have life and have it to the full.

"I am the good shepherd. The good shepherd lays down his life for the sheep. The hired hand is not the shepherd who owns the sheep. So when he sees the wolf coming, he abandons the sheep and runs away. Then the wolf attacks the flock and scatters it. The man runs away because he is a hired hand and cares nothing for the sheep.

I explained that if you are going to be the leader God has called you to be, you can't just be a hireling, you've got to love your flock. That includes the children, the congregation, the community, the world God has entrusted to you.

Then I talked about the necessity of Christian education. I have been convinced for many years of this next statement:

- You can't do in one day per week what is undone the other six days.

Trip #3: Croc Waters, a Machete, Bat Guano, and Minnows

The next point is one that I have stated in nearly every meeting I have conducted, and then read the quote from one of my heroes, Dr. Howard Hendricks:

- Christian education is the hope of the world.

Secular education seeks to make better, more effective, more successful, more intelligent people. The Christian educator aspires to nothing less than the transformation of a believer into the image of Christ. [9] *–Howard Hendricks*

This is the heart of Proverbs 22:6:

Train up *a child in the way he should go, and when he is old he will not turn from it.*

I then asked everyone one in the room, including myself the following question and used Deuteronomy 6:5 as the basis for the strength of the question:

- Am I doing Christian education with all my heart?

Deuteronomy *6:5:* Love *the Lord your God with all your heart and with all your soul and with all your strength.*

I quoted from the great theologian Michael Jordan.
Actually, I had to explain who he was and explain what a great basketball player he was.

Heart is what separates the good from the great.
– Michael Jordan

I concluded this first workshop by talking about one of the things that has concerned me about American Christian education. It seems that we get more caught up in setting an external image than we do reaching the heart.

Am I changing the heart or merely dressing up the outside? Do they still have a chimp's heart? Then I used one of my own quotes:

I am convinced that I could shave a chimpanzee, put him/her in a school uniform, and tuck a Bible under their arm, and most people would say, "My, my, what a fine Christian young man or woman this is!" There is only one problem... they still have a chimp's heart.

This year, I felt like I needed to spend more time reaching out to the leaders in the various ministries. The second workshop was on leadership. That session was followed by a talk called, *The Most Important Task of the Headmaster,* where we discussed the ten most crucial things a headmaster should do.

Other topics that were covered that day, and each of the subsequent days, were topics that would help both teachers and administrators. These included, *Building Strong Christ-Centered Curriculum; Tests and Measurements; Bloom's Taxonomy; and Discipline and the Christian School.*

I concluded this year's sessions spending some more time addressing leaders. Leaders of Ugandan churches, orphanages, and schools all face crisis daily.

Death is all around them.

Financing to meet the needs of the thousands of children that must be cared for and the daily strife of teachers living in poverty conditions make our crisis pale in comparison. So, I closed with a talk called, *Leading Through Crisis.*

The conferences this year were going to be great if today's discussions were any indication. I had forgotten how few hours of sleep we were running on, but as soon as I finished speaking, I was very aware of it. I could barely stay awake on the drive home. The bumpy road helped keep me awake, but what Timothy told us next really awakened me.

Timothy said, "Tomorrow, we are planning to baptize fifty or more people in Lake Victoria. At the end of the service, we are going to walk through town and end at the lake. We want people in the village to know what we are doing."

I said, "I would be honored to help with that." As those words were coming out of my mouth, I thought, "Wait, don't you remember that there are crocodiles?! There are crazy microscopic parasites that crawl up any body opening they can find and eat your brain!" And my next thought was, "Oh ye of little faith."

We didn't get to do the radio show as we have in the past because it took so much time to cover the material in the conference.

The next morning, we were off to church. I was excited about having the opportunity to see some old friends, to speak, and then to baptize more people than I had ever baptized at any one time. As we entered the church, I was extremely excited to see that the congregation was much larger than it had been the year before. The place was packed!

The place was packed!

Honestly, I can't recall what the message was that Sunday because I was so excited about the baptism to follow. As the service was about to end, a thunderstorm, like we often have in South Florida, came roaring in off the lake. I thought, "Well, that might do the baptism in," but not for Ugandans.

With thunder and lightning striking all around Mukono, the church emptied out, and the people moved toward the lake. I stopped by my room to get a change of clothes and borrow a pair of Timothy's tennis shoes. As I was changing, the lightning seemed to be right outside my room and at waters-edge. I was sure everyone would have run for cover, but as I started making my way to the water, I could hear singing over the blasts of thunder. As soon as I could get a glimpse of the lake, I could see that it didn't look like a single person had allowed the weather to weaken their resolve to be baptized. As Timothy and I talked at the shoreline, people began to form a very long line, and I noticed that one lone man had waded 50 yards or so out into the water. He was facing away from the shore, so I asked Timothy what he was doing? Timothy's response was a little unnerving, "He's watching for crocodiles."

Trip #3: Croc Waters, a Machete, Bat Guano, and Minnows

Neither crocs, nor lightning, nor parasites could keep them from being baptized.

Two of the pastors from Timothy's church and I waded out to about mid-thigh depth (remember the parasites. I wanted nothing in the water that they could enter!) I looked around. I thought, "This isn't the Jordan for sure!"

The line of praising, clapping, dancing Ugandans went on forever. I actually think we had other people line up to be baptized once they saw what was going on.

I looked to see when Timothy was going to join us. But he just smiled, stood on the bank, and waved. Some of those baptized would come out of the water, flaying away. I thought it must have just been such an overwhelming experience that they were almost out of control. That may have been true for some, but I was told that many of them had never been in the water before, especially under the water. Think of how much faith it must have taken for them to fight against their fears and be obedient to God's prompting.

We finally finished in the ceremony that I would guess took over an hour to complete, and finally waded back in. When I got to the beach, I whacked Timothy on the arm and asked, "Why didn't you come in?" He responded in typical Timothy Kakooza fashion, "No reason for both of us to get wet." I muttered under my breath, "Chicken."

From there we went back to Cross City Hotel to eat some lunch together, but I had to go change clothes first. I could feel that my socks were full of little back snails that live in the lake. They were very uncomfortable, but more than that, I remembered reading that the secondary host to many of the parasites was a snail. I don't know if there were parasites in this kind of snail, but I didn't particularly want to invite them in. The only thing that I've had taken in Uganda was this snail-filled pair of socks.

I shook out as many snails as I could, rinsed them out and hung them on one of the hedges right outside my room.

The next morning, they were gone.
I was more than happy to let those socks go.
Monday was going to be a jam-packed day. It started with Timothy taking us to a brand-new baby ministry called, *Happy Child House*.
The plaque on the wall read:

25 JUNE 2013
HAPPY CHILD HOUSE
WAS BUILT IN MEMORY OF SHIRLEY JOHNSON
DEDICATED TO THE GLORY OF GOD BY BISHOP
TIMOTHY AND JANEPHER KAKOOZA

Another of the endless projects that emerge because of God's blessing and Timothy's vision

This facility was truly a beautiful safe haven for abandoned babies. The caregivers were a joy to watch as they provided the first loving environment that many of these babies have ever experienced. Timothy took us out into a large section of the property, where he dreamed of planting a large garden. It would provide food for these babies as well as children at Winners Home in Katosi. I knew that this would be one of the places that would become a cow recipient at some point in the future when they are ready to care for it.

We spent about an hour visiting Happy Child House and then split up. I was off to do another teachers' conference in the Kayunga District, and David was off to buy cows.

I knew I was really going to have to hustle to get the same workshops covered on this second day. But I also knew that these teachers were eager for every bit of training they could get.

I later learned that David and his team had delivered the very first cow to an orphanage. He shot a video of one of the most joyful celebrations I have ever seen. It has become my classic video for showing the joy the orphans and teachers have when they find that they are getting a cow. When the children and teachers realized that this cow was to be theirs to keep, they erupted in celebration. They exploded in celebration. They cheered, they sang, they danced! At one point, it looked like the classroom was turning into a mosh pit. I have often said, "Can you imagine that level of excitement and joy from a cow being given in an American school?" Frankly, I can't think of any gift that you could give that would generate that much excitement.

I have shown this clip nearly every time I have spoken to groups about Uganda, and the response is always the same – joyful tears and more tears. At the time, I wondered if this was a one-time occurrence. I have now come to recognize that there is a similar celebration almost every time a cow is given.

As David headed off to buy cows, I headed toward the Kayunga District to conduct another teachers' conference. It would be a repeat of most of the material I had given at the first conference on Saturday. But, as it turned out, this was going to be a very different setting. Most of the meetings had been in well-equipped churches or auditoriums in larger cities. This was a very rural location. I was led to a wood-slatted building, with a dirt floor, open windows, and no door. There were twenty or so eager educators expectantly waiting in the room. Having no idea how long they had been sitting there waiting for my arrival, I passed out their study pages and began as quickly as possible. It was a challenging setting. I was going to have to move very quickly, the teachers had very little formal training, and it was nearing a hundred degrees in the room.

Every sentence had to go through a translator, plus the heat and lack of training made my audience pretty sluggish.

At one point as I was teaching, a goat walked into the room, stood there watching me train for a moment, and I would swear that he snorted, shrugged his shoulders, and walked out of the building.

I couldn't help wondering if that is the way my audience was feeling. The audience was gracious as usual, but I knew this had been a long day for them. Even though we were only about 50 or 60 miles away from Kampala, it was in a remote area, and it was going to be a long, slow journey back to Katosi. As usual, it was nightfall when we made our way back to Cross City. David was anxious to share the video clip of the excitement of the giving of the first cow. With my heart filled with gratitude and joy over the video, it made falling asleep very pleasant. The next day was going to be another long, remote location for me. It was also going to be a day that was going to require some wisdom that had been passed on by King Solomon.

If I thought Monday's journey into the bush had been long, I was about to discover how long a day trip in Uganda could be. The problem is that once you leave the main roadways to connect Entebbe, Kampala, Mukono, Lugazi, and Jinija, the roads turn into dirt trails. They are often muddy and full of potholes large enough to swallow a small car or at least break an axel. Traveling these routes can be long, dusty, and downright painful.

As you travel through the jungle, you see chilling signs that say things like "Stop child abduction," or "Help prevent child sacrifices." Other signs warn against leaving the roadway because Kony and his army have planted landmines and explosive devices in various places. You are hit with the reality of how remote and dangerous things can get in a hurry.

On this day, we traveled past all the places that I thought had been long distances before. We were now moving into a region that was much further and seemed even poorer than the other areas. My initial thought was that this is going to be a repeat of yesterday – only a handful of teachers that really needed months of educational training, not just what could be taught in a single day. As we pulled into the village, a man with a giant smile as broad as the Nile greeted me and was anxious to show me his school and all the guests who were waiting. Joshua would soon began to call me "Papa" and I would call him "Son." We will talk more about Joshua in a later chapter, but for now, we will simply let him show us his school.

The school was in the village of Buwenge, which on a good day is at least three hours away from Katosi. It is a dry and dusty place.

Most of the plants are low-lying shrubs, and they are pretty sparse. The buildings are mainly one floor, wood, or baked brick structures that all communicate a community in severe financial need. This is such a contrast to Jinja, the Source of the Nile, which is just a short distance away and is an incredibly fertile, green region.

As we neared a long, narrow, wood-slatted building (typical for remote Ugandan schools), the sound of joyful singing could be heard. As we entered a room with dirt floors and a light bulb or two hanging from the ceiling, my eyes had to adjust from the bright sun. When they did adjust, I realized that the room was packed with expectant teachers, administrators, pastors, and children. It was clear that this was an important day for them. There was a high level of expectation for the things that were about to take place. This was going to be a conference like none of the others. They had planned several student performances with children representing some schools/orphanages from around the district. Many factors make this day and this conference one that stills stands out as an exceptional experience. The way the day was set up was that I would teach a session and several children's groups would give their presentations, then I would teach another session.

My translator was a young man that I have seen each year I have returned to Uganda, and each time we greet one another, we break into smiles.

I have given him a new name, "Arsenio" because he looks so much like Arsenio Hall. He seems to enjoy his new name (I don't know if he even knows who Arsenio Hall is), and it has become a connecting point between us. He is a very bright young man that I always look to for intelligent, constructive involvement in the workshops he attends.

The children's presentations went beyond the usual, "Let's impress our American guests," to more of a performance with a message. The messages were not all the same. Some said through song and dance, "We are proud of our Ugandan and tribal heritage." Others said through dramas and recitations, "We are a generation that has been neglected, abandoned and abused." Still others sang of God's goodness and provision to them. These presentations were another reminder of the vital role the Church is playing in providing a safe haven for the children they rescue. It is not a perfect rescue, and much still needs to happen in many areas to be sure the children are appropriately cared for and are not abused by the very ones that are supposed to be caring for them.

In some of the faces, especially the older children, you see a hardness that seems to set it. I think it may be a feeling of hopelessness that says, "My condition will never get better. Life is just about surviving!"

It is going to take far more than posting a photo of a child on a refrigerator in America and sending a $30/month check to really make a significant impact in the lives of these children. I must repeat here that this is the reason I believe that the work of IACCS is so essential. We are attempting to educate the educators and to train the next generation to break the bonds of poverty

Trip #3: Croc Waters, a Machete, Bat Guano, and Minnows

and exercise those biblical principles that will equip them to be the leaders of their nation in the future (enough preaching, back to the story).

As the day went on, the crowd continued to grow. It became apparent that we were soon going to be out of room. As the next group of children started performing, I began to hear loud noise in the room adjacent to us, and boards began to disappear from the wall. Soon we were in one much larger room.

It was time to break for lunch, but I had planned just to eat a protein bar and invite pastors and administrators to meet in another room. After they had grabbed their food, the room filled with leadership from various ministries throughout the region. I addressed several issues I thought would be specific to leaders. I then opened it up to questions and answers. As time went on, they began to discuss the cow that was going to be given that afternoon. Our policy concerning the cows has been pretty simple: 1) it is to be a healthy milk cow, to be used only for milk and reproducing; and 2) if a calf is born, it must go to another orphanage caring for infants who need the milk.

Here is where the wisdom of Solomon comes into play. As they began to talk about receiving the cow, they began to speak in Lugandan, and their voices increased in volume. Lawrence, the pastor and driver that I have now spent hours traveling around Uganda with, leaned over to me and whispered, "I don't think this is going very well! You may need to speak." To my own surprise, I said, "Gladly. I was hoping you would ask." Lawrence quickly told me that they were arguing over who would make the decision of who would get a calf if it were born. I stood to my feet and said, with as much authority and grace as I could mix together in the moment, "Ladies and gentlemen, the people back in America that have given this money don't care who I give this cow to, they simply care that it is going to be used for milk. Now, if you can't figure out how to solve this problem, I can take the cow and give it to a group who can." I then looked back over my shoulder to Lawrence and said, "Or, you can go find me a big machete." He interrupted and questioned, "A machete?" I said, "A BIG KNIFE!" His and everyone else's eyes in the room got much bigger. I continued, "You can figure this out, or I will chop the cow up right here, and we will all have a big steak dinner!" It only took a few more seconds of conversation before the problem was solved, and we were able to move on.

I, like King Solomon, was relieved that I didn't have to cut anything apart.

The policy that emerged from this incident was that the executive board of UCCS-U would make the decision about which ministry would get a calf when it was born.

The lunch ended, everyone seemed to be satisfied with the decision that had been made, and I went back to teaching.

At the end of the last session, we all gathered outside for several gifts to be given out. By this time, Timothy and David had arrived, bringing the items we were to give away and to celebrate with everyone. We started things off by giving away several soccer balls.

You would think when you give a ball to a school that you had supplied their entire athletic department. Next, we presented several bicycles to school heads so that they could get to and from school with more ease. Finally, was the big event! A very healthy, energetic, long-horned cow was brought into the courtyard.

There were hundreds of people gathered around, the cow was led in by a young man holding an old rope, and the cow was very excited by all the people. I was sure someone was going to get trampled or gored before the presentation was complete, but no one was, and all ended with another grand celebration.

Arsenio translates while I teach

As we made our way back to Katosi, I reflected on the contrast between the three days of the educators' convention. The first day had been in a large city setting with a group of educators who were clearly more professionally prepared. Their participation was active, and the interaction in the workshops was very healthy. There was a genuine sense of hunger to learn more. The second conference was in a smaller, rural area where the teachers had less formal training. At times it was clear that they did not fully comprehend many of the educational concepts being presented. The third stop, the furthest, most remote region was full of vitality and an eagerness to learn. What seemed to be the difference? I thought of a quote from one of my mentors, Dr. Lee Robertson. He often said, "Everything rises and falls on leadership."

Where there was good leadership, the spirit was high, where it is lacking or absent, the spirit is depressed.

Where the leadership has cast a compelling vision, where a picture of hope has been painted for a brighter future, children, parents, and staff are all inspired to accomplish so much more.

When we arrived back at Cross City, I found I had a difficult time going to sleep because I was so excited about what was to happen the next day. Among a full day of activities and visiting orphanages, we were going to travel back to Sangaalo Babies Home and give Damalie her cow. This was the cow that started it all! We were giving away ten cows this year, but this one was special. God had used Damalie's dream of being self-sustaining with the help of a milk cow to touch Pete Reynolds' heart back in America to launch the cow ministry that is currently supplying milk to nearly 12,000 orphaned babies each day; and the number is growing yearly.

Damalie and her cow that started it all

Before we got to Damalie's though, we had several key stops at other orphanages to hear the children, to give away cows, bikes, and balls. David had also brought along a suitcase full of flip-flop sandals to give away to an orphanage designated by Timothy. This was the first time to bring any footwear to Uganda, and so this was somewhat of an experiment. Timothy had suggested that the children needed a very sturdy school shoe that ran about $20.00/pair and that flip-flops would not last. I told him that as I looked around, I saw thousands of children with no shoes at all (many have never had a pair of shoes), and it seemed that since we had flip-flops, they were better than no shoes at all. Also, I had seen hundreds of children in flip-flops that appeared to be working. This issue will come up again on future trips. I will explain when we get to those trips, but for now, we were giving away flip-flops.

Additionally, David had brought along enough toothpaste and toothbrushes to supply a village, and we had to pick a location of the appropriate size to give them to. We have learned that we have to provide strong instructions to the children not to eat the toothpaste. There are some serious side effects from eating an entire tube of toothpaste. With the lack of medical care in most regions, it is a warning that should be given and heeded.

Our first stop was going to be at Goshen Land, the school/orphanage I described earlier as the ministry on the top of a hill overlooking the city.

The staff and children always go to great lengths to put together presentations to demonstrate their desire to honor us as guests. But they also want to show their pride in the quality of their program. We were escorted to a large meeting room where the children and adults were already making presentations.

As I watched the children perform, there was an important realization. I had been trying to put my finger on the differences between the presentations given by American children and these

Ugandan children. American school kids are usually showing off academic skills or a talent they have worked hard to master. These children were giving presentations about their life and culture. They were more tragedies than anything. The good news is that most of them had a happy ending that involved God's intervention and rescue. My prayer as these children made their presentation was, "Lord may their rescue be true. May you protect these precious lives, and may you give them hope for a better future."

The closest I have come to actually bringing a child home with me was during these moments. Four children were preforming a drama about a young girl who was taken into a place where she was supposed to be safe. But instead, was she was horribly abused by the person that was supposed to be her protector. But a hero appears on the scene and she was rescued. I spoke of this drama in an earlier chapter, so I will not go into more detail here.

The point that I want to make at this moment is that the young girl who had the lead role was far too young to have to know about or experience this kind of abuse. However, it is a harsh reality. Abuse and neglect are a part of the life of so many Ugandan children. This young girl was an exceptionally bright, articulate, young lady. Not long after their performance, there was a short break, so I asked if I could video this young lady and if she had a message for the American Church. She agreed, and I nodded that the camera was running. I said, "What would you like to say to the Church in America?" Her response surprised me because it was so short and to the point and absolutely on target. She said, "Pray without ceasing. Never stop praying."

I waited for her to continue, but she pursed her lips together and just looked at the camera. I stopped filming. Then she said, "I would like to say something else." I started the camera again. She looked past the camera, into my very heart, and said, "I wish to go to America." Then she smiled a sweet smile and just stood

Trip #3: Croc Waters, a Machete, Bat Guano, and Minnows

there waiting for a response. Tears welled up in my eyes. I had no reply other than a very inadequate response of, "Thank you." Each year that I have gone back, I have looked for this young girl at the children's events but have not seen her again. It may be a good thing because she might end up on a plane with me heading back to our home in Florida!

Our next stop was at a gathering of several schools for a special luncheon feast and children's performances. There were perhaps a thousand children at this gathering, along with their teachers and administrators. They had prearranged the order in which each group of children would perform, and they came one after the other. David and I were seated in special guest of honor seats near the front and to the side of the room so that we could see all the performances clearly. We were served lunch and were to watch the children's presentations as we ate. I glanced down when we were served. I did not look closely, but it looked like many other meals that I had been served in Uganda. I knew that it was a special meal and represented sacrifice on the part of our hosts.

I was focused on watching the children and eating without looking down. Suddenly I felt something plop on the top of my head. I thought, where did that come from? No one had moved. I didn't see anyone squirt anything, and we were indoors. I put my hand to my head and brought a blob of what looked like sunscreen down to examine it. As the blob got close to my nose, it was evident in a fraction of a second that it was not sunscreen. I looked up and hanging from the rafters were several bats! Now, this all took place in seconds, but it felt like hours.

It is tough to look like a distinguished guest of honor with a head full of bat guano. Apparently, no one had noticed, or everyone was being very gracious not to break out in laughter. I leaned over to David and asked, "Do you have any wet wipes with you that you can easily reach?" When he saw what had happened, he was not as gracious as our Ugandan hosts.

Fortunately, he did have some wipes and slipped them to me under the table. As he did, he whispered, "Have you looked at your meal?" I thought I better look down at my meal. At first, I just saw beans and rice (very normal), but then I looked again, whole minnows were looking back at me. I mean "looking back at me!"- heads, guts, fins, tails...

I wondered how many I had eaten and if any exotic parasites were introduced into my digestive tract. With that thought in mind, and my head recently cleansed of bat poop, I decided I was no longer hungry. I looked around and made eye contact with one of the boys who had an empty plate and was looking longingly at my mine full of food. I used universal sign language that any child anywhere would understand – I pointed to my plate, pointed to him, and acted like I was eating with my fingers and pointed back to him and his empty plate. He was a quick read and nodded, "Yes." I slipped my plate to him, and he slid me his empty plate. Then I watched something I've seen several times with Ugandan orphans.

The young recipient of my plate didn't just start chowing down. He took the plate and gave equal shares to the children around him. I am deeply moved every time I see this act of kindness.

I have asked often, "What do you do to teach this to your children?" The response is always the same, a shrug, and the reply, "It is part of our culture. It is just what we do." Don't get me wrong, you do see acts of selfishness, but these acts of kindness so overshadow the selfish behaviors.

To be completely honest, I have seen adults act in stingy, greedy ways that I think is a learned behavior born out of years of poverty and despair.

Trip #3: Croc Waters, a Machete, Bat Guano, and Minnows

After all the children's groups had made their presentations, we moved outside, where we participated in the often-repeated celebration of the giving of our gifts. At this spot, we gave cows to the schools, accompanied by the wild celebration, bicycles–more wild celebration, and soccer balls – even more wild celebration. We have seen this over and over again and it never grows old.

These celebrations are not rehearsed, but instead, they are outpourings of extreme gratitude.

Friday, our last day, was another day packed with activities, focused primarily in Katosi and the children at Winners Home. Every second of the day was filled with activities before we boarded our plane late that night to begin our journey back to Florida. High on my priority list for the day was a visit to the clinic. If it was in the same poor condition it had been in the year before, I was going to have to do some explaining when I got back to the States. Timothy would also have some explaining to do. As I approached the clinic, I held my breath, but my fears were relieved when I saw that the clinic was in very good condition. The floors had been tiled, there were new examination tables in place, and the medical supply closet was well stocked. Additionally, there was new fencing around the entire compound, and the building was clean and freshly painted. It was a relief to take this news back to the donors from the year before.

From there, David and I returned to Winners Home to prepare to feed close to a thousand kids. I have learned that Timothy likes to use my visits as opportunities to feed the children a special meal. The "special meal" usually means that some kind of meat, either fish or beef, is added to the mix of beans, rice, and posho. We stand behind large kettles with plastic plates, which we dip into the mix of rice and beans, dump it on a child's plate, and another helper puts a ladle of the meat and broth on top. The children line up in what appears to be a never-ending line and wait patiently to be served. Occasionally, some of the children from the village will also sneak into the line, and I am more than happy to serve them. But if they are spotted by school staff, they will often be pulled from the line and escorted away. That saddens me, but I understand that there is just not enough food to feed the entire village.

After feeding the children, we are invited to a side room where we are served the same food and talk with the school leaders and other officials who have gathered for the event. These are always enjoyable Q & A times that I try to use to strengthen the IACCS cause in Uganda.

After our meal, we moved to an open field where Timothy and the children of Winners Home finally received their cow. We had been successful in giving away all ten cows and had learned some things to help in the process in the years to come. Here are a few of the takeaways from this process:

1) Always be sure you have a trustworthy Ugandan to do the negotiating for the price of the cow. If they see an American, the price automatically goes up.
2) Get a receipt and be sure that the cow is actually their cow to sell.
3) Inspect the cow to be sure it is a good milk cow.
4) Be sure you have calculated the price of transporting the cow.
5) As the cow project began to take shape, we were discussing how to buy a bull. How do we get it around the country to be introduced to our cows so that calves would begin to be produced?

We knew that bulls would be expensive, and the logistics of transporting them from orphanage to orphanage could be cost-prohibitive. But, thanks to the Lord's natural wiring patterns for cows and bulls, they have been able to figure this out on their own without any help from humans! No bull purchases have been necessary!

With full hearts, empty pockets, and empty suitcases, we headed to Entebbe for our return trip to Florida. David prayed, got a seat all to himself. I prayed and got stuck in a middle seat all the way home.

The Lord has a wonderful sense of humor!

Chapter 6
Trip #4 Unto the Least of These

When we Christians behave badly, or fail to behave well, we are making Christianity unbelievable to the outside world.
 – C.S. Lewis, "Mere Christianity" (1952)

It is a passage you see on many walls in orphanages in Uganda, and it is at the heart of the work of IACCS. The passage is Matthew 25:40-45 (NIV)

> "The King will reply, 'Truly I tell you, whatever you did for one of the least of these brothers and sisters of mine, you did for me.'

> "Then he will say to those on his left, 'Depart from me, you who are cursed, into the eternal fire prepared for the devil and his angels. For I was hungry and you gave me nothing to eat, I was thirsty and you gave me nothing to drink, I was a stranger and you did not invite me in, I needed clothes and you did not clothe me, I was sick and in prison and you did not look after me.'

"They also will answer, 'Lord, when did we see you hungry or thirsty or a stranger or needing clothes or sick or in prison, and did not help you?'

"He will reply, 'Truly I tell you, whatever you did not do for one of the least of these, you did not do for me.'

Whatever you did for one of the least of these... We were about to experience in a new way what it means to care for the least of these.

It is now 2015, and this is trip number four for me. The team for this year is made up of two guys from our church. Pete Reynolds, the one who gave the money for the first cow; I mentioned him earlier and told you that he had been in the British Special Forces and he was a skydiver. He was also a Harley-riding, tattooed rascal with a heart as big as gold, who would cry at the drop of a hat and would give his last dime to someone in need. The second friend was Gary Mace, a highly qualified SCUBA instructor, dive shop owner, and techie guru. He never hesitated to use his own resources to meet the need of anyone he perceived with a need.

Each of these men is great to travel with. They both bring a unique mix of talents to the table. These talents will allow them to help the people of Uganda in many ways.

With Gary's techie background, he wanted to make sure we were prepared for any and all emergencies, so we had to find a company in Miami that would rent a satellite phone. I tried to reassure him that everyone in Uganda had cell phones, and we would never be stranded in the bush and need a satellite phone rescue. Still, it was reassuring to have it along just in case. I always make sure to double-check with the State Department regularly for months before leaving on a trip and register with them right before we leave. Additionally, I make contact with the American Embassy, both precautionary measures that are recommended.

I have found a travel group that specializes in negotiating reasonable prices for missionary and humanitarian aid airfares and started using them on this trip. One of the significant advantages is that each traveler is allowed to check three large bags, plus all of your carry-on is still allowed. I have learned to pack everything I need for the trip in my carry-on and one large suitcase, so I have two bags to fill with things to give away in Uganda.

I was excited about this trip because of the excitement of these two men and their huge, compassionate hearts. We loaded 450 pounds of stuff in the back of Gary's truck and were off for the airport. When settled in on the plane and had just touched off, I leaned over to Pete and said, "Hey Pete, I didn't want to worry you before we left, I don't know what we are going to do about your tattoos. I understand they eat people with tattoos first!" I tried to keep a serious face and remain relatively expressionless. Pete's eyes widened, and he nervously put his hand over one arm in a failed attempt that covered about 1/5 of the tattoos. Of course, I couldn't keep a straight face and began to laugh, and Pete also laughed, but his was an expression of relief. Now, we do see a lot of strange things in Uganda, but cannibalism is not one of them. A little later on in this chapter, we will be looking at a practice that still takes place in Uganda that is every bit as horrific as cannibalism. We have talked briefly about it in other chapters, but it needs a more in-depth look.

I held my breath as we cleared Customs with our 450 pounds of stuff, but we made it through and were greeted by Timothy's warm smile and bear hugs.

As usual, we got to our rooms very late and were pretty fatigued from two days of travel, so we were asleep very quickly.

The next morning, Timothy and Janepher were both there to greet us with a Ugandan breakfast. Everything is cooked in a kitchen right off the little room where we gather to eat and stage all the activities and giveaways for the day.

When you think of a kitchen, what comes to mind, stoves, sinks, microwave, freezer/refrigerator, and a toaster oven?

That is not a Ugandan kitchen.

Their kitchen is more like firewood, open fire on a fire pit, large pots, and a hose. Sometimes the kitchen is entirely separate from the house, but it is certainly always a small separate room away from the main living area.

The little room where we gather does have a refrigerator in it, which Timothy keeps stocked with water and Mountain Dew while we are there. And, there is a small toaster oven in case we want to toast bread. Most of the time the breakfast consists of some type of egg, pineapple, bananas, jackfruit, papaya, flat bread called chapati, and always a supply of peanut butter and jelly. There are fertile fields of tea in Uganda, so there is always hot tea in the morning to be made with water they have boiled and mixed in with some ginger. It has a bit of a kick to it that takes some getting used to, but it really clears the sinuses out! At breakfast, Timothy told us that the first thing he wanted to do was to show us the site where he was building a children's church. Pete and Gary were full of excitement, but I was a bit more reserved in my excitement because I knew that I was going to have to tell Timothy that IACCS money could not be used for projects that were not related to the UCCSU/IACCS projects that would benefit all of the ministries in the association. I did not express those concerns because I wanted to see what was going to happen. So, off we went to the site, which was right next to the main church at the top of the same steep hill described earlier.

The road was so steep and bad that I wondered how any building materials, let alone construction trucks and equipment, could get to the site. When we arrived, there was an elderly gentleman who I later learned was the project manager and could build anything anywhere out of nothing. He had a group of young men with machetes, shovels, pickaxes, and posthole diggers; all hand tools, with hand-made handles made out of sturdy limbs that had cut and shaped to fit the tools. There was not a power tool or piece of heavy construction equipment in sight. Most of the young men were barefooted but had feet calloused like construction boots. The underbrush and trees had been removed, and the rich red clay had been leveled to perfection. A trench had been dug by hand, which was to be filled with large granite boulders. This would serve as the footer for the building. This was going to be a large building! I wondered how long it was going to take and how much it was going to cost.

I asked Timothy what his plan was. He said he would build it as God provided the funds and as the materials were available. I had just finished completing a gymnasium complex for our school that had taken several years to complete and cost 4.3 million dollars.

So that was the frame of reference I was working from. Construction in Uganda is very different from building in America – no architect or engineering fees, no permits, no landscape mitigation, and no sewer hookup. In other words, it was going to cost far, far less to build in Uganda. Pete and Gary were ready to start building right then. Pete's knowledge of construction was extremely helpful but made him even more prepared to dive in. It didn't take long for Pete and Gary to huddle up, talk about what they could afford to spend out of their own money to help get this project out of the ground. They asked me if I minded and I of course was delighted at their hearts and their desire to help the children of Katosi. A number of people from Island Community Church had given me money and given me permission to use it wherever I felt it could best be used. I also had some money that I had from weddings and other things that I had done since last year's trip that I planned to use in Uganda.

We told Timothy what we had to spend, and he quickly had a list of materials to get things started. He promptly sent Gary and Pete off with his foreman to purchase the materials to get started. Timothy and I were off to Mukono to the bank to exchange the money we had brought with us and get it distributed to the various projects we were scheduled to keep. The money IACCS projects had come in throughout the year as more and more people were buying into the mission. The cash for cows was especially attractive to donors. As we were making initial preparations to return to Uganda, the same gracious gentleman and Rotarian friend that had given the tremendous gift for cows the previous year approached me again and said, "I want to give you $12,000." In addition, a Christian travel group for students, Joshua Expeditions, gave a check for $3,000. I have served on the Joshua Expeditions Board for several years, and it is thrilling to see their heart for missions. With those gifts, as well as a number of other miscellaneous gifts, we were going to be able to accomplish several important tasks. BACK home, it had become the norm that whether going to the gym, to lunch, the store, or to church, someone would walk up and hand me money and say, "Use this in Uganda." With these resources, our plan was to buy at least 15 cows, as many bicycles as possible, and distribute 20 soccer balls and air pumps that we had brought with us.

Once we had finished at the bank, Timothy and I headed on to Kampala for another radio show. It was the same type of program we had done in the past. We were able to give a report about the growth that had occurred in the UCCS-U over the past year. The intent was to generate enthusiasm for the educators' convention, which was going to take place the next week. This year, we had an open mic and received several phone-in calls talking about how UCCSU had benefited Christian education.

When we got back to Katosi, Peter and Gary were also just returning after a long day of negotiating and purchasing building materials for the children's church. I expected to hear about jackhammers, nails, concrete, bricks, etc. but what I heard about was a bunch of steel and wooden posts. It is so hard to translate our view of construction projects into Ugandan methodologies. The steel posts were going to form the necessary support structures, and the wooden posts were going to be the support for the walls and the roof. A large number of bricks were also purchased but had to be fired and delivered when the site was ready for them. We had already spent all of the money that we had committed to the project. Still, it was well underway, and over the next three years we would see money continue to come in and the building completed.

Sunday morning was once again going to be a special morning of worship and celebration. The celebration this time was going to be over the launching of the Children's Church Project. In the back of the auditorium were two huge piles of the steel and wooden poles, along with a wheelbarrow full of tools. These were all there for two purposes – to keep them secure and to generate enthusiasm for the project.

Timothy, Gary, Pete, and I began the worship time standing in the middle of the site where the church was to be built.

Surrounding us were bright, smiling, singing children all excited that this was going to be a place just for them.

The children loved to get as close to us as possible, and several of them were rubbing and trying to pull Peter's tattoos off (no one attempted to eat him!) I later asked Timothy about how Pete's tattoos were culturally received. His response sounded about like we would expect to hear back home. Rural communities, where they are seldom seen, would be a little uncomfortable or not know what they were. It the city and among a younger crowd, they would be seen as "cool." In actuality, they have never been an issue, mainly because they see Peter's tender spirit before they see the tattoos. The kids almost always want to touch or rub the ones on his arms. He is like the Pied Piper with the children – wherever he is walking, he is surrounded by a crowd of happy Ugandan children.

We moved from the children's church site into the main service. After about thirty minutes of singing, praying, and children's presentations, Timothy called Gary and Peter up on the platform. Timothy began to tell the story of Peter and Damalie's cow and how that started everything in the giving of cows to different schools. He pulled the number ten out of his hat and said that we were giving that many away this year. We were actually shooting for at least fifteen. I was grateful that he had understated, not committing us to more than we could handle. As Peter was being honored by Timothy, I was videoing and managed to zoom in on Pete's face as his eyes filled with tears. One of the things I love about this brother is that he is so humble and always wants all the credit to go to God, even when he has been used in a major way. Timothy then turned to Gary, and in a way that only Timothy can do, said that Gary is here to help build our children's church. I had to chuckle and thought, "Well, whether Gary knew it or not, I guess that is what he is doing now!" Timothy has undoubtedly done more for children than most in Uganda. I believe it is because he is always dreaming, casting vision, and getting you to commit, even when you are not sure you can. But I also think that because the need is so great, he has to do it.

I once again had to chuckle at God's sense of humor. Pete, the guy who could build anything, had been relegated to being the "cowboy," and Gary the "techie" was the builder.

Pete's tears as Timothy tells of the Cow Project

I was once again given the honor of bringing the message. It was primarily an evangelistic message about how living according to the principles that Jesus taught and demonstrated was the hope of the world.

After the service, Timothy, Gary, Pete, and I walked through the village and down to Lake Victoria. It was quite a sight to see Peter walking along with his crowd of children tagging along. At one point, I saw a young boy with a book that looked very familiar. It was a Bible from Operation Christmas Child, a program sponsored by Samaritans Purse and the Billy Graham Association. Our church and school have participated in OCC for many years. We have packed shoeboxes full of gifts for children to be sent all over the world. We mail them to Samaritans Purse, where a Bible, along with a very clear Gospel presentation, is placed in each shoebox. It was so very encouraging to see that this program had reached such a remote location in Africa.

Operation Christmas Child reaching the uttermost parts

Making our way through the village of Katosi, I marveled at how much more this village resembled a community from biblical times than it did the 21st century towns and cities back home. I purposely lagged behind to watch the guys' reactions to their first experience in the village, and to watch Timothy's interaction with the people he had committed his life to.

Let me see if I can describe the scene in a way that will help you get a glimpse of typical Ugandan village life. We walked past two young women, one dressed in the typical long gomesi, and the other was in a Western-style blouse and clam-digger jeans. The one in the gomesi was sitting on a rock and the other was standing over here doing her hair. This rock appeared to be one of the many beauty spas. Behind them was a wooden, three-sided, open front structure where there were several handmade clay and metal cooking pots for sale. This type of booth was the norm in most villages, and everything from a rich array of vegetables and fruits to furniture, steel gates, and cell phones were sold from them. Open fires were burning next to most of these stalls and some even out in the roadway. Walking a little further down the street, Timothy stopped to talk to a guy who pulled up about a dozen tilapia from a bowl. They were all tied together through their mouths and gills and were about to become our dinner. It seemed that Timothy was negotiating with the man, but he did not seem to strike a deal. I thought, "Well, maybe they aren't for dinner after all." As we moved along onto the busy main street (all roads in Katosi are dirt or gravel roads), I looked over and was surprised to see several old Yamaha outboard motors in various stages of repair. The only tools they had were hand tools, and most of the parts were cannibalized from other old outboard motors. I was thinking about how this outboard repair shop compared to ones near my home in the Keys. Just then, we heard a very raucous group coming down the street. They were speaking Lugandan, and waving limbs full of leaves around in some type of celebration. One of the men looked at me and gave me a big grin and a thumbs-up.

Timothy explained that it was some type of local political rally.

That group had barely moved by when I glanced over at a group of guys, probably boda boda drivers, waiting for someone to hire them.

One of them made eye contact with me. I am not sure whether he thought I was supportive of this political parade or what, but he put his hand to his throat and made a cutting motion, imitating cutting my throat. No one else saw it, and I decided it was probably a good time to keep moving! To this day, I don't know what that was about and have never had it happen since.

Almost every group of children we encountered on the street was carrying some type of water container. It was a reminder of how vital just getting water is for their survival. Most of these children would, unfortunately, simply dip water from the lake. Many do go and get water from the water system that we put in at Winners, but the "Ugandan way" is to draw water from Lake Victoria; pollution, parasites, and all.

On almost every available board or wall, there is a poster promoting some sort of revival or concert. Most of the three-sided stalls are simply bare wood, but occasionally you will see a painted one – almost always a lime green.

Based on the color of many of the buildings, I am assuming that there must have been a real bargain on green paint at some point in the past. An amusing site was a lady outside her little booth cooking on an outdoor fire, selling some type of hot food. The humorous part was that despite it being in the high 80s or low 90s, she was wearing a red flannel Santa's hat with fluffy white trim around the bottom. I wondered if she had any idea Christmas was still four months away, and if her hat did anything to increase sales – it certainly got my attention.

Later, when we got back to our usual eating area, I opened the refrigerator. To my surprise, there were several of the tilapia just lying whole on the bottom shelf.

The next morning, they were part of our breakfast offerings. I am not sure how it was prepared, but it was delicious.

This Monday was going to be a very memorable one.

We were going to do and see several things that would make this day stand out more than most. We were headed to an orphanage somewhere out in the bush to give away our first cow, but had to stop in Lugazi to get the printed copies for the educators' convention. We had decided to see if it was better to get things printed in Uganda rather than lug them from the US. Apparently, one of Timothy's assistants had dropped off the pages to be printed several days before. A young man that I did not recognize walked up to the van window and our driver, BJ, handed him some money. We were in sort of an open, town square area. As usual, there was a large crowd milling about. Timothy told us to just remain in the van. I have been asked on occasion if I have ever felt uneasy or threatened in Uganda. I must admit that this was one occasion that made me a little nervous. Our van was suddenly surrounded by dozens of men.

They walked up and were looking in the windows as if to size us up or to see if we had anything worth taking.

Timothy and BJ spoke very sternly to those peering in, and they backed away. I told the guys, "Don't look so Mzungu!"

I was glad that I had two native Ugandans in the van with us. I am not sure what they might have done, but the group just sort of melted away. I was glad I had Peter along as a personal "bodyguard." I have joked with him about that on occasion, but I hope I never have to see him exercise any Special Forces skills. After a few minutes, the man who had been given the money for the printing returned with a stack of papers for the conference. The print quality was not quite as good as copies that I make and bring with me. After the encounter with the men that morning, I decided I would just print the workbooks and bring them with me each year. The study sheets were handed off to someone else to be collated and put into workbook form.

From Lugazi, we traveled back out into the jungle to a rural orphanage with excited, cheering children waiting for us to arrive.

Gary and Pete got the honor of giving away a cow to this joyful, celebrating crowd.

The next stop was one of those stops that amps your understanding, awareness, and compassion to a whole new level. This stop was at an all-girls orphanage. The orphanage was run by Bernard Bogere's son.

You will recall that Bernard was the well-spoken gentleman that had been raised by American missionaries and had been captured by Idi Amin. As we pulled into the compound, the children were prepared to greet us with several songs. Before we got out of the van, they were already singing and walking toward us. I would guess there were fifty or so children in this choir, and there were probably a hundred or more children in classrooms or in dorms. I was filming the children and noticed two things that got my attention. The first was a cow tied to a nearby post. Clearly, this was going to be the next of our cow-receiving orphanages. What really got my attention was that there were two white children in the midst of all the other children. If you looked closely at the two, it was evident that these children still had Ugandan features with white skin.

When we asked Stephen, Bernard's son, about them, he said they were albino children. I asked how they would fare if they were not in his orphanage.

His response was alarming. He said they would have very little chance of surviving and that they had been abandoned by their parents because they were albinos. I asked what he meant by "they wouldn't survive?" He said witch doctors would have probably killed them because they were cursed or because they thought their death and dismemberment would bring wealth to the village. That was hard to believe, so I did some homework on albino children in Uganda.

Here is some of what I found:

Albinism is known to be widespread in Uganda, necessitating the creation of organizations such as Source of the Nile Union of Persons with Albinism (SNUPA). However, to date there have been no large-scale prevalence studies, nor any other sources of empirical data to capture the lives of people with albinism in the country. Hence, the need for the study reported in this article.

In Africa, lack of the usual dark pigmentation found in indigenous populations makes the visible appearance of those with the condition markedly different to those in their families and communities without albinism. They are in effect what Phatoli and colleagues describe as 'being black in a white skin'. This has significant, negative psychosocial and cultural impacts brought about by perceptions of 'otherness'. Their lives are often marred by stigmatization and rejection, lack of acceptance and limited social integration. As a result of their perceived difference, people with albinism are feared and viewed with suspicion, while simultaneously considered to have mystical powers. There is a misconception that their body parts can bring good luck, success and easy wealth but on the other hand, they are believed to be a curse, bringing bad luck.

In extreme (but not infrequent) cases, superstitions and traditional beliefs about albinism can lead to violent assault and murder. Body parts of those with albinism are used in witchcraft-related rituals that typically involve them being made into charms that are believed to bring wealth and good luck. Attacks take different forms, such as forcibly shaving off hair, mutilation of fingers, limbs, ears and genitalia, and murder. In sum, otherness poses a significant societal risk for people with albinism and a direct threat to their human rights. Underpinning this are deep rooted, culturally embedded beliefs about people with albinism that simultaneously hold them as enigmatic and frightening. To date however, such beliefs have been understood largely through anecdote, rather than empirical investigation.[10]

It is an amazing thing to see these children under the protection and care of this orphanage. But it was not just the adults giving the care, it was the children looking after and loving them. What cultural barriers were being broken down by this example?

In subsequent trips, I have seen these two at the Children's Day events. They seem to be healthy and safe. On the 2018 trip, I traveled to one of the most remote regions I have visited so far and saw another albino child. But this time, the child did not just have albinism, but also Down syndrome and limited mental capacity. This child would have never survived without the loving care and protection of this orphanage. This child's almost every move was cared for by the children that surrounded him.

This is a harsh reality of being different and living in a culture where superstition has such a strong foothold.

This is another of the many things that show the importance of Christian education and training children and adults to live by biblical principles.

This issue helps to make a point. I am occasionally asked, "Why do you put so much emphasis on education being the answer to the world's problems?"

My answer is always the same, "I don't! My emphasis is on Christian education and the truth it holds." This shows the contrasts between the philosophies and values that come from the Prince of Darkness and the Lord Jesus Christ. The Evil One comes only to steal, kill, and destroy, while Jesus has come to give life to the full (John 10:10). Men like Bob Goff or Gary Haugen and International Justice, and a host of other brave men and women are living out "caring for the least of these." As they and the pastors of Uganda take on the witch doctors and abusers of children in various forms, the culture is slowly changing. If we don't train the next generation to follow Christ, there is little hope.

As we gave out the cow to this orphanage, it began to rain, really rain!

We gave the cow away and quickly piled back into the van. We were on the way to another location in which several schools/orphanages had gathered to receive cows, bicycles, and other gifts. It was even further into the jungle, and the roads were getting increasingly worse and muddy. We had barely made a turn onto a side road when we were forced to stop. In front of us was a power pole that had fallen directly across the road. The heavy rain had washed its base entirely away. The power lines were still attached and live. Water and electricity don't go together very well. But there were people on foot who were climbing over the pole and walking on down the road. Guys on boda boda were running out into the jungle with their motorcycles and coming back on the road when they had cleared the downed pole.

But, as we tried to get a game plan for what to do next, we could see at least two more power poles down, all connected to live electric wires. It was still pouring, and it seemed to me that the logical plan was to turn around or find another route in. Timothy said there was no other route and that there were too many people waiting, with high expectations. Turning around was not an option either. He walked away for a few minutes, had a conversation with a couple of men, and walked back to us, and said, "Go ahead, climb over the power poles (all three), and someone will meet us on the other side. With great caution, we worked our way through the maze of downed poles and hot power lines. When we cleared the third pole, there were men on boda bodas waiting for us to hop on. So, the one caution that I had made an effort to heed – don't ride boda boda – had now gone by the wayside. Timothy, Gary, Pete, and I were all headed down a very muddy dirt trail. I was trying to film from the back of my motorcycle, but there was so much mud flying, that I finally had to give up.

After several mud-slinging miles, we finally reached our destination. There were children and adults everywhere. I don't know how many, 250? 500? I couldn't tell. I was just grateful we had made it alive.

This group was such a memorable gathering because their celebration and gratitude were so genuine. They seemed to sing and dance with every ounce of energy they had.

They formed what I know only to call a conga line and danced and sang around their cows and us for the better part of an hour. They would stop, someone would speak, we would give a cow or a bicycle away, and they would start celebrating again. It was getting dark, and I wondered how we were going to get home.

I was beginning to anticipate a very long, wet boda boda ride back, but about that time, our van showed up. I have no idea how many miles BJ must have had to drive to get to where we were. We boarded the van, and I assumed we were heading home. You would think by now, I would have learned never to have that assumption. Instead, Timothy announced that we still had three more cows to give away that night.

Any attempt to try to guess where we ended up in the jungle would be useless. We drove deep into the wilderness; it was almost so dark that you couldn't see. Still, occasionally you would see a shadowy figure walking along the road carrying water jugs, or sticks of sugar cane, or a bundle of clothing on their heads.

Off the side of the road, you could still make out mud huts with thatched roofs. There were usually no doors or windows.

Often, a sheet hanging in the entranceway was the door. Some of these homes had a fire going outside. Many of them had various vegetables and fruit for sale. Which begs the question, who in the middle of this jungle was there to buy their products? I guess someone forgot to tell them the old business phrase, "Location, location, location."

We finally arrived at a clearing in the jungle, and there once again was a crowd of people ready to greet us. No matter what time it was or how long a group had been waiting, they always wanted to sing and dance for us and express their gratitude. Usually we would be seated, and some fruit and water would be presented to us, and the children would perform. Then Timothy would get them excited about receiving their cow, and the wild celebration would begin. This night, using the light of our cell phones, we were able to give away three cows.

I had been looking around for the cows, and they were nowhere to be found. Then coming from somewhere in the jungle, I heard the sound of a truck. It pulled up, and we had the exciting adventure of off-loading three very anxious cows amid cheering children and adults. No one was stampeded, and we added three more cows to our rapidly growing herd.

What a day it had been! You see why I said that this was a day that would stand out in our memory? It started in the morning with the encounter with the group checking out the mzungus in the van, then the downed power poles and live power lines, the albino children, the boda boda ride, to off-loading three cows in the pitch-black jungle. It was nice to have an uneventful, although bumpy, muddy ride home.

The next morning was the beginning of the two-day Christian Educators' Convention. It was evident that a lot of preparation and planning had gone into this convention. It was in one location,

Mukono, rather than several areas out in the jungle. I can't tell where Mukono ends and Kampala begins. It is one massive conglomerate of humanity. The conference was at a large facility that had a Bible College as part of its ministry.

The 2015 UCCSU Christian Educators' Convention

The convention had very good attendance and was made up of more administrators than at some of the past conventions. There was even a very knowledgeable educator from the Ugandan Department of Education. He kept responding to questions and gave valuable input in the conversations. He did not let me know that he was with the Department of Education until well into the second day of the conference. He told me that his primary responsibility was oversight of the state testing that all schools in Uganda are required to take. He seemed to be pleased with the conference and the things we were discussing. I am sure he reported back to the department and that it added to a favorable attitude toward UCCSU and IACCS.

There is a noticeable difference between the level of professional training and professionalism with the teachers and administrators that come from these larger city schools. That is understandable for two reasons. First, as I mentioned earlier, teachers can find it easier to live in the cities and can earn more money. The other reason is they have access to better training and resources. That, of course, is not always so. I have encountered some highly effective, skilled teachers in some of the most remote and poorest schools. But they are in those schools because of their calling and conviction. These exceptional teachers in the rural schools remind me of the teachers I hired in the first year of the school I started in 1974. They were all young, right out of college. Our enrollment and tuition were so low that we couldn't afford to pay very much. We opened with a total of 54 children, and the maximum tuition anyone paid was $500 per year.

I had to meet with all the teachers and say, "I believe God has called us to this, but we can't pay what I had hoped we would be able to pay. All I can do is promise that we won't starve to death. Many of the teachers lived together in a dormitory setting. We settled on paying each teacher $8.00 per student per week. In the beginning, most teachers had less than ten students. Enrollment did grow to 154 by the end of that year, but the teachers all made huge sacrifices to get the school open. The teachers in rural Uganda make almost nothing – some as little as $3,000 per year. They often live in tiny rooms at the school or in the dorms with the orphans and eat the same food as the children. They are living Spartan lives out of the conviction that what they are doing is making a difference.

This, in no way, should diminish the role of any teachers who are in the larger schools in city centers. They are also sacrificing and making a difference in the lives of the children they lead. This was demonstrated so clearly during the conference. When we entered the auditorium, there was a children's choir up on the stage singing and performing. The first song that I recognized was, *My Hope Is Built on Nothing Less*, or *On Christ the Solid Rock I Stand*. It was spectacular, so much so that I asked them to sing it again. I found out that these children were all orphans and had not had any chorale experience. They had responded to the guidance and instruction of an excellent teacher who believed in them and saw their potential. These children could hold their own with any of the traveling groups that come to America to sing in churches to raise money for orphanages back in Africa. That is not a slight on these groups. They are great, but it is a statement of how outstanding these children are.

As mentioned, this convention was a two-day conference I had been so involved in the teaching at the conference, I had not seen Gary or Pete for two days. I was not sure what they had been up to.

At the end of the conference, Timothy had Gary and Peter join us at the meeting, and the cow story and the building of the children's church were shared with the conference. Again, their involvement was enthusiastically celebrated. At the end of the day, we headed back to Katosi to see the progress in the children's church project. As we pulled up to the project, it was a sight to remember for a very long time. The ground had been completely cleared and leveled (remember, no heavy equipment of any kind). A group of ten or fifteen young men was carrying huge granite rock, weighing anywhere from twenty to I would guess seventy-five pounds. They were walking along a narrow strip of soil above a ditch that ran the length of the building. Not a single one of these young men had shoes on. They were doing this backbreaking work barefoot! I watched for several minutes

– they would carry their load about twenty yards, drop their rock in the trench, and turn and walk back to pick up another rock.

Not once did I see anyone slack off or try to pick up the smallest rock or lag back to let others carry more rocks.

They worked equally and shared the load evenly. It wouldn't be long before this building would come up out of the ground.

No shoes and lots of muscle

It was time to grab a bite and get packed up to head home. Gary, Pete, and I gathered in the little dining area. A young pastor named Moses (lots of biblical names in Uganda) joined us.

While waiting for dinner, I decided to video Gary and Pete and ask them about their thoughts about the trip. Below is an excerpt from that interview:

Pete and Gary interview
(have to read hearing a strong British accent):

Tony: "Peter, here we are, the last day of our trip to Uganda. I know you haven't been very emotional during this trip (said sarcastically).

Pete: Chuckles

Tony: Tell me what this trip has meant to you and what has been the most impacting or most meaningful thing to you.

Pete: The most meaningful thing has been how grateful the people are while having nothing. Reminding me that we should be grateful for the air we breathe and the water we drink, instead of worrying about the things we buy... the trash.

Peter then deflects our attention to meeting Pastor Moses, a young Ugandan pastor, who was sitting next to him, sharing in the breakfast we were having. Pastor Moses was a very humble young pastor who had been pastoring his church for eight years. He was quick to let us know that he "had but one wife" and four children.

Tony: Gary, what about you? What has impacted you?

Gary: Such a wide range of emotions. It is humbling; what people who have nothing can accomplish. It is amazing what people can do and how they can love. The people of Uganda are some of the most humble, gracious, kind people I have ever met. They get by with whatever is around and making do. There is no new iPhone, new computer, new tennis shoes – they just get by; whatever they get, they just live with it. We saw that when we handed out the cows. Having fresh milk is a luxury, and some of these kids really needed it and enjoy it.

He then added: I want to thank Tony for inviting us to come, it really changed my life.

Tony to Gary: Tell us about the conversation you were having last evening and what the exponential growth rate is supposed to be.

Gary: Right now, there are about 34 million (actually approaching 46 million as of 2019) people in Uganda and with the mortality rate going down (it was around 20% and now has dropped significantly).

That means that by 2030, Uganda could have over 64 million people. Everywhere we went in the last few days, we would see people in little villages; we would see houses that have actually been condemned and are going to be torn down.

Have no idea where they are going to live (This is actually part of the road expansion. The people simply come by and put a large "X" on the side of the house. That basically lets the owners know that their home is in the way of the new road and is going to be torn down).

If you double the population, it is just going to add to the amount of need.

> I think education is the key. Breaking the cycle and the more that we can do to break that cycle, that when 2030 does come, we will see those numbers reduced.

Whether these numbers are entirely accurate, only time will tell, but Gary said it well. The answer is education; education that is accurately taught and heeded. Sometimes the Church and Christian organizations get a bit squeamish talking about sex education and population control, but if we don't, we will be dealing with much more significant problems in the future.

Statistics show that the average age of Ugandan women for giving birth is just over 18 years of age. The birthrate is one of the highest in the world at 5.8 children per woman. Here is the statistic that should cause pause – actual fertility exceeds women's desired fertility by one or two children. As gains are made in reducing the mortality rate (the area where the most significant gains are occurring), it gives us a new problem: the population grows exponentially. There is unmanageable increased pressure on and already stressed, and fragile infrastructure. Clearly, the solution is not to let more babies die. There is a delicate balance that must be walked in addressing this. We cannot inflict Western standards on the Ugandan culture. You can stress biblical truth, but it must be done in the context of the culture.

For example, we would teach that it is never right to have a child and abandon that child or leave them on the curb because you have had more children than you want or can care for. The Ugandan Church is standing in the gap and addressing these issues well. Here are a few of the things that they are addressing actively: sex outside of marriage is wrong. Remain monogamous (as mentioned earlier, their symbol of being a committed Christian is to say, "I am the husband of but one wife"). Have only those children you can adequately care for (which involves teaching on birth control). Do not have children to simply increase your work force.

I ended the interview as Timothy and Janepher joined us for dinner. They presented us with several gifts, some made by the children, and a traditional Ugandan dress to take home to Colleen.

The next morning, we took a quick spin by Winners Home.

I took a quick trip over to the clinic to see what its condition was compared to previous years.

Unfortunately, the supplies were not what they had been the year before. It was still clean and being used, but it clearly needed some restocking.

It strengthened my belief that I need to find a Christian doctor who would join me in this mission (it would be another two years, but a young Christian doctor started attending our church and has joined me on two trips).

Next, I walked over to check the water system.

It had been improved. Two large holding tanks had been installed next to the main tank, and many people were filling up their yellow water cans.

It was clearly working well for the orphanage and for the village of Katosi as well. Timothy came to me and said we had one more cow to give away on the way to the airport. He sent Peter and Gary off in one direction and me off to give away another cow. We then met back in Mukono at the conference center, loaded our luggage and were off to the airport for another late-night flight out of Entebbe. As we were saying our goodbyes in Mukono. I commented to Janepher that we had really covered some ground on this trip, and then I recorded her response.

Trip #4 Unto the Least of These

She laughed and said, "Hooo! You came to Entebbe, from Entebbe to Kampala, to Mukono to Katosi; from Katosi to Gesaga; from Gesaga you went to Beuenge; from Beuenge you went to Jinja; from there you crossed the Nile; and you crossed the Nile again and came back to Jinja and went to Kayunga; from Kayunga back to Mukono; back to Katosi; then today you have been in Nakifuma." Then she laughed her big, delightful laugh and said, "Welcome back. God bless you. Thank you for sending them to Uganda. Bye-bye." And waved a big goodbye wave to the camera.

And, with that wave, we were off to the airport to close out this very memorable trip.

On the way to the airport, Timothy decided we needed to stop to get a bite to eat. We pulled into what would be comparable to a Ugandan shopping mall. We pulled into a shopping area parking lot surrounded by a concrete fence about eight feet high. The gate had a guard standing at the entrance, and you had to let him look in your vehicle to make "sure of"…I am not sure of what! I looked around to see what kind of exotic Ugandan restaurant we might be getting ready to visit. This, after all, was Entebbe, the hub where almost everyone flying in or out of Uganda had to come. They must really have some interesting, good places to eat.

And there it was in all its glory, a real exotic Ugandan restaurant, a Kentucky Fried Chicken! We had to chuckle. We are on the other side of the globe, and Timothy's big treat was a KFC.

It was good, and it was fast.

As you approach the airport, you have to clear security. There is a checkpoint with an armed military guard. Typically, what happens is that your vehicle is inspected to make sure you are not taking weapons or explosives into the airport.

All passengers get out of the vehicle and walk through a security screening area. Typically, that was what is done, but this time, Timothy called the guard over, and I heard him say something about the President. The guard looked in at us, and I started to get out to walk through the checkpoint, but he put his hand up and said, "No, no." I am not sure what Timothy told him I was the president of, but it was the one and only time that I have not had to walk through security. In any case, the President and his two guards, (Peter and Gary), where shortly boarding a plane and heading back home.

Chapter 7
Trip #5 Rick Strong and the Mayah

"Aim at heaven and you will get earth thrown in. Aim at earth and you get neither."-C.S. Lewis, "Mere Christianity" (1952)

Before we begin to talk about trip #5, I must first give some background information to lead up to it. The backdrop of this story is a story of deep friendships. The first friend is Rick Moeller. Rick is a wonderful friend who was a great Islamorada, backcountry fishing captain. He had been born and raised in the Keys. A well-educated, thoughtful Florida Gator. For years, Rick and I had been having spiritual conversations, and on several occasions, he had said that he accepted Christ as his Savior. But he was also a man with lots of doubts and questions. I loved that about him. He was a lot like the guy in Mark 9:24, who said, *"Lord I believe; help me with my unbelief."*

I so appreciated his honesty and loved to spend time answering his questions. His wife had been a Christian for several years, and his daughter, who was in college, was also a Christian. His oldest son was and is a lot like his dad. He believed, but had lots of questions. One day well into the journey, I received a call from him, and he said, "Both kids are going to be in town in a few days, and

I was wondering if you would be willing to baptize all of us." I was thrilled! This was a significant faith move on Rick's part. In a few days, we met at a long dock running out into the Atlantic, waded out several yards off the dock, and Rick and his two adult children were baptized.

He and Karen, his wife, attended our church regularly and Rick continued to grow spiritually, but thankfully continued to ask tough, compelling questions.

One afternoon, I had finished up at my office and was heading home when I received a tearful call from Karen. She said, "Tony, we need you!" That was about all she could get out. I was about two miles from their home. I whipped my car around in the middle of US 1 and darted back to their home. When I walked in, they were both in their upstairs living room. Even though it was a bright day, the room had a sad darkness that had descended on it. Before I could even ask what was wrong, they began to tell me that they had just gotten back from a doctor's appointment, where Rick had been diagnosed with stage-four lung cancer. Rick's Dad, Dickie, had died from lung cancer but had been a smoker. Rick, on the other hand, had never been a smoker and was stunned by the news. They knew painfully well what this disease could do and the painful road that they were facing.

All of a sudden, the hope and promise of heaven became very real. Rick and Karen determined that they were going to fight with everything they had to beat this terrible disease. They had the typical highs and lows, the successes and the defeats of families that have to battle cancer. My own Dad had died from lung cancer in 1971, so this was especially painful to me. But I was also trying to encourage the entire family by telling them that I was hopeful because they were fighting cancer now, not back in 1970. With the advances that had been made in treatments, there was far more hope. Rick battled for several years, but slowly cancer began to drain his life away from him.

We are going to step away from this part of the story for now to tell you about the other friendship.

When I am finished, all the pieces will fall into place, and you will see why this trio of friends is so tightly woven together.

The second friend is a man named Mike. There are only a handful of men in your life that you can genuinely say you love, but Mike is one of those men that I can say I love like a son. But we didn't start as friends. In fact, quite the opposite, and most people today would probably say, "I don't know how those two guys could be friends!" Here is the story behind all of that. Our community had recently been incorporated into Islamorada, Village of the Islands. Like many new governments, we were dealing with some of the growing pains associated with a new community. The first meeting that involved an encounter between Mike and me involved the establishment of Founders Park. It is a beautiful park with baseball, softball, and soccer fields, tennis courts, a marina, fitness area, Olympic pool, and a government center. The park had one of the only beaches in the area. The park had been a resort before the Village had purchased it, so there was a small beach pavilion that served food and drinks by the beach. A discussion was being made to allow alcoholic beverages be served at the beach stand after the park opened. At the time, I was president of the Upper Keys Athletic Association. I had been approached by several parents who were concerned that this would be a bad idea.

I agreed because I felt that allowing parents to drop their children off for a ball game or practice and then go to the beach and have a few drinks was a horrible idea. I argued this before the council and said, "We have enough problems with parents behaving at ball games without alcohol being involved. There are plenty of places to have a drink in the Keys, Founders Park does not need to be one of those places."

What I didn't know was that Mike was the vendor who was attempting to get the contract for the beach concession.

Suffice it to say, we had words about this issue. In the end, the beach concession was voted down.

Then a second issue came up. The newly formed village council called and asked for my help in addressing a problem that had surfaced. There was an adult bar that had nude dancing as their major calling card. There was no ordinance in the Village to address adult entertainment in our community. The council asked if I would come and address the issue as a pastor.

I agreed to do some homework and then speak at the next council meeting on the issue. When I arrived for the council meeting, the room was already packed with people representing both sides of the issue. I was introduced to two men, the man who would manage the establishment, and the other, a man whom I had already met, Mike; the same guy from the beach concession debate. He was a well-known community figure and was supportive of the establishment.

I addressed the issue and basically said that without an ordinance, this establishment seemed to be grandfathered in. But unless we wanted to completely change the family-friendly environment of Islamorada into an adult entertainment island, there needed to be an ordinance in place. A lot of conversation and debate ensued, centered around the fact that we were known as the Fishing Capital of the World and a diving center. We were trying to attract and maintain a place that would have a broad appeal to families coming to Islamorada. The other side said this would add another layer of entertainment to people visiting our island.

Mike spoke in support of the establishment. After the meeting, we had a civil conversation, and we went our separate ways.

The ordinance was put in place that would prevent further development of adult entertainment in the Village.

Fast forward a few years, Mike and I had interacted on several occasions, and he had been very supportive of our school. Mike decided to run for Village Council and eventually became Mayor. He was a very successful owner and operator of a popular restaurant, Mangrove Mike's, in the heart of Islamorada. I ate lunch there fairly regularly and began to get to know Mike and see a different side to him. Mike was and is deeply committed to our community. He has a special place in his heart for the disenfranchised or people with special needs. I have rarely known anyone more willing to help anyone in need. If he had been in the biblical story of the Good Samaritan, he would have been the Samaritan who stopped and cared for the injured traveler. On a fairly regular basis, some need, or crisis would involve Mike, and he would call me to step in and help him with the problem. Because of this, over time, a genuine friendship began to develop. Mike knew of our Uganda trips and, at one point, said he would like to go with us.

I told him that I would love for him to join us.

Now, to tie Rick, Mike, and me together; Rick was also a very good friend of Mike's, so as he began to battle cancer, the three of us walked together with Rick's family through those tough days. In fact, the picture below was taken of the three of us at Mangrove Mike's, showing our Rick Strong bracelets that we wore in support of Rick and his battle. My second book, *Bone of My Bone, the Journey Continues*, is dedicated to Rick.

Three friends and Rick Strong bracelets

That is the background information that needs to be kept in mind as we prepare for Trip #5 to Uganda.

After returning from Trip #4, I went to Mangrove Mike's and was telling Mike about the trip and showing him pictures. He said, "I've got to go!"

I said, "If you are serious, I will make it happen." He said, "I'm serious." Several months had to pass before the next trip. But I continued to work on raising money for cows and the other Ugandan projects, and giving Mike information about the trip. Peter had also told me that he wanted to go again.

In the meantime, Rick's battle with cancer continued. There were times that it looked like he was going to beat it, and at times like he was not.

Mike was running for Village Council again. The election was in early November, and so we scheduled the Uganda trip to occur in the middle of November, so the election would be over. He was re-elected and was selected as Vice Mayor. He had some campaign funds leftover and asked me to think of a unique project we could do to benefit Ugandan children.

A day or two before we were to depart for Uganda, Rick and his family had asked me to come to visit them at a cancer center on the Florida mainland.

I drove up, knowing that this was going to be a tough visit. When I went in, the family was with Rick in a room specifically designed for people battling cancer. His wife, two children, and his sister were all together. Rick was struggling, but upbeat, as usual. We talked very frankly about his battle and the days ahead, and we dreamed about tarpon and bonefishing together. At one point, he said he wanted to pray. I had never heard Rick pray, but as he began, I knew that this was going to be an extraordinary moment. The words that came were from somewhere deep in his soul. He expressed love for his wife and family that could only come from a man who understood the depths of the love of God. I was in tears and speechless for several minutes. It was time for me to return to the Keys, and I still had to pack for the trip, so I said my goodbyes to Rick and the family, headed back home with the hope that this was not my last visit with Rick.

On November 14, 2016, I received a call from Rick late in the evening. He knew that Mike, Pete, and I were leaving for Uganda the next day, and he wanted to talk. I could tell his breathing was labored, but he said to me that he still intended to beat this thing and stand up in front of church and tell everybody how he had kicked this thing's butt! I told him that I looked forward to that day; then the conversation turned to talk about heaven and being with the Lord.

He was very confident that when he died, he would be with the Lord. At one point, I said, "Rick, you know that one way or the other, you are going to kick this thing's butt." I don't know whether it is going to be in this life or when you are looking back from heaven, and you have the ultimate victory over death. But you are going to beat it!"

On the morning of the 15th, Mike, Pete, and I boarded the plane in Miami headed for Uganda. We had a layover in Atlanta that was going to prove to be a game-changer for this trip.

Sometime after 5:00PM, we had boarded the plane and were settling in for the long trip to Uganda. Mike and I were seated together, and as we were settling in, my phone rang. I answered, holding my breath, because it was from Rick's sister, Julie. She said, "Tony, Rick is in heaven." I asked her if she knew that we had talked the night before. And she said that she didn't, but that that was the only call he had made that night.

I knew I had to tell Mike but had to get myself together first. I am sure that he had a good idea about what had just happened, but I leaned over and just whispered, "Rick is gone."

Mike didn't speak.

Instead, he put his jacket hoodie over his head and disappeared under a blanket. It was about two hours into the trip before Mike surfaced again. When he did, he said he wanted to use his leftover campaign funds to do something in Rick's honor and ask me to try to think of the best way to do that. I told him I would, and we went back to silence.

I thought of the usual areas that I had seen with needs – cows, food, beds, insect netting, computers, building materials, the clinic. None of these seemed to hit the sweet spot for Mike, so we kept talking and thinking.

We had arrived in Entebbe a little earlier than in past years. After clearing Customs, we met Timothy and his entourage and introduced everyone to Mike. I began to explain that Mike was the Vice Mayor of the Village of Islamorada. I could tell that the word "Vice" was not registering correctly. I was afraid they were afraid he was involved in something illegal or sleazy. I settled on just calling him the Mayor! That title has stuck with him each year that he has traveled with me. But Ugandans don't call him Mayor. They say it more like "Mayah," with two short 'a's and an "h" at the end as almost a separate syllable. After some laughs about the "Mayah," we loaded all the gear in the van and were off to for the exciting ride to Katosi. I knew it was going to be fun to watch Mike's face and reaction as we hit the bumpy road and then entered Katosi. After we had been driving a few minutes, Timothy asked me if I knew I was speaking at his daughter's wedding. I said, "I know she is getting married and we are attending." He said, "No, I want you to speak. It is a great honor to speak at a wedding, and I want you to do the honor." I said, "Okay." And began immediately to work on what I was going to say at a Ugandan wedding. The road had not gotten any better since the year before, and Mike's reaction was as I hoped it would be, amazed, shocked, and apprehensive.

All of the activities of arriving, the introductions, and the bumpy ride had served as a bit of a diversion from the sadness we were feeling about Rick.

Before we settled in for the night, Mike asked, "What do you think about a park or playground to honor Rick?" I said I thought it was a great idea and that we should run it by Timothy.

I had a hard time getting to sleep because I kept thinking about what I was supposed to say at a Ugandan wedding, what building a playground would look like, and the grief that was hitting me about Rick. I finally decided on just talking about 1 Corinthians 13 and the qualities of love for my part in the wedding. But that was two days away. Before that, we had cows to buy, a huge launch celebration, and Children's Day on Friday. I was doing an educators convention for first timers in the Kiboga District on Thursday. Plus, we had a playground to plan. We talked with Timothy over breakfast and settled on a playground for all the children in the village of Katosi. Timothy lined up a crew to find, and purchased the best playground equipment that they could find, and gave them an idea about the types of equipment to buy. Mike and a team were off to find playground equipment. It was going to take all week for all of the equipment to be built and put in place.

Mike discovered his favorite Ugandan delicacies, chicken-on-stick. Any time you go through an area where there are street vendors and have to slow down, they will rush your vehicle selling water, sodas, fruit, and chicken-on-a-stick.

Timothy first bought some and shared it with Mike and Pete. They were sold on this as their go-to food when traveling around the countryside.

Side note: I am the only one who has not eaten chicken-on-a-stick. But I am also the only one that has not come down with a stomach bug...any correlation? I don't know, but I don't plan to find out.

Day two involved two significant events, the teaching of three sessions at a Christian Educators' Convention in the Kiboga District to educators who were attending for the first time. This meant I was reviewing much of what had been covered in 2011 and establishing a strong philosophy of Christian education presentation. The second event was the giving of several gifts – cows (Mike's first cow give away), soccer balls, and bicycles in the same district. Oh, by the way, my Rotary friend had increased his gift to $15,000 for this year!

Each year that he gives me the gift, he does so with tears in his eyes and is so gracious with his words about what we are doing.

These gifts and the conference were crucial for this district. The Kiboga District is located in Central Uganda. It is primarily a rural district and so most of the population is involved in some sort of agriculture. I mention this because one of the great challenges that is being addressed is keeping children in school when they reach secondary school age. Strong, young, able-bodied workers are needed for the fields. While many parents understand the need for education and would tell you that they see education as the means for their children to have a better life, the immediate need to have workers for their land is always creating tension.

One of the things that Uganda has done to address this issue is to join the UN initiative of the Universal Primary Education (UPE) program launched in 1997. Among other things, the stated goal was to "Ensure that, by 2015, children everywhere, boys and girls alike, will be able to complete a full course of primary schooling." It must be kept in mind that the UPE is a global initiative of the UN, not just a Ugandan program. But Uganda has experienced more success in achieving this goal than other developing countries. The following data from the UN will help to clarify this statement:

- Enrollment in primary education in developing regions reached 91 percent in 2015, up from 83 percent in 2000.
- In 2015, 57 million children of primary school age were out of school.
- Among youth aged 15 to 24, the literacy rate has improved globally from 83 percent to 91 percent between 1990 and 2015, and the gap between women and men has narrowed.
- In the developing regions, children in the poorest households are four times as likely to be out of school as those in the richest households.
- In countries affected by conflict, the proportion of out-of-school children increased from 30 percent in 1999 to 36 percent in 2012.[11]

Those numbers should concern us! They show the reason for the mission of IACCS to be carried forth. The fact that there are

57 or 58 million children of primary school age that currently do not attend school worldwide and leaves them condemned to extreme poverty.

As Uganda strives to maintain a democratically elected government, they have, under the UPE, waived school fees for government-run primary schools. As a result, far more children are remaining in primary school. As mentioned earlier, the government is responsible for educating two children per family. That means that the other children in the family either remain uneducated or are enrolled in one of the faith-based or other private educational programs. I can't stress enough, the dynamic role that church and parachurch organizations are playing in providing education and care for those children that would otherwise be neglected. According to Timothy Kakooza, the president of UCCS-U, there are 216 member schools from 14 districts, with 54,236 students in these schools.

Compared to American private schools, fees are very small, as low as $75.00/year, with a more upscale school costing up to $900 US per year. But the thing that must be kept in mind is that when the average person is living on a dollar or two per day, these are astronomical expenses. Many schools/orphanages are dependent on finding outside support for the children they are trying to minister to.

An American-based organization, known as E3, gives an excellent primer in Ugandan education. I have included it here to help readers gain a clearer understanding of the educational system.

Government-run schools range from Primary 1 (P-1) to Primary 7 (P-7), and secondary schools ranging from Secondary 1 (S-1) to Secondary 6 (S-6). Students take their major exams at the P-7, S-4, and S-6 levels. If a student's score is not high enough, they are not allowed to continue in school. In this case, a student would then consider vocational training (if they can afford it) or dropping out altogether.

Ugandan School Level Equivalents

USA	Uganda
Kindergarten	*P-1
1st Grade	*P-2
2nd Grade	*P-3
3rd Grade	*P-4
4th Grade	*P-5
5th Grade	*P-6
6th Grade	*P-7 with Primary Learning Exams
"O" Level Ordinary	
7th Grade	*S-1
8th Grade	*S-2
9th Grade	*S-3
10th Grade	*S-4
"A" Level Advanced	
11th Grade	*S-5 with Certificate of Education Exams
12th Grade	*S-6 with Advanced Certificate of Education Exams

Since 1998, the Ugandan government has stated that they will allow three children from each family to attend primary school while paying only minimal tuition. These schools, in which classrooms can have more than 100 children to one teacher, are called UPE (Universal *Primary Education*) schools. This "rule" does not necessarily apply across the board and students who should be eligible for a "free education" are not. In these cases, a student must pay whatever fees the school charges.

There are generally two levels of schools in Uganda: Higher Standard and Lower Standard.

- It is nearly impossible to enter a Ugandan university without having gone to a Higher Standard school.

- *Higher Standard schools generally teach in English, often have a religious affiliation and are non-discriminatory toward girls.*
- *Higher Standard schools have a much higher percentage of their students successfully passing Leaving Exams than those of a Lower Standard school.*
- *Higher Standard schools generally pay their teachers a decent wage and may provide housing. Lower Standard schools often have a reliability problem with teachers not showing up for class and taking on second jobs.*
- *Higher Standard schools generally have smaller classroom sizes as compared to Lower Standard schools and generally have much better building facilities.*

There are three types of schools in Uganda: government schools, private day schools, and private boarding schools.

- *Government schools tend to run in the Lower Standard school arena.*
- *Private day and boarding schools will generally be in the Higher Standard arena.*
- *Boarding schools offer the following critical assets for a rural student to successfully complete their education:*
  - *They are Higher Standard schools.*
  - *Students have a safe place to sleep, unlike at government or day schools.*
  - *Students do not have to walk two hours or more to school in the morning, which is very often the case when attending other types of schools.*
  - *Students have 24/7 supervision and scheduled study time, unlike most would have if they lived in their rural villages.*

- *Students receive adequate daily meals and a school uniform, which is often not available to them otherwise.*
- *Sponsored students don't have to work to provide for their tuition and can dedicate more time to studies.*

(Please note: the term "private school" may conjure up visions of an exclusive preparatory school to U.S. readers, but be assured that "private" here simply means not government-run.)

Why are there school fees?

The student must pay for a uniform (required), shoes, sports uniform, school supplies, exam fees, and other "minor" items. Each school requires that a student brings their own mattress and bedding materials. Secondary boarding school fees typically range from $650-$850 U.S. per year. This is usually not affordable with a rural family earning an average of less than $2 a day; it is rare that they can support the secondary education of one child/teen, let alone 4-5 children. It is easy to see how this can be unattainable for a youth from a poor clan or village.

What happens if school fees are not paid?

If school fees are not paid, the student cannot enter school until they are paid off. This is a frequent event, seeing how the majority of students are coming from very poor families. They miss some school, pay the fees and go back, fall behind on fees again, miss more school, pay the fees...it is a vicious cycle that takes a toll on the child, which eventually leads to a slow decline toward the bottom of the class, and ultimately, they will have to drop out of school. Jobs are incredibly hard to find, so it would be unusual if a child could actually find a job to earn the necessary school fees. Most students are extremely poor, and many are orphaned with no means of support. Without assistance, the *likelihood of them ever obtaining an education is almost non-existent. There are children and teens trying to do whatever they can to earn money, and praying that somehow their school fees will be paid.*

How do they get to the university level?

To advance to a university, a student must successfully pass all three Leaving Exams (see Ugandan school level equivalents). To acquire a government scholarship to study in a university, a student must pass with a perfect score in their S-6 exams. Only a very small percentage of Ugandan students have the opportunity to receive internal assistance by means of a government university scholarship. If they're in the top one-third of the examinees, they might qualify to enter a university, but they would have to pay the tuition themselves. A year of room, board, and tuition at a university typically costs around $1,600 U.S. Most university study programs last three years.[12]

I felt that this lengthy sidebar was necessary to really get a grasp of education in Uganda, and for that matter, much of the remainder of the developing counties in Africa.

Now back to our trip. When I arrived at the conference, I recognized the building.

It had been one of the places we had visited on trip number one in 2011. It was encouraging to see the growth that had occurred in this district.

The building was painted a dark red/amber color, unlike most others we had visited, so it was easy to remember. It was also a more substantial, solid, brick building, indicating that this ministry had significant influence in this community.

When I arrived, there was considerable celebration as if old friends who had not seen each other for some time were being reunited. One of the things that set this group out was the fact that they had clearly considered the conference an important event. As I have mentioned, Ugandans always dress up, but the teachers and administrators at this event really dressed up! They were ready to be challenged and encouraged. The conference was well attended with over 200-300 eager new teachers, with a deep desire to become the best teachers they possibly could. The teachers in rural areas need more encouragement because of their limited resources and the daily challenge of just keeping their students in school.

When we do a conference in a rural area, I intentionally spend more time cheering the teachers on. I try to affirm them and tell them how valuable and vital to the next generation they are. They need to know that they are making a difference.

As the conference was wrapping up, Mike and Pete joined us. They had been out making the purchases for our giveaways. In this case, it was to be cows and bikes. This was going to be Mike's first cow! I was anxious to see how this affected him. Mike's heart is so tender towards helping others that I suspected he would be deeply moved, and he indeed was; so much so that he has returned to Uganda with me every year since!

We gave away three cows at this location and a number of sturdy bicycles to several of the administrators. A friend of mine back in the States was selling soccer balls, but they weren't just your everyday soccer balls; they were wordless book soccer balls! For those who are not familiar with the wordless book idea, it is a book, or in this case, a soccer ball, with no words, just colors; red, black, white, gold, and green. The colors are used to explain God's love and His plan of salvation through Jesus (I will let you Google it to see how the story is told). I had purchased as many of these as I thought I could and brought them with me. The entire time we were on this trip, we were giving out the soccer balls and using them to share the Gospel.

As we left the Kiboga District, Timothy began to talk about how we would see many of these teachers the next day at what UCCSU was calling an official launch event. He explained that this was a more significant event than any we had ever had.

He said that the Minister of Education, Janet Museveni, was to be in attendance, along with several other dignitaries, and that most of the schools both teachers and students would be at this event. Keep in mind that his daughter was getting married the next day. I was amazed at the organizational ability and perseverance of Timothy to pull these events off with a wedding the following day.

He was right; this launch celebration was far more than I could have imagined. The event was held in Lugazi, at Bernard Bogere's large school/orphanage. As we arrived at the front gate, we were warmly greeted by a uniformed officer who escorted us to a parking area. The first thing that got our attention was a small herd of five cows tethered to large shady trees. We were delighted to know that these were going to be given to orphanages at some point in the day's festivities. The next thing we noted was several brightly colored, festive tents that had been erected in a large square. They set up around the perimeter with an expansive central open area where all of the activities would take place. As we were being escorted across the campus to where we were to be seated, there was indeed a sense that this was indeed an extraordinary event. There were probably two thousand people or more seated and standing around the perimeter.

At one corner of the courtyard there was a very skilled band of high school students lead by a young conductor, who himself was playing a trumpet. I later learned that they were a group of high school students from a Christian school in Kampala. As soon as the band finished playing, another group of young girls began to sing. One of the older girls was singing and dancing around the edge of the crowd. She would stop at specific places in front of those of us seated, and with great expression, a captivating smile, and engaging voice drew us into the celebration. Her singing was followed by another, and then another. There had obviously been a great deal of rehearsal and preparation for this event. I noticed from time to time that some of the people who seemed to be responsible for the guests and speakers would come and whisper something to Timothy. There was always whisper in low tones, with serious looks on their faces. He would say something, shake his head, and they would move on. At one point, I asked Timothy if everything was okay. He shook his head and said, "No! The Minister of Education has called and is stuck in traffic in Northern Uganda. That is not good, the people will be very disappointed!"

He explained that she was trying to get back but that she was a very long way off. There were other dignitaries from various branches of the government. But the people had high expectations for Janet Museveni to be with them. They wanted her to see first-hand what a good job they were doing. The group remained in contact with her team throughout the day, with the hope that she might be able to make a brief late appearance. But that was not to be. Before I had left the United States, I had contacted Bob Goff, author of L*ove Does* and *Everybody Always*. I told him that it looked like we were going to have an opportunity to meet Mrs. Museveni, First Lady to Uganda and their Minister of Education. I asked him how I should address her. He said, "Excellency." I asked, "Your Excellency?" He replied, "No, just Excellency."

Then I asked if there was anything else that I should know. Bob told me that she had written a book and that I should read it.

I made sure that I had a copy and read it before this meeting.

I asked, "Anything else?" His response surprised me. He said, "Bling." I thought I had misunderstood and said, "What did you say?" He repeated, "Bling. She likes bling. And it would be nice to take some for her aide as well."

My Mother-in-Law, sweet Anne Cullen, had been living with us for the last three years of her life. She was an elegant lady. When she passed away, she had left behind quite a bit of jewelry. After her family members had taken what they wanted of it, there were still several beautiful pieces left behind. I decided to see if there might be anything there that might be appropriate for the First Lady of a nation. I found a perfect piece for both First Lady Museveni and her assistant.

As the day wore on, it became increasingly evident that the First Lady might not make it. It looked like I was going to have to give the jewelry as a wedding gift to Timothy's daughter and to his wife, Janepher.

About an hour into the celebration, Timothy called Peter and Mike to a microphone. He introduced Mike as the "Mayah." Mike addressed the group and gave Timothy a government pin from Islamorada. He began to speak as a film crew filmed and I made a video. His words were very affirming and appropriate for the moment.

He said, "I have never seen so much love and compassion for one another. That's what our children in American need to learn. I do believe what was said earlier, that 'education begins at home.' Then it goes to school, and God's going to help you."

Then he got a wry smile on his face and pointed to the children in the large crowd and said, "I tell you, if all the kids are missing after this event, it is because I took them home. I love you. Thank you." With that, he handed the microphone back to Timothy.

Then it was Peter's turn (or Peet-a, as he is called in Uganda). Timothy had Peter stand next to him in front of all the people. He told the story of how Peter had given for the first cow. Then he explained how that had started the cow ministry. I loved Peter's response. He had tears in his eyes as he always did, pointed his finger toward heaven, and gave all the credit to God for starting the cow ministry.

Then Timothy turned to me. He briefly told the story of how IACCS and the UCCS-U had come to be, thanked me, and turned the microphone over to me. I had been asked to speak to the group about IACCS and the future of Christian education in Uganda. I spent about twenty minutes challenging the adults and children with the value of Christian education and encouraging them to continue to strive for excellence. This was a valuable time because I knew several government officials were there.

There were representatives from each district, members of the Parliament, and the Department of Education. They needed to see the strength of these schools and the association. I believe that this day went a long way in solidifying and legitimizing the UCCS-U in the minds of the government officials, and that it strengthened the resolve of the schools for the future.

When I finished speaking, Timothy had the UCCS-U Board of Directors and a couple of students representing all the students come forward. An enormous cake was decorated as a Bible. On top were three large Roman candle, sparkler-type fireworks. The "Mayah" and "Peeta" were called up to join us in the celebration. After prayer and several minutes of cheering, a young student with a carving knife as big as he was began to cut the cake. Being an old school guy and dad, I was more concerned about the young boy with such a huge knife, and the fireworks than about cutting the cake. I kept pulling his hands back to keep him away from the flames and from chopping off any fingers. It all worked out fine, no one got injured, and no one went up in flames. I am not convinced that in the next few minutes we didn't witness an event like the feeding of the five thousand, because there was enough cake for all who wanted it…and kids always want cake!

Cake and fireworks! Yikes!

The next big event was to move to the other side of the campus where the cows were tethered. As each of the schools/orphanages was called up to receive their cow, there was great cheering and celebration, and a film crew filmed each of the groups receiving their cow. Once again, I was struck by the celebration and gratitude that was demonstrated as each cow was given away. As these celebrations were coming to an end and the day was winding down, it became clear that the Minister of Education was not going to make it. She had made a great effort but was simply too far away to get back. I asked Timothy about it and he said, "That was not good. Our people were very disappointed that she could not be with us." I encouraged and suggested that we try to set up a meeting with her on one of our future visits.

This day had come to an end, but now we had to prepare for the enormous Ugandan wedding of Katumba Crown Steven and Mighty Kakooza. Officially named Kitiibwa Glory Kakooza, but

Mighty is the name everyone calls her. Mighty, what an appropriate name, for she indeed is mighty. Bright, spunky, talented, I am sure she could run for President and win. Each of the Kakooza children are amazing and talented. Their parents have done a good job in giving them a desire for life and leadership. Each of the children has taken an active role in their parents' ministries and continue to do so as adults.

When we got back to Cross City in Katosi, Janepher came into the dining area and I asked if I could give her a gift. I explained my conversation back in the US with Bob Goff and his advice to take Janet Museveni some "bling." I told her that I would be honored if she would receive the necklace, I had brought for her. She was delighted, and when she opened the gift she exclaimed, "This is beautiful! I will wear it to the wedding tomorrow."

The next morning when I saw her, she had the necklace on, and it was a perfect match for her wedding outfit. I had to smile and think about how pleased my mother-in-law would be that this gift was so appreciated.

The wedding was held at the same facility were the UCCSU had formed and where the first and largest Christian Educators' Convention had been held. It was a large church, and was filled with several hundred people when we arrived.

A Ugandan wedding is something to behold. I don't mean to sound like I'm writing a socialite column here, but describing what a Ugandan wedding is like is worthy of a conversation. Remember that early on in this book I mentioned that one of the first things that a Christian man in Uganda will do is state that, "He is the husband of but one wife." This is because outside of the Christian community, polygamy is very common. It is also not uncommon for a man and woman outside of the church to live together long before there is a formal wedding ceremony, simply because there is not enough money for the elaborate wedding ceremony that Ugandan weddings are. What I will be describing here is the Uganda Christian wedding and courtship. Traditions will vary from region, tribe, clan, and cultural group, and by how much the couple has been influenced by Western culture. Some of the groups that will have varying cultural traditions specific to them would be Buganda (I'm most familiar with this culture because this is the region I stay in), Ankole (cattle are very much a part of their culture and traditions), Jopadhola, Bagisu, Lango, and Lugbara. The traditional Ugandan wedding is called an arranged marriage, but that does not mean that the couples don't know each other or have a say in who they wed. It does mean that the families must be included in the wedding process, and at least ceremonially agree. Traditionally, the elders must agree to the couple being wed. If a young man and woman are interested in one another, it must be the prospective groom who initiates the request for the hand of the woman. If the woman was to let the man know that she wanted to court or even hinted of the possibility, he would have to say, "No," because it would mean that he was "not a man" if he agreed to the relationship.

The Ugandan wedding ceremony, customs, and festivities have roots that may date back centuries into African culture and convey tribal, district, and clan traditions. The events leading up to the wedding engage the entire extended family, reflecting their heritage and honoring their ancestors. It would be rare for the wedding to just be about the bride and groom. It is truly about two families (term used loosely) becoming one. Because of this, most Ugandan weddings are three or four times larger than most American weddings. It is not uncommon for entire villages to participate in a wedding celebration by the time it concludes.

There are some key steps that take place under the banner of what we might call "the wedding." The first is the *Kwanjula*, meaning the "wedding proposal." It literally means, "to introduce."

The groom would have a spokesperson known as *Kateraruume*, most often an aunt/*senga* that would serve as his negotiator with the bride's parents. Their primary function would be to represent the groom's interest with the bride's family. The groom's family must make a payment, called the *Mutwalo*, to the bride's family, symbolizing the groom's ability to take care of his future bride. The size and amount of this bride price will vary, but the father may ask any price he desires. A cow is in some regions a customary gift. In Northern Uganda, the price may be as high as a hundred cows. For that reason, there are not many people from Southern Uganda marrying those in the North. When the cow or goat is received, it is a symbol that no other suitors may ask for the daughter's hand. In some cases, if the bride's family asked for a very large gift, it probably should serve as a hint to the suitor that they do not approve of this marriage. In today's culture, in some regions, these gifts are largely symbolic and may include Bibles, hymnals, walking sticks, or some other gifts of spiritual or cultural significance. If they are not just symbolic, they may be a cow, goat, or several of each. Along with the *Mutwalo* required by the bride's family, there are other required gifts in some cultures. They might include a variety of fruits and vegetables (eggplant is not considered an appropriate gift in some of the clans). These are usually carried in a traditionally-made, specifically designed basket. Other gifts might include bread, paraffin, cooking oil, spices (curry), sugar, salt, soap, and other related items. Meanwhile, the bride brings *emihingiro*, gifts for the groom's side of the family.

Once the proposal or bride price has been accepted by the girl's family, both families begin to discuss and plan the wedding ceremony. If there was agreement, the bride-to-be's parents would set a formal date for the *Kwanjula*. The *Kwanjula* includes an enormous feast for all, and a huge celebration that lasts close to six hours, and includes many cultural customs and traditions. It usually takes place a few weeks before the formal wedding ceremony. This is where the family formally becomes one. Many of the customs that are followed during this festivity represent this happening. The bride and her attendants, called *enshagariz*, are in separate quarters and do not see the groom until after a meal is shared with the groom and the bride's family. Prior to the meal, the men meet in a circle in a separate room and ceremonial bride price rituals and other customs are shared. After this ceremony concludes, the men are escorted to a table for the serving of the feast. This meal takes place about two hours into the ceremony. After the meal, the bride is presented. There is usually a festive dance of the bride and the *enshagariz*. One of the things that occurs throughout the celebration is that the bride changes dresses multiple times, and each time the dress get more extravagant and usually more colorful. Gifts are often presented from the groom's family members and group of friends to the bride and her family. The women wear beautiful dresses called a *gomesi* (pronounced *gomas*), typically a brightly colored silky dress with pointed sleeves and tied around the waist by a large cloth belt, and the men wear a kanzu, a long white tunic, with a suit coat over it. There is usually a great deal of traditional dance and songs, all choreographed to communicate various messages associated with the coming together of the families and the bride and groom. Full audience participation is expected with lots of clapping and joy.

What we would typically think of as the wedding ceremony is called the *Okuhingira*. In addition to many of the customs we would expect in an American wedding, this is when elders bless the bride and give her away to the groom. The *Okuhingira* is much about the bride's family. One of the major differences in a Ugandan wedding is that the bride and groom never kiss during the ceremony. They can hug, but anything more intimate is not considered proper for the formal ceremony.

After the church portion of the ceremony, there is an amazing feast. It is what we would think of as a wedding reception. The events usually are held in an open-air setting with festive tents, walkways, and a covered structure with two large throne-like seats just for the bride and groom. All of the wedding guests travel to the location of this event. Once seated, the meal is served. It includes a sumptuous feast for all invited. It is common for the menu to include *matooke* (mashed plantains) and *kalo* (millet paste), served with delicious accompaniments, mashed beans or peanuts, and a healthy serving of meat (beef or chicken). After the meal, a roving DJ makes various announcements and introductions and leads the festivities through a series of carefully planned, very carefully orchestrated, colorful processionals of the wedding party, songs, dances (by performers), and the other usual wedding merriment. During the event, gifts of all kinds are presented to the bride and groom (at the one I attended, even a mattress was given with a great deal of hooting and cheering). The *Okuningira* lasts for many hours. After the *Okuhingira*, the bride is not supposed to do any work for the next ten days. At that time, the cultural initiation takes place. During this tradition, the bride lights fire for the first time in the groom's kitchen, symbolizing that she is assuming the home-making responsibility for her new family.

I have done hundreds of weddings in America, but none more elaborate than this one. I was escorted to a platform and invited to take a seat in a large high-backed chair off the side of the platform. There was the usual seating of the parents and the recessional with groomsmen entering, followed by the bridesmaids. The elaborate and colorful suits and dresses were exceptional, and not colors that you see in weddings in the US. The men's suits were a bright royal blue, and the bridesmaids' dresses were a bright red (almost fluorescent) on the bottom that faded into blue tops with a flowered embroidered print. I have never seen more elaborate dresses, *gomesi*, and couldn't imagine the amount of craftsmanship it must have taken to produces these very special dresses. Instead of going to the stage, the groomsmen and bridesmaids were all seated in the front row. Just before Mighty and Timothy entered, two little flower girls entered, dressed in all-white dresses. After Timothy had given Mighty away and several words in Lugandan were spoken by another pastor, the couple, wedding party, certain family members, and others that had been designated earlier, gathered around the bride and groom up on the stage. The bride and groom knelt, and an extended series of prayers were offered for the couple.

After everyone had prayed, and certain gifts that had particular meaning in Ugandan culture were given, the entire group returned to their seats back in the audience. I was then summoned to come and speak. Steven and Mighty took seats directly in front of me in the front row. My message was simple. I opened the Bible to 1 Corinthians 13 and taught, as I do at most American weddings, on the elements of *agape* love. I challenged Steven to be a model of the love of Christ to Mighty. I challenged Mighty to love and honor Steven as the Bride of Christ, the Church.

After I concluded my portion, there were several more elements to the ceremony that were done in Lugandan, so I did not know much of what was taking place. At the conclusion of the formal church service, the wedding party, along with their families, and the three Mzungus (the three of us), gathered on the back steps of the church for photos. One of the things I remember most about this moment was that the photographer and videographers were almost identical to those I was used to back home. In fact, in some ways, they were ahead of the curve. At one point, I looked up and realized that there was a drone overhead filming everything that was taking place. Since this wedding, I have performed several weddings where drones were used, but this was a first for me.

After the photo session finished, we headed as a group in car caravan to a beautiful garden-park. Once again, there were the brightly colored high- pinnacled tents and open-air tables spread around the grounds. There was an arched walkway with a red runner for the wedding party to walk/dance down to their designated seats. As described earlier, the bride and groom's area was an elevated covered gazebo-type structure with a large seating area just for them. After seeing the spread and variety of food, I understood more fully what Scripture is talking about when it talks about a wedding feast. This was way beyond the typical wedding reception meal that I was used to seeing in America. This was a kill the fatted calf, pull out all the stops feast. I knew that the three of us (Mike, Pete, and I) were now officially being treated as Ugandan when we were given no silverware to eat our meal. It was fingers or fast! Needless to say, there was no fasting on this day. It was very enjoyable just watching Timothy and Janepher celebrating as proud parents. Throughout the afternoon, people would come and give various gifts to the couple, exchange a few words and hugs, and go back to their seats. I had wrapped the other piece of "bling" that I was going to give to the First Lady but decided it would be a good gift to give to Mighty, instead. I took it to her and told her how honored I had been to be a part of their wedding. In the center of the courtyard, I had noticed an enormous wedding cake that was going to feed this entire crowd. It was time for the bride and groom to do the honors of cutting the cake. Even this was a celebration in itself, with dancing and songs, and then the cutting of the cake. There was enough for everyone with some left over (I will explain why this is important in a moment).

The event was clearly going to last for hours, more into the evening, and Timothy very graciously offered to let us return to Katosi for some rest. We took him up on his offer and slipped away so that I could look over my message for the Sunday service the next morning.

Three Mzungus, a proud father and Mighty's wedding

Sunday morning was going to be exciting. Mike came from a Jewish family, but would probably not say he was a practicing Jew.

He grew up in Virginia Beach, next door to Jim and Tammy (the Bakers). Needless to say, that had left him with more than a little cynicism toward that flavor of Christian behavior. I must admit that I am also more than a bit cynical of that flavor! I wasn't sure how Mike was going to do with this church service. It can be Ugandan, wild and woolly! But whether intentional or not, Timothy made a smart move when we arrived. He took us straight to the children's church and straight to the core of Mike's heart. From that moment on, I had few worries about how Mike would feel. The children won his heart. This was the children's church that Pete and Gary had gathered materials for the previous year. We had seen the foundation being formed. Now the building was up as high as the walls, up to the tops of open windows and doors. It was ready for a header and a roof, but the children didn't care, they were anxious to have children's church without a roof. The roofing would take another two years, a couple of more trips, and more generous people to make it a reality. For now, a tarp tied off to the sides of the building to provide shade and some protection from passing showers would have to do.

One of the things that impresses me about many people in Ugandan culture is their ability to make do with whatever they have. And, it is not that they are just making do; they are finding contentment, satisfaction, and joy in the midst of it all. I have seen men put a new truck tire on a rim alongside the road with hardly any tools at all – no air tools, no jack, just a lug wrench, a pry bar, a wedge of wood, and several sturdy logs. I'm not talking about change a flat tire; I am talking about putting a new tire on a rim and then getting that on a truck. I see this in their schools as well. I have not seen a store-bought chalkboard in a classroom. They are boards painted with green or black chalkboard paint, and their chalk is usually a big chunk of soft limestone. No "Smart Boards" here! In fact, from time to time, I have had a teacher or administrator who knows something about the technology that is available in other parts of the world, ask about it and how they could get it in their school. I try to answer as kindly as I can, but also try to help them understand the quantum leap that has to occur before this is even a possibility. Many of their classrooms have no electricity, no Internet connection (or it is so slow that it would not accommodate their needs), no hardware, infrastructure, or support services to run their systems… it is an issue that requires nation-wide advancement, not just something that can be solved by sending old computers and school equipment to them.

This is, of course, truer in rural schools than might be found in Kampala or Entebbe, but it would be true for the vast majority of schools.

But, back to our conversation about Mike and the children's church in Katosi. Like in America, there are some Sundays when the church is packed and other Sundays when attendance is a little sparse. This Sunday in Katosi, the children's church was packed. Many of the children recognized Peter (his tattoos) and me (my bald head), and immediately came to greet us. Mike jumped right in, and the kids showered him with their love as he communicated his warmth and acceptance. As I shot video, Mike danced and sang with the children. In the back of the open room, three boys played drums that were really old water jugs turned upside down.

Mike was enamored with the way a young child was using a typical African broom to sweep up rocks on the dirt floor. These brooms are used by everyone. I have never seen a broom with a handle on it. They are basically made of straw bundled together and are only a couple of feet long. When they are used as this child was, people bend at the waist and sweep back and forth, bent the entire time. Mike couldn't believe how the child stayed bent over and was concerned for his back.

He was convinced that he was going to start a market for long-handled brooms. It allowed me to talk to him about the phrase "that's just the Ugandan way." Certain customs are followed and run so deep in the culture that even when a new method is introduced, the majority of the people will continue to use the old ways. Timothy's daughter, Glory, was leading the children's church as she does most Sundays.

When it was time to teach the lesson for the day, she invited two children to come to the front. They were near the same age as the children sitting in front of them that they were teaching. The boy and girl each took turns teaching. One would speak in Lugnadan and the other would translate in English. One of the first things I noticed was that both children were using Operation Christmas Child Bibles. As I looked around, I noticed that several children in the group also had OCC Bibles.

It was the second time I had the joy and affirmation that Samaritan's Purse was reaching deep into cultures that might otherwise be ignored. While these children were teaching, Timothy motioned to us that it was time to go into the adult service. We walked several yards from the children's church toward the main church building. We walked past two outhouses with stick figures, one of a man, the other of a woman. I nodded at Mike and said, "Hope you don't have to go!" Ugandan outhouses do take some getting used to (it's the Ugandan way).

We entered the church from the back and were escorted to a group of seats in the front row.

In a few moments, a Ugandan woman came and knelt before us with a basket of water bottles that she handed to each of us. The singing was all in Lugandan, as were the prayers. Even though we did not understand what was being said linguistically, we fully understood the joy and sincerity of their worship. I am not exactly sure of all that made this Sunday such a special Sunday, but it was filled with energy and joy. Perhaps it was because of the Children's Day launch ceremony, maybe it was because of Mighty's wedding, but it was a special Sunday service.

The men were all wearing kanzus instead of their usual, more casual wear, and the women were in their gomesi.

One little guy that I had seen in past years came over and climbed up on Mike's lap, then over to my lap, then to Pete's lap, and back to Mike's lap. I had to keep an eye on him because I was sure that Mike was going to smuggle this little guy back to the US in his suitcase. It turned out that this was the son of one of the pastors and administrators of one of the very good schools that we had visited on my first visit.

Timothy called the three of us to the platform (the little guy came with me) and told the cow story once again, and how Peter had been the catalyst to launch an entire herd.

He introduced Mike as the "Mayah" of Izzlamarder (a Ugandan way of pronouncing Islamorada). He then reintroduced me and handed the microphone over to me to preach once again. When I finished speaking, Timothy came back up and asked a young woman to come forward.

I am not sure all that was taking place because it was all in Lugandan.

It had something to do with this young lady's upcoming marriage and her commitment before the church to maintain purity until her wedding day. Some symbolic gifts were given to her, and then she spoke to the congregation. During the entire time that she spoke, she was in a kneeling position.

After she finished speaking, the leftover wedding cake from the night before was brought in and cut into small bite-size pieces. That was so everyone in church that day got to celebrate the wedding and enjoy a small piece of the cake. After the cake had been given out, Mike, Pete, and I watched something that made tears well up in all of our eyes. There was a piece of cardboard and wrapping leftover from the cake. It was full of little cake crumbs that were just so inviting to all the small children. When the service ended, the children rushed to the leftover crumbs like a school of hungry piranha. It took about ½ a second for the bits to spill all over the dirt floor or end up in a child's hands or on their face. What happened next was the part that was so moving. The children picked up the crumbs that fell to the floor and began to eat the tiny bits. But the children didn't just pick up the pieces and eat them. They shared them with all the other children who had not gotten any yet.

Even the pieces from the trampled-on dirt floor were devoured. It was another reminder of how entitled and selfish our culture can be. On a side note, though, remember I talked about the outhouses being just outside the church? Now imagine people going to the outhouses, then walking straight into the church, walking around on this same earthen floor that the crumbs had fallen on, and the children are eating crumbs off of it! If they survive childhood, they must have iron stomachs and bulletproof immune systems!

After the service, food was served to all. I assume it was food from the wedding the day before.

The next big event was that we were driving back into Mukono, where Mike was scheduled to teach a business conference for men and women. His assignment from Timothy: give them some business pointers. I joined Mike at his workshop to provide moral support. When we arrived at the conference site, I had to chuckle. This was the same resort I had stayed in on my first trip, the one I had fondly named Hotel California. As it turned out, they had made several key improvements. They had become an often-used conference center for events in Mukono. There were probably 30 or 40 businessmen and women in attendance. Mike was very relaxed and spoke from his heart about the way to treat staff and how to strive for excellence in whatever business you are involved in. He also talked about serving and caring for the community you live in and work in. I was impressed and realized why Mike was such an effective businessman and council member. I was glad I had gone along because the questions turned to questions about church and school administration and leadership. Mike was more than happy to deflect those questions over to me but was also able to share general business and managerial insights for these topics.

Monday was another Christian Educators' Convention and cow give-away day. I would travel out to a village in the jungle outside of Jinja. We would cross the Nile and take a series of country roads until we reached the village somewhere north of Jinja. It took a good three to four hours to get to our final location. I had conducted UCCSU conferences in a variety of settings — larger auditoriums, churches, and schoolrooms that looked more like livestock barns. But I was not exactly prepared for this one. When we arrived, there was a very large crowd of teachers, administrators, pastors, village officials, and schoolchildren. I had seen this type of gathering at many of the other meetings. What made this one so unique was that it was outside. A few tents were set up where the people were seated, and a few shaded trees that others had found for some relief from the scorching heat, but where I had to teach was in the open sun. I had failed to bring sunscreen or hat but knew that I had to spend several hours teaching and giving out the gifts, which would be delivered later in the day by Mike and Peter. As I taught throughout the day, I had built-in pauses where I would give out various gifts — the wordless book soccer balls, curriculum materials, and teaching aids. Each time I gave a gift, I marveled at the joy and gratitude that the recipient showed. It was a reminder of how grateful the teachers are of even the simplest of gifts.

Another thing that stands out about this day was a group of young teachers sitting around a picnic table. Whenever I would ask a question that required some though or creative response, they were the first to fire out the correct answer. I was encouraged that a group of young Christian schoolteachers was being trained up to lead future generations.

We broke for lunch, and three of the leaders asked if they could share something with me. I wondered if there was a problem, but when we had walked to another set of buildings, they brought out a shirt that had been made exclusively for the UCCS-U. They were to be given to all the attendees and leadership of the association.

They were well made, with embroidered logos on them. They wanted me to put it on right then and there and wear it for the rest of the day.

I was certainly willing to do so, but it didn't take long to realize that they were heavy and did not wick well.

They were also short sleeves, which I hardly ever wear, because of the need for sun protection in South Florida.

I knew I was going to pay the price for no sunscreen on a hairless head and very white arms! But I also was reminded of the gratitude that I had seen with every gift that had ever been given to the people of Uganda. This was my turn to be grateful.

I taught throughout the day, with a timeout here and there, to have a group of children make various performances. Near the end of the day, Timothy, Peter, and Mike arrived. They had visited the Source of the Nile, purchased more cows and bicycles, and had checked on the progress of the playground equipment construction. As usual, the celebration and gratitude for receiving the gifts moved us to tears.

After the gifts had been given out, we had an extended time to just play with the children. It was such a pleasure to see these children so anxious to play and be loved by their new Mzungu friends. It was nearly pitch black, and it was time to begin our ride back to Katosi.

We piled in the ever-faithful Toyota van (it must have 900,000 miles on it). As we loaded into our usual seats, children began to pile into the seats behind us, and more children, and more children, and more children. Without exaggeration, there were probably twenty kids in the van along with us.

I found out that these were all orphans who needed rides back to their respective orphanages, and Timothy had agreed to take them before we headed home. Just before we pulled away, two young girls came to the side of the van and tapped Peter on his arm. I thought they were probably asking him for money or email address. That is a pretty common occurrence as we met individuals that felt connected to us in some way.

But instead of asking for money, they handed Peter something. He looked down at what they had given him and began to cry. When he pulled it together and we were heading down the road, I asked him what they had given him. He still had the gift in his hands. He opened his fingers and there in his palm – as tears welled up in his eyes, he was gazing at several small coins. Kids who had nothing wanted to share what they had just to say thank you for loving us!

Lord, may I never lose this image.

After we had dropped all of the children to their orphanages, we started the long trip back to Katosi. It was going to take several hours, and we still had to stop for some food. Timothy decided we needed to stop for some Kenyan cuisine. We stopped at a little restaurant in Jinja that almost had a Starbucks feel to it, except they were serving Kenyan food. I had no idea what to order, so I let Timothy do it for me (that was a bold faith move). I was exhausted and certainly was not thinking clearly when the food came. It was served over a small open flamed pot.

Without thinking, I reached out with both hands to pull mine closer to me, not realizing that it was red-hot. Everyone around the table looked at me like I was crazy. I had two pretty good burns on my hands to remind me never to do that again. The burned hands matched my burned face, bald head, and arms from teaching in the sun all day. By the time we got back in the van, I was out of gas. I guess the teaching, sun, and cooked hands had all taken a toll. I was sitting upright and kept falling asleep, as I would doze off, my head would fall forward and hit a metal bar between our seat and the front seat.

Pete watched my head bounce off the bar several times and told me the next morning that he had spent the rest of the trip, catching my head every time I was about to hit the bar. Thanks, Pete!

Tuesday, November 22, was the last day, and it was going to be a monumental, community-changing day. This was the day we were going to set up the temporary playground and dedicate it as the Rick Strong Playground in honor of our friend, Rick Moeller. When we arrived at the front gate, there was a line of children that was probably a quarter of a mile long and three or four children deep. They were on either side of the roadway into Winners Home, and were cheering and repeating over and over, "You are welcome. You are welcome."

We walked past two sets of classrooms on either side of the road. We rounded a corner to see even more children singing and greeting us and playing on freshly delivered playground equipment. Mike and Timothy had managed to turn unused campaign funds from Mike's election into slides, swings merry-go-rounds, seesaws, monkey bars, a swinging chair, and several other pieces of equipment. I could not believe how many items they had been able to buy. They were set up at the top of the hill, just behind a building that was being completed at Winners Home. This location overlooks Lake Victoria and would be a beautiful setting for a play area, except that there was not enough room for all of Timothy's plans. The final plan was to move all of this equipment down the hill to a site next to the lake. Timothy's plan was to fence it in but to have it accessible to the children in the community, as well as the orphan children at Winners. Also, his bigger dream was to put in an entire athletic compound that would include a soccer pitch.

But this day was the dedication day. A young man was leading the other children in singing and praising God for their new playground. As soon as they were allowed, the children rushed to their new gifts. Every piece of equipment was filled to overflowing with children. It was such a joy to watch and hear the laughter of pure joy coming from these children. I was proud of Mike and very grateful for his heart. I was called upon to offer a prayer of dedication for the playground and this celebration.

The Mayah climbs the construction to get an overview of the Rick Strong Playground

While the children were still climbing all over their new playground, Mike, Peter, and I were escorted to the base of the hill so Timothy could show us the plan for where everything would be located. Holes were already being dug, and large concrete poles were being set for the fence.

While we were there, we walked to the lake, where several of the wooden fishing boats were pulled ashore. While we were watching, a young child, certainly no older than preschool age, did something that made Mike say, "That broke my heart!"

The little boy waded into Lake Victoria with one of the large yellow jerry cans to fill it with water for the family. Despite the risks – drowning, parasites, bacteria, and crocs, the child waded into the water. Mike asked, 'Why would he do that with a water system just over there?" as he pointed toward the tank and system for the town's people. The only answer I had was not a good one, "That's just the Ugandan way!"

"That's just the Ugandan way."

One of the things I have learned is that It takes a long time to break many generations of habits. I have also learned and am still learning that just because it is not the way we do things in America, does not make their methods wrong or inferior.

We were summoned from our lakeside explorations to come back to Winners Home. When we arrived, we were handed flat plates or large ladles for scooping food. By now, we knew the routine well. In front of us were seemingly endless lines of very hungry children, and some of our money had gone to help buy a feast for them.

One by one, they stood in front of us as we scooped rice and beans, posho, and a stew mixture. This exercise had its funny side, as Mike, who had managed successful restaurants his entire life, was scooping his helpings of rice to the children. He had two adult supervisors giving him opposing instruction. A lady would look at his serving and say, "More rice, more rice! The children are hungry!" and a man on the other side would say, "Too much rice! Less rice!"

This went on for the majority of the time we were serving. Mike handled it very diplomatically, he ignored them both and just kept serving.

One of the treats of the day for me was that I got to meet and spend a few moments with Sharon (Colleen and my Ugandan girl). It had been over a year since I had seen her, and she was now an older teen about to finish school at Winners. I had noticed that each year there was an increasing level of aloofness about her.

I didn't blame her. A visit once a year or so and a few gifts certainly didn't communicate a deep friendship.

That led me into some serious thought about what some Americans call adopting an orphan. What they really mean is that they provide some type of monthly support for an orphan or group of orphans. Putting a picture of a child on your refrigerator, saying you will pray for them regularly (which we frequently forget to do), and sending small gifts that do little to meet the needs of these children is not adopting an orphan! To really make a difference, there must be more. It must be more than just a token of passive sympathy. It must be more than actions to make us feel better because we feel overwhelmed by the magnitude of the problems these children face every day.

Andrew Stanley, the son of Andy Stanley, is a wonderful young Christian comedian making a living by poking fun at some of our American Christian practices and attitudes.

In one of his routines that I recently had the privilege of hearing, he talks about his family vacations always being missions trips disguised as vacations. He talks about how they would visit the children they sponsored in other countries, "or as I like to call them, our refrigerator family." He tells about one trip where his younger brother (about six) had been bothering him the whole trip – kicking the back of his seat on the airplane, breaking his iPod.

Here is how he tells the rest of the story:

(Andrew) "I was really mad at him. So, on one of the first nights we were there, we were sharing a motel room and I waited until it was really late. I said, 'Hey Gary, you awake?'"

(Gary–the younger brother) "Yeah."

(Andrew) "You know the real reason we came to Kenya, the reason we are at this orphanage is because when we go home on Sunday, we are going to leave you here. And Ramamani is going to come home with us and he's going to live in your room. He's going to play with all your toys, and we are going to give him your inheritance. But don't worry, because we are going to send you $38.00 per month until your eighteen. We'll write you a letter like every six months (at least for the first six months). I don't know what to tell you buddy. I voted for you..."

Now as humorous as that was, it pokes fun at a very real truth. The attitude toward missions and the constant stream of appeals that come rapid-fire at us is often to ignore them completely.

Sometimes the need seems so overwhelming that we throw a few dollars toward the cause to hopefully satisfy our conscious concerning missions and the plight of "the least of these" in the world.

One of the things noticed when visiting many of the orphanages is that you often see a hardening and skepticism settle in on many of the older children. They are beginning to figure out that $38/month and a few gifts are not going to make much difference in their overall life circumstance.

I have tried to stress to our American school kids, my own family, and those traveling on any mission trip with me. "If you are looking for a Christian vacation and calling it a missions trip, don't bother to come." There is joy all around you as you pour yourself into service and the culture. It will be a thousand times more rewarding than just a vacation. You will return home spent. Your heart will be broken and overflowing at the same time. You will probably think differently about how you spend your money in the future."

This had been a great day. I watched Pete attract kids like the Pied Piper, and I watched Mike's heart fill to overflowing as he watched the children enjoying the Rick Strong Playground. One particular little guy captured his heart. I first saw him on the swinging chair apparatus as Mike pointed him out and said he had seen him earlier and that he had a voice like an angel.

He looked like he was dealing with severe scoliosis or some other disease that had left his body twisted, but his spirit was captivating as was his personality and smile. I found out on the flight home that Mike had given him a pretty significant gift. He never told me how much, and I never asked.

The next day was going to be our last day, and we still had a lot to get accomplished. I had one more teachers' conference to conduct, some more cows to give away, and Timothy was very insistent that we stop by the UCCS-U office in Mukono on our way to the airport.

Trip #5 Rick Strong and the Mayah

This final day was going to be another of the days where Pete and Mike would go off in one direction and me in another. We were scheduled to meet back in Mukono at the church where the wedding had taken place, and then head to the airport. I was off to teach at the conference, and Mike and Pete went off to give away some more cows, bikes, and whatever other items we still had left to give away.

I can't recall the location of this last conference, but what I do remember is that it was hot, it was outdoors, and it was again in the direct sun. This was the third day of getting cooked by in the Ugandan sun (the reason for mentioning this will become evident a little later). This was another of the conferences where it appeared that the teachers had not had as much training as those from city centers. It was again a reminder of the need for providing training in the outlying areas of the country. As tricky as some of the trips into the bush can be, they are still essential until some of the Ugandan teachers can begin to lead them on their own.

That is one of my ultimate goals.

I am striving for the day when all I have to do is come in, be a cheerleader, an encourager, and let the Ugandan administrators and teachers lead the conferences.

We finished the conference early afternoon and headed back to meet with the team. We gathered at the church, said our goodbyes to the people who were there to see us off, and headed to the UCCS-U office in Mukono. The office had been forced to relocate from the original site. It was now located in a busy main street of Mukono. It was far from elegant and was going to take some time to get to the standard I would like an IACCS office to have. It was in a warehouse-looking compound, with stores of all types surrounding it in every direction. Timothy had pressed us pretty hard to use some of the IACCS money to buy new office furniture to make the office more suitable. He wanted us to see these purchases and to see that the office was getting reestablished. I was glad we had spent a little money on this. If we were going to have a legitimate presence and have a voice in Ugandan education, we needed a place that would communicate that we are serious, that says we are an organization here to stay, to make a difference in the education of the nation.

When we arrived at the office, most of the UCCS-U Board of Directors were there to meet us and bid us farewell. But there was also another reason for their gathering.

They had purchased several plaques and awards for us as a way of saying thank you, for as they say it, "loving the people of Uganda" (I shared these at the FACCS Christian Educators' Convention back in Orlando, so that our schools in America would know how appreciated they were).

From there, we were told that we had one more stop that we needed to make on the way to the airport in Entebbe. We returned to the school that in the first year had the students that had waited so patiently for us to arrive when we had been running hours late. I remembered the school because it is so well kept, and the students were so sharp.

There is clearly a great deal of school pride and extra care to detail here. When we arrived, there were children gathered on the lawn with their teachers waiting for us to arrive. The same little guy that had climbed up in our arms at church came running to us and piled up in our arms again. This was the first time I had connected all the dots. This same little guy from the church in Katosi was the son of one of the pastors at Timothy's church and the headmaster of this school. We were introduced to the children gathered around. We then all walked down to another area of the campus where there was a very healthy looking cow waiting for us to give her away. We did so with the usual exuberant celebration.

Then very quickly, Timothy said, "We must go." In moments, we were off and headed toward Entebbe.

When we hit Kampala, the traffic was at a standstill. There were thousands of people, cars, boda boda, bikes, and trucks all packed more tightly together than anything I have ever seen. You got a clear sense of how densely populated developing countries can be.

Timothy looked back and told us to roll up our windows. That was his way of warning us that someone could reach in and grab anything they could get their hands on – camera, cell phone, backpack, anything. We sat and sat and sat some more. I wasn't sure we were going to make our flight. I asked Timothy if we were going to make it. He said, "Yes, we have time." But he did not sound very confident. We sat and sat some more. We were stuck. At one point, I really began to worry because I heard Timothy say, "Dear Jesus, help us!"

I interpreted that to mean that without a miracle, we were not going to make our flight. We finally got to a place where BJ could turn down a side street and began to weave his way toward Entebbe once again. It was dark when we arrived. As we pulled into the parking area, there was something very different about the look of the airport. I had never seen it like this. There were far more people than usual, and there were white high pinnacled tents set up in almost every open space. We asked Timothy what was going on. He replied that the Muslims were returning from their pilgrimage to Mecca. We made it to the security area, said our goodbyes, and arrived at the gate with just a few minutes to spare.

We got to our seats, and as I lifted my carry-on bag to the overhead storage compartment, I rested it on my head for a second (this is where the discussion about the being in the sun for three days comes into play).

When I picked the bag up off my head, a giant layer of sunburned skin lifted with it. I closed the compartment and tried to sit down as quickly as possible without making a big deal of it or making anyone throw up because I looked like I had just been scalped. I grabbed some wet wipes and began to try to clean up as much as I could. Wet wipes and raw flesh are a painful combination! But it was necessary just to safeguard against infection. I knew this could make the trip a very long, painful ride home. After we got in the air, I told the guys I was going to go get cleaned up. Have you ever tried to shower in an airplane bathroom? It is not an easy task, but with water and wet wipes, the mission was accomplished. Surprisingly and thankfully, the scalping was not too painful, and the exhaustion from the trip made falling asleep pretty easy.

Reflecting on the trip made me grateful for the things that had been accomplished. But more than that was the thrill of the things that were happening in Mike and Pete's hearts. I am so grateful for their love for people. In terms of the tangible accomplishments on this trip, there had been many. We had been a part of a fantastic launch ceremony, increased the Minister of Education's awareness of the work of UCCS-U, and performed a Ugandan wedding. I was able to conduct several Christian Educators' Conventions in some very remote regions of the country as well as a larger conference in Mukono. We were able to buy 15 more cows, 5 very sturdy bicycles, 20 soccer balls, food for 700 orphans, and furnishings for the UCCS-U's office. We now have five calves that have been birthed over the last two years. That is important because that means that five more orphanages have gained a cow. We have only lost two cows over the previous three years, so the total cow population has grown to 33. It is our hope that by next year this number will more than double.

CHAPTER 8
THE TRIP THAT ALMOST WASN'T

"God whispers to us in our pleasures, speaks to us in our conscience, but shouts in our pains; it is his megaphone to rouse a deaf world."-C. S. Lewis, "The Problem of Pain" (1940)

2017 was to be the sixth year of IACCS trips to Uganda, and it almost became the trip that wasn't. In late August, we began to monitor the track of a tropical storm moving across the Atlantic. There was no need for alarm, but it required the usual diligence of keeping an eye on it. This was a normal routine for those of us living in the Florida Keys.

Tropical systems marching off the coast of Africa are the norm for this time of the year. This time, the system turned into a hurricane, then into a super storm, and it was headed right for the Keys. We made all the necessary preparations, and they ordered a mandatory evacuation of the Keys for Wednesday morning for all visitors, and that evening for all residents. By the time all the evacuation orders had been given, nearly seven million Florida residents had been ordered to evacuate. This would ultimately be the largest or certainly one of the largest evacuation orders in US history. Our school was usually turned into a shelter-of-last-resort for people who could not or would not evacuate or who had waited too long to try to leave.

But the potential impact and strength of this storm made Emergency Management close all shelters. Colleen and I drove to our son's home at Fort Jackson, Columbia, in South Carolina. Hurricane Irma made landfall as a category 3 storm at 9:10 AM on Sunday, Sept. 10, 2017, at Cudjoe Key. Big Pine Key reported the highest peak wind gusts of 150-160 mph, with No Name Key being entirely covered by the storm surge. I was on the phone constantly with Corey Bryan, Police Chief for Islamorada, and Captain Terry Able, with Monroe County Fire Rescue, about conditions and their needs. Mike Forster (the Mayah) had decided not to evacuate because of his position in the Village, and because he cares so deeply for the community.

I spoke to Terry just after the storm had passed on Sunday afternoon, and told him I was headed back south just as soon as the weather cleared enough to get out. He said, "Yes, probably a good idea, people may need you as much as they need me right now." I spoke to Mike and echoed the same sentiments. With those words ringing in my ears, I loaded my car with a generator, chain saw, bottled water, tarps, and cans of gasoline, and tried to hit the road. Irma was not cooperating and had hugged the coast of Florida, Georgia, and South Carolina.

As I was trying to leave, the storm was at its worst over us. I had to turn back after just a few miles. I waited it out, and at about 3:00 AM, the wind and rain slacked off enough to let me get on the road. Other than an occasional wind gust dodging debris, blowing across the interstate, and sheets of rain, driving was pretty easy. There was absolutely no traffic! As the sun began to shed enough light to see along the roadway, it was becoming increasingly apparent that this storm had been one of the most significant storms to hit the lower east coast. Trees were uprooted, buildings damaged, and all exits off the interstate were closed. There was no power anywhere up the coast. Even the rest stops were closed (no bathroom stops). There were no gas stations open because there was no power. When I first started driving, there was no traffic. As the day went on though, I began to notice that all the vehicles on the road were emergency response vehicles or convoys of utility trucks headed to the aid of those south of me. Due to a lack of traffic…and my speed, I arrived back in the Keys by late afternoon. There was a roadblock on the mainland in Florida City to prevent people from returning to the Keys. I had been on the phone with Cory and the Monroe County Sherriff's office about what I needed to do about the roadblock and the passcode to get through. Cory told me not to worry about it, to just call him when I got there. I never had to make that call. When I arrived at the roadblock, they just waved me through. I didn't have to stop or identify myself or show any ID. I literally drove right through while everyone else was being stopped.

To this day, I have no explanation for this other than the Lord simply paved the way.

When I arrived in the Keys, my first stop was at my house. I felt almost guilty; there was no damage. I walked into the house and it felt cool; my A/C was on, which meant I had power. I opened my freezer, and there had been no thawing. I turned on the TV, and the Weather Channel was on. It didn't take long, however, to discover that I was very fortunate and that almost everything on the oceanside of the islands had been destroyed or severely damaged. As you got into the middle and lower Keys, the damage was increasingly worse. I was feeling a little guilty because my house and property had fared so well. I expressed that to a friend, and they said, "I think that was so you could focus all of your attention on helping others." Whether that was true or not, it certainly did allow for that.

I drove south to our church and school. It didn't look too bad. The buildings were all still standing! But on closer inspection, I found that the bottom floor of our high school building had been flooded. The more I explored, the more damage I found. All signage was gone. Fencing was all down. Many of our A/C units were completely blown off of the roof. A water pipe on the roof ruptured, so water was gushing out. The gymnasium/Family-Life Center had received no damage. It would very shortly become a vital resource for the recovery effort in our community. I drove a block south to where the main church campus was. In 1960, Hurricane Donna had hit Islamorada with a direct hit, and the building that was now our church (the Cinemorada Theater at the time) had become a giant swimming pool. It slopes from ground level to several feet below ground level. When the water from the Atlantic poured over US Highway 1, it flooded the building, leaving the water at about six feet in the lowest area.

Had not some local residents who had to ride the storm out in the building, managed to swim down, and open the back doors, I am sure the building would have collapsed.

As I pulled into our parking lot, I was afraid that the same thing had happened again in Irma. I walked to the front of the building and could see seaweed and debris right up to the front doors. I opened the doors; the tile floor was wet, and thought, "Oh boy, this is not going to be good!" I opened the auditorium doors, and to my surprise and joy, there was no water! The sea had come across the highway, but the increased elevation of the road (and the Lord's protection) today compared to the way it was in 1960 had prevented the flood. From there I went to the second floor where my office is located. My office was in what had been the old projection room of the theater. It was directly facing the Atlantic and the brunt of Irma. It had not fared so well. A section of the roof had peeled back. The wind and water had made my office look like it had been in a hurricane (oh, that's right it was!) Stuff was blown everywhere! I begin to take pictures of all that had been damaged, but honestly had bigger concerns about the rest of Islamorada and the Keys below us. I started getting reports from down south that painted a very bleak picture. Because of that concern, I drove south to Mangrove Mike's Restaurant, where I knew all of Emergency Management would be gathered. Mike had opened his place and was providing free, non-stop food, even though the restaurant had received considerable damage.

When I walked in, Mike announced, "Pastor Hammon is here," and everyone began to applaud. When natural disasters strike, many people find themselves crying out to God, and at that moment, that is whom I represented. Several important things happened in the time I was there. The first thing that happened was that the on-duty commander of the fire station asked if we could have a church service the next morning. I said, "Absolutely. Where?" He said, "How about the fire station, at the shift change in the morning? If we do it, then we can cover both shifts." But before I could say yes, he changed his location idea. He said, "Better yet, how about the Hurricane Monument?" I said, "Great idea!" The Hurricane Monument was a memorial and crypt to honor those who had perished in the 1935 Hurricane. The official count of those who lost their lives in that storm was 485. That number was made up of local families with names of Russell, Pinder, Parker, Lowe, Albury, Dalton, Thompson, and a host of others that were pioneers of the Florida Keys. The Russell family alone lost 61 family members, leaving only 11 survivors.

Their official count was divided up into two groups, a total of 259 civilians reported to have perished, and 257 veterans that had been sent to the Keys under the WPA after WW One.

So, this seemed like the most fitting of places to hold a service. As we gathered at the monument that next morning, it was a somber reminder of how grateful we should be for early warnings and accurate predictions from the National Hurricane Center and all of the services from Emergency Management. The service was brief, but a necessary time of prayer and encouragement.

The second thing that happened while meeting at Mike's was that Emergency Management asked if we could make our gymnasium/Family-Life Center, a Red Cross shelter. People were finding that their homes in the Lower Keys were destroyed or unlivable. We, of course, agreed, and the center became home for 30 or 40 families and a staging area for supplies being sent south.

The third happening from Mike's was that I learned that we had housed law enforcement officers from Marathon during the storm because their homes were too damaged to live in and that they needed to be accommodated for days to come.

It was pretty clear that we were not going to be able to get the school open for some time to come. We had been damaged; we were a Red Cross shelter, and we were housing Marathon Law Enforcement officers and their families in several of our classrooms.

Between our two buildings, there were several thousands of dollars in damage, but that was just the beginning of the financial hit that we would face. We had teachers who were not working, families who had lost their source of income, and, in some cases, their homes, and we had no way to generate the tuition income needed to pay bills. Churches and Christian schools from all over the country began to reach out and send assistance our way. I was facing an internal personal struggle. I knew how great our need was, but I also recognized that the demand in the Lower Keys was far, far higher than ours. I felt like when people called and asked how they could help, that I had to tell them about the need south of us. The churches in Big Pine Key really stepped up for the families in the Lower Keys. Steve and Alice Lawes from Big Pine

The Trip That Almost Wasn't

Key Vineyard Church became two of my heroes. They turned their church into what lovingly came to be known as Vineyardmart. The Vineyard is a larger metal frame building about the size of a gymnasium. People could go in find what they needed to survive and rebuild and just take it. That included food, water, blankets, diapers, bedding, clothes, first aid supplies, even generators, and about any other necessity needed. Steve, Alice, and the church were dealing with their own loss but were models of the love of Christ to the people of the Lower Keys. I think God honored the fact that we sent relief efforts south by meeting our needs as well. Because of gifts that came from individuals and other ministries, we were able to pay our teachers and provide scholarships to several school families.

Now let's get back to our Uganda trip.

At some point on the drive back to the Keys from the evacuation, it hit me that we were going to have a difficult decision to make about this year's trip. The need was going to be great right here at home. Would the team members have suffered so much damage that they couldn't go?

The team had a collective decision to make. Do we go to Uganda or not? We still had two months to decide, but we had mixed emotions. Our tickets had been purchased. Large amounts of money and items had been given, and the program had been set for the trip. We decided that if we could get things stabilized and the community and our families did not need us, we would go. I went to each of the team members privately and had conversations allowing each of them to decide to go or not.

We kept working on the Keys' recovery effort. It was a day in, day out effort, and it became clear that this was going to be a long, slow recovery.

But as we got closer and closer to our trip, each of the team members spoke with an increasing resolve that they felt they should go. So, by the end of October, all team members were fully committed to the trip.

Chapter 9
Trip #6 Care from Head to Toe

This was the reason why you were brought to Narnia, that by knowing me here for a little you may know me better there. -Aslan
"The Voyage of the Dawn Treader" (1952) - C.S. Lewis

Momentum for what IACCS was doing, especially in Uganda, had really picked up. The local press had written two or three major articles. I had been invited to be a keynote speaker at the Regional Rotary International Conference. I had spoken at several other locations and conducted radio interviews. People began to really buy into the purchasing of cows and the Shoe That Grows projects. More and more people began to ask about going on this next trip. I felt like the Lord wanted me to take anyone that had a desire to go, and that could make a contribution to the work while we were there. However, as mentioned earlier, I wasn't looking to provide "a Christian vacation" for people just wanting to travel to Africa. If they had a gift or talent, and they wanted to use it to really serve, I was anxious to have them join the team. When the dust had all settled, we had a team of seven signed up and committed to the trip. It was quite an eclectic group. The veterans on this trip included Peter, Mike, and me. The rookies on this trip were Dr. Miguel Diaz, Patty Cook, Wendy Aguirre, and Dorothy Stathis. I was a bit nervous with a team this size, and with three women on the team – not because they were women, but because I wasn't sure how they would be seen and treated in Uganda. The role and demeanor of American women is extremely different from Ugandan women.

This concern never became an issue, and the ladies jumped right in and began to serve with great enthusiasm. Patty was a seasoned missions-experienced lady who had worked in some extremely high-risk situations with some of the most vulnerable people on Planet Earth. She had spent time in Asia rescuing young women, some not even in their teens yet, who were being forced into prostitution. She would be a good fit for anything we might encounter in Uganda.

We will tell Wendy's story a little later as we travel together on this journey. For now, let me just say that she was, at this point, still a seeker trying to process all that she was hearing and seeing about Jesus. Dorothy was a free spirit, willing to take on just about anything this mission brought her way. She rapidly earned the nickname Dory, from the *Finding Nemo* movie, because we kept having to track her down, as she wondered off seeking her next adventure. I guess Dorothy liked her new moniker because she began to use it on her Facebook account.

We made our usual late-night arrival into Entebbe, and there was an eager team of Ugandans waiting to give us warm greetings.

The logistics of loading luggage for seven people was challenging enough. Besides, we also each had identical large, black duffel bags filled with 50 pounds of the Shoe That Grows.

We almost did not clear Customs with these bags.

As we were going through the normal exiting process, we were stopped and escorted to a separate examination area.

There, Mike and I had to do some serious convincing that we were not going to sell these shoes on the streets of Kampala. We had to convince the Customs agent that we were going to personally ensure that they were put on the feet of orphans. I think I even said something crazy like, "I pledge my right arm that these shoes will be given as gifts to the children." The Customs officer didn't quite get the jest of my hyperbole, but I guess he figured I was serious if I was willing to give up my right arm! I briefly wondered if we were going to be given a shakedown and have to come up with some additional money to get the shoes into the country. But after a polite scolding, we were told that the next time we would have to obtain permission to bring the shoes into the country. I asked, "From whom?" He didn't know, and we have never been able to find out. We have chosen a different method for subsequent trips. We now pack all the shoes in bags that look like the rest of our luggage. We also stuff shoes in with our other items. So far, they have gone through without a hitch.

In any case, getting all these bags plus people loaded into vehicles in the middle of the night to go a couple of hours through the jungle was a bit of a challenge. We loaded most of the luggage through windows on an old Mercedes bus that I had seen parked at Winners Home on past visits. I had assumed that it didn't run because I had never seen it move.

But here it was ready to take us to Katosi for a very short night's sleep. Timothy and his team had clearly spent some time making sure the rooms were prepared for the ladies when they arrived. But it had been a strain to get everything completed for them in all the rooms. The first thing that I saw in the morning was a man work outside our accommodations. With just simple hand tools, he had made a new door for Wendy's bathroom.

His tools that I saw included a small hand-held plane, handsaw, hammer, and glue. It was impressive to watch this craftsman at work with such skill with very simple tools. I never cease to be amazed at what can be accomplished without the use of the tools we would typically think of having to have in America.

Wendy's Door – An example of Ugandan ingenuity and craftsmanship

This was Wednesday morning on October 11. I wasn't sure what the day would hold for us, but I knew Timothy would have it packed with ministry opportunities for the team. When I walked into our little dining room and meeting area, most of the group had already found coffee and were chatting with the excitement of what was in store for them. Timothy and Janepher arrived, and we were treated to our Ugandan breakfast, egg, Chapati (a flatbread served at most meals) and lots of fresh fruit–pineapple, mango, and banana. There was always hot tea with ginger added to the water for a little kick and a little purification.

The breakfast team day 1

After breakfast, we had some extra time to walk around the area just outside the compound.

It had been raining through the night and into the morning, so it was a muddy mess. But that didn't slow the team down. They were anxious to make some hands-on contact with the people of the village. Timothy always got a little concerned when we went outside the walls of Cross City Hotel, I think, for two main reasons: the first was our own safety. We could have been overrun just by people wanting whatever we might have to give away. The second reason was that every time we gave a gift to someone outside the compound, we were giving away something that could go to one of his orphans. That is just speculation on my part, but it makes sense. There are hundreds of children running around and would literally be impossible ever to bring enough gifts to give to all the children of the village and the thousands of children in the orphanages. That is tough to see and deal with, but a reality.

There is clearly an unspoken protocol associated with the children in the orphanages and those who, for whatever reason, are not in an orphanage or school. Some of them obviously have parents or families that they live with, and so most of their essential needs are being met. Others are street kids (especially in the larger cities) and have learned to "hustle" for survival. In any case, the unspoken rule is that we give to the orphans in school first, which cycles back to the safety factor. In some regions of the country, you have to be aware of your surroundings and the people around you. You get a sense of this when you walk outside the compound at Cross City. Directly across the street, is a row of mud huts–open doors, sheets covering to keep critters out, and open windows with no screens.

Some will have electricity, and some will even have a satellite dish on the side of the mud building for TV. I am not sure what they watch – soccer, soccer, more soccer…and one channel that has a tribal version of a soap opera. But, surrounding most of these homes is a fence made of mud and brick. Each is about five or six feet high, and on their flat tops are large chunks of broken glass embedded in the concrete. It works as a pretty strong deterrent for any unwelcome intruders. That and the gated compound where we stay suggests that there are always security concerns.

We were not planning to enter any of their homes, but the team did want to give some toothbrushes and other small gifts (candy) to the children passing by. It was always a treat to walk outside and to watch the life of the village. There was a steady stream of foot and boda boda traffic down the muddy trail that separated the Cross City Hotel from the huts on the other side. I marveled once again at the items people carry, either on foot or strapped to a boda boda. This particular morning, a boda splashed down the trail, mud flying in all directions with a cloth bag of food and a whole large Nile perch strapped down with a bungee cord. A young boy playing with a soccer ball got a full splashing of mud from the boda as it dropped down into a deep puddle. Instead of yelling or being upset, the little guy just giggled and kept on playing, now a little wetter and muddier than before. A lady carrying an enormous bag of grain or rice on her head came walking swiftly by.

She didn't look up or acknowledge us, but walked as if she was focused on a mission to be accomplished. A young girl, probably not more than eight years old approached us, and someone in our group handed her a small piece of candy. In an instant, she did what women in many African cultures have done for centuries. She dropped to her knees and bowed to show respect to us. The pathway was muddy and sloppy, and she was nicely dressed, but that didn't matter. She instantly and instinctively dropped to her knees. Pretty humbling to experience, and I always feel so unworthy of such a display of respect.

A very humbling sight

Another young girl, I would guess 14 or so, came walking by, a baby of about 6 months strapped to her back. The girl was barely big enough to carry herself, yet it looked like she was the primary caregiver for this infant. It made me reflect on how that scene is repeated in Uganda. It is no wonder that so many children are left abandoned on the streets. When children have to care for children, there can be and often are horrific consequences.

Girls as young as 12 or 13 (I am sure some even younger than this) are giving birth and/or are given in arranged child marriages. The downward social and economic consequences leave little opportunity for these young mothers, which put added financial strain on the nation of Uganda. The pattern is seen over and over. The girl gets pregnant. The girl drops out of school to care for children. The girl has no specific skill set, the girl sees little hope to gain marketable skills. The girl lives in poverty. The children live in poverty.

Take a look at this excerpt from an online article by WorldBank from 2017:

> Annet _____ is only 18 years old, but she is a mother of two boys, aged 4 and 3. At 13, she fell pregnant and dropped out of school after her mother, a widow, decided she was better off married to the father of her child to secure her future.
>
> Towards the end of last year, she left her sons in the care of her mother, bought a one-way bus ticket from the eastern city of Mbale, and found work as a housemaid in Namugongo, a residential suburb of Kampala, the capital of Uganda.
>
> *"Life got unbearable,"* she says of her marriage now, a note of determination in her voice, *"as there was not much to eat, and the man would come home drunk and sometimes*

beat me up. I don't regret leaving him because I am now earning some money, which I send home to my mother to look after the children."[13]

Child caring for child

This is probably another good spot to take a sidebar from the trip and talk about what I will call the "Dark Side." This falls under the broad category of human rights. It is not intended to be all-inclusive, and I would never claim to be an expert on the subject. This book titled, *On the Edge of Eden* and my subtitle *A Story of Beautiful Land and Beautiful People in the Midst of Brokenness*, is chosen intentionally. I want it to point to the fact that even though Uganda is a spectacularly beautiful land and the people are so kind and humble, it is also a land that is fractured. I would only be telling half of the story if I did not address some critical issues as head-on as possible. Admittedly, I am speaking from the outside looking in and am still in the midst of a huge learning curve. Human rights and their violation could fill volumes.

Numerous books, articles, and documentaries have been written addressing the subject. I will not attempt to deal with every area and certainly will not deal with those areas that are a reflection of societal mores or convictions that may differ from America.

Most of the quotes below come from a 2018 report from the United States Department of State Bureau of Democracy, Human Rights, and Labor.

Sadly, most of the reports confirm the fact that the abuse and neglect are inflicted on the most vulnerable individuals. Here are just some of the examples and associated reports:

- **Children who are abandoned** and infants left to the elements to die or be picked up and cared for by others.

  Sangaalo Babies program is made up almost entirely of babies that local authorities and others have found abandoned and brought to her facility for safe care (See Ch. 2).

- **Handicapped** and those deemed different are subjected to unspeakable abuse, neglect, and in some cases, are murdered.

  According to local media, some parents of children born with disabilities killed them in what the communities referred to as "mercy killings." Local media reported that some parents who gave birth to children with partially formed limbs and deformed body structures killed them to wash their families of curses. Local police reported no knowledge of these incidents.[13]

  Persons with disabilities faced societal discrimination and limited job and educational opportunities. Most schools did not accommodate persons with disabilities. The UNFPA (UNITED NATIONS FUND FOR POPULATION

ACTIVITIES) reported that violence against persons with disabilities was common, especially in school at the hands of staff, but most cases went unreported. The UNFPA also reported that neighbors and family members who knew they were alone with persons with disabilities sometimes sexually abused them. Local media reported that some families killed children born with physical deformities and that employers often denied jobs to persons with disabilities or paid them less than nondisabled persons for the same work.[14]

- **Widows** who have no one to fend for them, being forced from their homes and properties by thugs who go unpunished.

    I have encountered this firsthand while in Uganda. Widows have told of being forced to abandon their homes and small gardens because thugs came and forced them to leave. Then the punks staked claim to their property, all because there was no one to advocate for them. There is not enough law enforcement to force them to hand their property back over, and in some cases, even the officers fear what the thugs might do to them in revenge. In other cases, there is corruption within the agencies that should be providing the protection.

- **Mothers, rape, and childbirth,** sometimes as young as 12-years old, being forced to deliver babies in the most unsanitary conditions simply because they don't have the money for adequate medical care or care is not available.

Even though the sentence for rape is the death penalty, it is seldom enforced. A problem that arises is that if the parents don't like the guy their daughter is with, they can accuse him of rape, and he can be locked up for years with little hope of a fair trial. Because of this, it is easier to allow the accused to remain locked up without a hearing. *Rape remained a common problem throughout the country, and the government did not effectively enforce the law. Local media reported numerous incidents of rape, often involving kidnap and killings of women, but the authorities were very often unable to investigate and hold perpetrators accountable. Local media often reported that perpetrators of rape included persons in authority, such as government ministers, MPs, judicial officers, police officers, teachers, and university staff. According to local media and local CSOs, rape victims often felt powerless to report their abusers, in part to avoid stigmatization. CSOs reported that, even when women reported cases of rape to the police, UPF officers blamed the women for causing the rape by dressing indecently, or took bribes from the alleged perpetrators to stop the investigation and pressure the victims into withdrawing the cases. According to CSOs, UPF personnel lacked the required skills for collection, preservation, and management of forensic evidence in sexual violence cases.*[14]

- **Disappearance**

In addition to child abduction done by Joseph Kony and the LRA, there are children abducted and forced into slave labor. Then, there are boys and girls sold into prostitution. We've already talked about the murder and sacrificial rituals by witch doctors. Of course, there are still those disappearances related to adults a community has deemed to have committed a crime or have disagreed with the governing authority.

- **Child Sacrifices**

Media and local NGOs reported several cases of ritual child killings, violence against widows, and acid attacks. According to local media, traditional healers kidnapped and killed children to use their organs for ancestral worship. Local NGOs reported cases in which wealthy entrepreneurs and politicians paid traditional healers to sacrifice children to ensure their continued wealth and then bribed police officers to stop the investigations. On August 14, local media reported that the UPF arrested traditional healer Owen Ssebuyungo after it found an infant's skull buried in his shrine's compound. The state charged him with murder on August 19, and the case continued at year's end.[14]

- **Child abuse**

It is difficult for many Americans to come to grips with the fact the practices that are found here still occur anywhere on earth. Or that such wickedness could even exist today. But rest assured, it does. There is a category of abuse that we would call exploitation. Some of the more common forms include forced and harmful labor, sexual exploitation in many forms, forced and child marriages, use of a children for armed warriors, force of youth to engage in illegal activities, debt bondage, slavery or servitude, human sacrifice, the removal of organs or body parts for sale or for purposes of witchcraft, and harmful rituals or practices; *The law prohibits numerous forms of child abuse and provides penalties of 2,400,000 shillings ($640) or five-year imprisonment or both for persons convicted of abusing children's rights. The law defines "statutory rape" as any sexual contact outside marriage with a child younger than the age of 18, regardless of consent or age of the perpetrator, carrying a maximum penalty of death. Victims' parents, however, often opted to settle cases out of court for a cash or in-kind payment. The Children Amendment Act made corporal punishment in schools illegal and punishable by up to three-years' imprisonment. The amendment also sought to protect children from hazardous employment and harmful traditional practices, including child marriage and FGM/C.*

Despite the law, a pattern of child abuse existed in sexual assault, physical abuse, ritual killings, early marriage, FGM/C, child trafficking, infanticide, child labor, among other abuses. Local media reported that the vast majority of schools used beating with a cane as the preferred method of discipline, and a UNICEF report released in August stated that three in four children had experienced physical violence both at home and in school. Government statistics also showed that more than one in three girls experienced sexual violence during her childhood, and that most did not report the incidents because they feared they would get into trouble or would be shamed or embarrassed. The Ministry of Gender, Labor, and Social Development also noted that corruption in police and health response services discouraged victims from reporting.[14]

Then there is a category of injustice and corruption in law enforcement, the judicial system, and the penal system. The US State Department describes in detail abuse and corruption in these main categories:

- **Torture** and other cruel, inhuman, or degrading treatment or punishment of those imprisoned or awaiting trial (52 percent of the country's 49,322 inmates were pretrial detainees.).

- **Conditions of prisons and detention centers**

    Physical Conditions: Gross overcrowding remained a problem. The UHRC reported in June that "some prisons housed twice or up to three times their designated capacities," especially prisons holding male detainees. The Uganda Prisons Service (UPS) reported that it held 49,322 inmates, yet its capacity was 22,000. The UHRC reported that it found the 250-person-capacity Arua Government Prison holding 840 inmates and the eight-person-capacity Kamwenge Police Station men's cell holding 30 detainees.

    The UHRC reported that delays in the judicial process caused overcrowding in police cells. The UPS reported that overcrowding had increased the spread of communicable diseases, especially multi-drug-resistant tuberculosis.

    According to the UHRC, authorities violated the law by holding juveniles and adult detainees together in police stations it visited due to absence of specialized holding cells for children, ignorance of the law by UPF personnel, and failure to ascertain the juvenile's age. In at least five police stations it visited, the UHRC found juveniles aged 11 to 14 years detained in the same cell as adults. The UHRC also reported that authorities kept pretrial detainees and convicted prisoners together in all but two prisons.[14]

- **Arbitrary Arrest or Detention**

Security forces often arbitrarily arrested and detained persons, including opposition leaders, politicians, activists, demonstrators, and journalists. The law provides for the right of persons to challenge the lawfulness of their arrest or detention in court, but this mechanism was seldom employed and rarely successful. [14]

In some regions, nothing more than an accusation from someone ascribing a crime may warrant arrest and jail time that may last months, or in extreme cases, years.

- **Denial of fair public trial and unlawful trial procedures**, plus corruption and lack of transparency in law enforcement lead to overcrowded prisons, abuse to those incarcerated, and distrust and fear of the justice system.

On December 5, a federal jury in New York City convicted the head of an NGO based in Hong Kong and Virginia on seven counts for his participation in a multi- year, multimillion-dollar scheme to bribe top officials of Chad and Uganda in exchange for business advantages for a Chinese oil and gas company. According to the evidence presented, Chi Ping Patrick Ho caused a $500,000 bribe to be paid via wires transmitted through New York to an account designated by Sam Kutesa, the minister of foreign *affairs of Uganda, who had recently completed his term as the president of the UN General Assembly.*[14]

For further reading I would recommend the following books. Some of this reading is definitely not for the faint at heart!

- *Garden of the Lost and Abandoned*, Jessica Yu, Houghton Mifflin Harcourt
- *Half the Sky,* Sheryl WuDunn and Nicholas D. Kristof, Knopf Doubleday Publishing Group
- *Just Courage,* Gary Haugen, IVP Books
- *The Locust Effect,* Gary Haugen, Oxford University Press
- *The Teeth May Smile But the Heart Does Not Forget*, Andrew Rice, Picador, Henry Holt and Co.
- *Too Small to Ignore,* Wes Stafford, Waterbrook Press
- *Not for Sale,* David Batstone, HarperOne

Now back to the journey:

Eventually, we were herded back into Cross City and loaded the bus. Our first stop was a return trip to the infant care facility that was part of Community Concern Ministries. The team had visited this program the previous year, and it had quickly become one of our favorites. The facilities were all new, and the staff offered excellent care for these infants. Timothy had great dreams about planting a garden that would produce enough food for these children as well as help supply food for Winners Home. There was a plot of two or three acres of rich, fertile land that could produce a great deal of food if adequately cared for. It was inside a gated compound that would make it far less susceptible to poachers. The team quickly set out, giving toothbrushes and toothpaste to all the children and staff, with me shouting over and over in the background, "Don't eat the toothpaste!"

Eating toothpaste has apparently become a problem, with some children liking the taste and eating an entire tube, which I understand can make you very ill. I'm not inclined to try it, so I shout not to do it. We would return to this site later to distribute food, toys, and other items, but this was a quick trip just to let the team begin to get a feel for what they were in store for the next few days.

From there, we traveled to Winners Home in Katosi. This was a "first look" for about half of the team. I was aware because of my own first-time experience, that this place was going to leave them in awe and that they would be deeply impacted. I am not exaggerating when I say that this first-look experience is life changing.

The view of care and people and orphans forever embed their mark on your soul. I spent more time watching and filming the team's reaction than anything else.

Peter, who was by now an old friend to these children, was immediately surrounded by a gang of kids laughing, smiling, and hugging. And of course, rubbing his tattoos and lifting his shirt to see if they were there, too.

Mike immediately sought out his little buddy (the one with what appeared to have spina bifida) from the year before at the playground dedication. It didn't take them long to find each other, and it was a sweet reunion.

Mike reunites with his little friend

The Rick Strong Playground had been moved from the top of the hill to its permanent location by Lake Victoria. It was in full use! I couldn't imagine how the equipment had survived with the number of children that would pile on every apparatus. I had to chuckle at one sight. The kids were sliding down a slide, and at the base, they had dug out a square hole about 5 inches deep that was filled with water. The children were sliding down the slide and just lying out in the water, school uniform and all. Nobody seemed to care, and I dubbed it the Ugandan Water Slide. The fence, or should I say lack of fence, was just as we had left it the year before. The concrete fence posts were still sticking out of the holes we dug. The good news was that this allowed children from the village to use the playground as well as children from Winners. Mike and I saw this as a good thing because our original intent was for all of the children of the village to have access to the playground.

Playground in place and in full use

Ugandan Water Slide

The team also got to see the water system and Wilsie House in full use. I noticed that a group of children and young adults had gathered around Doctor Diaz.

As I got closer to the group, I could hear them asking a barrage of questions about what it took to become a doctor, and might it be possible for them to reach that goal. I had to take a second look because right in the middle of this group was Bernard Bogere and his wife. They had driven over from Lugazi School and were fully engaged in the conversation with Doc like they were old friends. It was good that these children were getting the opportunity to talk and spend time with these knowledgeable adults.

Doc talks about what it takes to become a doctor.

From there, the team was invited to do something that I had not had the opportunity to do other than a brief stop on the first trip in 2011. We were invited into a section of Winners Home that was the girl's dormitory compound. I mention this because it gives such a clear feel for how these children live while in an orphanage. There is nothing luxurious ,plush, or glamorous about these facilities. In fact, you might say they are Spartan with just the essentials for survival and a tolerable level of comfort. The compound is made of several buildings, each filled with rows of old bunk beds and well-worn foam mattresses (a problem addressed on a later trip). By each bed is a trunk or box with all the child's personal belongings.

As we walked about, there were a group of young ladies gathered outside one of the dormitories, braiding the hair of one of their teachers. They seemed unfazed by our presence and kept diligently working on their project. There were a few trees and shrubs in a central courtyard area, each being used as a clothesline or drying rack. There were several groups of girls working in small groups, bent over tubs of water, doing their laundry by hand. Many of the girls only had a couple of outfits to wear, so washing was a never-ending task. While watching, it was very apparent that these girls were family. They were moving about, carrying out various tasks, laughing, playing, but functioning very much as a self-sufficient unit. We walked through their midst, and it was almost as if we were outside observers. It felt as if we were an audience watching a high stakes drama being played out before us.

But the girls were not performing; they were living the only life they knew. I wondered if they would say they felt love for one another or if living in such a large orphanage had made love an abstract concept. For many, there seemed to be little hope for a future other than another day in an orphanage. But, stop for a second and think about how bad the alternative would be: a life on the streets, or sold into slavery, or perhaps abducted and mutilated…an orphanage sounds like a much better option.

Actually, as we were walking back to our vehicle at the end of the day, we got to see a real-life example of a Winners Home success story. A young man walked briskly to Timothy, and their greeting was the greeting that a loving father and son might share. They laughed and hugged and talked in Lugandan, and then Timothy introduced us to his young "son". This was a young man that had grown up in Winners Home, had gone to university, and then to medical school, and was now a dentist. I wondered what might have become of this young man had it not been for Winners Home.

TRIP #6 CARE FROM HEAD TO TOE

From orphan to dentist

The next day was to be another grand celebration, another Children's Day, as the association has started to call them. It was going to be a day of celebration, student competitions/performances, and cows to give away.

One of the really good challenges we had to solve this year was that we had been given enough money for cows that we weren't sure we had enough time to purchase them before we had to leave.

We had gone to the bank earlier in our trip. We had made the exchange of our money into Ugandan shillings so we could get our cow buying team out with the correct currency to by cows as soon as possible. I had not seen any cattle yet, but knew we should be giving away more animals on this day than any day in the past.

When we arrived for Children's Day, we were, as usual, escorted to a row of seats of honor and then were called to the front for introductions. Each member of the team was asked to greet this large crowd that had gathered from all across Uganda. This year, the Children's Day was being held at Winners Home in Katosi. I have no idea how many schools were represented or how many were in attendance. The crowd was so large and moving about so much that it was impossible to get a count.

The performances took the entire day, which represents the large number of schools that participated. The performances/competitions were divided into several types: choral groups, choral groups with dramatic presentations, dramatic skits, recitations, and preaching.

A panel of Ugandan judges listened to each performance, at times asked questions of the presenter, and at times asked them to repeat a portion of their presentation. There was a break for lunch, and we were once again asked to feed this sea of hungry faces. After lunch, the competition resumed. It became evident that the sun was going to set before the competitions were going to conclude. We determined that it was probably best to take a break late in the afternoon and give away the cattle that had arrived at some point during the day. The cows are usually brought in by truck, offloaded, and tied to a tree until time for the presentation. It was exciting to realize that we were going to be giving so many cows to such a large number of orphanages. One by one, we had the schools gather as their administrator would come forward to receive their cow for the children. A different member of our team would come forward and present the cow. The children and adults would break into wild rejoicing. This happened over and over as each cow was given. Some groups would burst into spontaneous songs of thanksgiving and praise.

Others would break out in prayer, thanking God for His provision. All totaled on this day alone, we were able to give away nine cows, a monumental accomplishment compared to past years. Once the cows were presented, the sun was rapidly sinking below the horizon, so we quickly moved back to the performance area where all the awards were presented. The night was entirely upon us by the time we finished awarding all the trophies.

No one seemed to mind, and within just a few minutes, everyone had climbed aboard buses or slipped away into the jungle.

Care for the heart and care for the teeth in children's church

Friday morning, we were awakened by the usual drone of the loudspeaker, showering their monotonic sound waves over the village of Katosi. Timothy says that it is just community announcements, but it sure sounds more like Islamic prayers to me. In any case, it is an unusual alarm clock.

This day, the team would be divided into several groups: Dr. Diaz and Wendy were assigned to the clinic; and Mike, Pete, Patty, and Dorothy were off to give away hundreds of pairs of the Shoe That Grows to several orphanages.

I was off to spend the day teaching at another of the Christian Educators' Conferences, and give away four more cows in one of the more distant regions of central Uganda.

Timothy thought that having me travel to these areas was more practical than having all the teachers and administrators go to the expense of traveling great distances. Their shillings were already stretched beyond their limit.

As hard as it was on me, I had to agree; and besides, it gave me opportunities to see lots of Uganda that I would not have been able to see otherwise. Besides, we were able to provide several more bikes to head teachers.

It was very late when I returned that evening. The rest of the team had already met, traded stories about their day and were all sound asleep. I was anxious to hear how it had gone because these were two of the big tasks that I had hoped the team would accomplish. My hope was that the work in the clinic would be very productive and could become a regular part of our work in the future, and Mike had poured his heart into the Shoe That Grows project. I knew that putting these shoes on the feet of children that had never had shoes before would be a life-changing experience, both for the children and for the team.

We gathered Saturday morning for breakfast. As we ate, the team began to share their stories and experiences from the day before. The shoe team described what it was like watching the children who had never had shoes on their feet try to walk. They said it was like watching a kitten that had little booties on. They would step high a gingerly. They also talked about washing all the children's feet before giving them their shoes (sounded pretty biblical to me), and described the scars, cuts, and gouges that they almost all bore. The team took numerous photos and videos of the day, which really captured the joy of the day.

The clinic team described a day of dealing with various respiratory infections, HIV patients, and both endo and ectoparasites. One of the frustrations expressed by Dr. Diaz was the fact that he knew that as soon as we left, the children would, for the most part, go back to their diseased condition. But there is some hope, there is a young volunteer doctor that visits the clinic weekly. He and Dr. Diaz have established a relationship. They will hopefully be able to work together to improve the health in Katosi. Quite honestly, this is our biggest challenge. To say that healthcare in Uganda is a challenge is an understatement.

There are enormous problems on several fronts: the lack of trained healthcare providers, the lack of up-to-date medical facilities, equipment, methodologies, and medications, the lack of sanitation and sterile environments, and the lack of income to obtain medical care. Add to this list the fact that there are so many poor public health practices, and you get a glimpse of a few of the glaring problems faced in Ugandan health care. In a report by a medical group in Uganda, called Bulamu Healthcare, they state the following in *The State of Healthcare in Uganda:* [15]

Uganda's Biggest Healthcare Challenges

The biggest challenge for Uganda is inadequate resources. Uganda has five medical colleges and 29 nursing schools training people in Western medicine. Even so, there remains a shortage in healthcare workers, with only one doctor for every 8,300 Ugandans.

With 70% of doctors practicing in urban areas, where only 20% of the population lives, the coverage in rural areas is much worse: one doctor for every 22,000 people. Programs are in place to train community health workers, forming Village Health Teams that operate at the local level, but coverage has been too limited to solve the problems. The Uganda Ministry of Health conducts annual surveys that assess health system performance, and these have shown significant shortcomings in availability and quality of service. Customers complain about poor sanitation, a lack drugs and equipment, long wait times, rude service, and inadequate referrals. This uneven service discourages patients from seeking out professional care, especially in rural areas with longer travel times.

In the 1980s and 1990s, Uganda had one of the worst healthcare systems in the world. But that story is different today. For example, HIV infection rates reached 30% of the population then and have fallen to 6.5% today. The maternal mortality rate has dropped by 40%, from 561 deaths per 100,000 live births to 343 today. The table below shows how Uganda compares to Africa, the World, and USA on key public health measures, according to World Health Organization data.

Uganda Key Public Health Statistics vs. Africa, World and U.S.				
Statistic	Uganda	Africa	World	USA
Life Expectancy	62.3	60.0	71.4	79.3
Maternity Mortality Rate[1]	343	542	216	69
Neonatal Mortality Rate[2]	18.7	28.0	19.2	3.6
Skilled Health Professional Density[3]	14.6	14.1	45.6	117.8
Malaria Incidence[4]	218.3	244.9	94.0	0
Suicide Mortality Rate[5]	7.1	8.8	10.7	14.3

1. Maternal mortality ratio per 100,000 live births
2. Neonatal mortality rate per 1000 live births
3. Skilled health professional per 10,000 population
4. Malaria incidence per 1000 at-risk population
5. Suicides per 100,000 population[15]

As you can see, the problem of healthcare is going to take a great deal of time and resources, and cooperative efforts to even begin to make a dent.

This cycles back to my purpose with IACCS: that of helping schools provide better education. When the youth are trained in good health practices and given the tools to make educated choices, the culture will continue to improve.

Breakfast ended, and Timothy announced with what has become our on-going call to action, "Okay! We go. Let's go, please." Over time, we have learned that at times the "Okay! We go." simply marks the beginning of the time that we should begin to think about loading into the vehicles with a thirty-minute to hour window. Then there is the more emphatic, "OKAY! WE GO!" which means it is really time to depart (almost always later than we anticipate – It's just the Uganda way!)

This Saturday morning, we were off to Lugazi again, where I would be teaching at another conference, and the team would give away several cows and bicycles.

The team had some extra time while I was finishing my last sessions. They began interacting with a number of the children that were hanging around the area where I was teaching. Mzungus tend to draw a crowd naturally. It is a combination of things that creates this: our white skin, Pete's tattoos, and the anticipation that we might have something to give them. If Mike is along, you can almost always be sure that there will be Jolly Rancher to be given away. If Patty is there, you can count on some type of Sunday School lesson and activity. If Dori is along, you can count on her wandering off to engage with children on some new adventure (usually involving finding her and rescuing her from a crowd). Wendy would typically be surrounded by a group, she would be firing off questions about their culture, and they would be asking her about hers.

This particular afternoon, the group had found someone selling ice cream. This is an incredibly rare treat for Ugandan children. The team decided it was a treat to great to turn down. They bought enough for all children who were gathering around. I never asked, nor am I sure I would want to know how much they spent on this impromptu ice cream feast! As usual, the children shared their ice cream, and the joy they expressed at this seldom-enjoyed treat made it more than worth the effort.

I finished my teaching for the day just about the time the children were finishing their ice cream. Some of them were wearing as much of it as they had eaten because the hot African sun makes short work anything frozen. But none went to waste! They licked up every drop that they could find.

It was about time to start our journey back to camp when we realized that Dorothy was missing again. It required an all-out search, but we finally found her inside a gated compound where she was surrounded by a group of excited children chatting away with her. We were relieved that she had not been abducted!

As we were preparing to return home, Timothy asked if I had an interest in doing another radio show in Kampala that evening and if Patty would like to join us. I was excited about the opportunity. With Patty's experience ministering and rescuing young girls who had been forced into prostitution in Asia, I knew we could not turn down this chance. So off we headed from Lugazi into the heart of Kampala, about a two-hour journey on a good day.

This was not a good day, as far as traffic goes, but we made it to the station with seconds to spare. I did my usual presentation, talking about IACCS and the UCCS-U, stay in school, your children are the hope of Uganda, only have as many children as you can care for, and the need to accept Jesus as personal Savior. I then handed the ball off to Patty to talk about child abduction, forced prostitution, stopping childhood-arranged marriages, rape, and waiting to have sex until married. As you can see, I let her talk about all the easy subjects! She did a great job, speaking from the heart, rather than just rattling off statistics (just a reminder, Timothy says that this show goes out to 6-8 million listeners). What an opportunity! As soon as the show ended, we were back in Timothy's car, headed to Katosi.

It was hard to believe that so much had happened in the four days we had been in Uganda, and we still had several more days to go.

The next morning, Sunday, a day filled with activities, usually centered around the church in Katosi. To my surprise, the entire group had come together for breakfast, all dressed in suits.

Sunday's best

I couldn't resist getting several pictures and teasing everyone for getting so dressed up, mentioning that the Ugandan culture of putting on their finest for Sunday was rubbing off on them.

We were all very excited to see how much progress had been made on the children's church. Because we had been involved with this project since it was a cleared piece of ground, we were anxious to see the work that had been done. We made our usual turn at the giant rock, just past the goats, and vegetable stand, and began the climb up the steep dirt trail to the church. It is always fun to watch the expressions of the first-timers on the trip as we start the drive up the trail. They are convinced that we are simply going to topple over and cartwheel all the way to the bottom of the hill.

On this trip, the van just couldn't handle the climb, so we all had to pile out and hike the rest of the way to the church. When we arrived, we could hear singing coming from the building just above us, which was the main church; and we could also hear singing coming from a building just off to the right. This was the children's church. The building was filled with joyful children singing and playing. There was no roof on the building yet, but that didn't stop them from getting full use out of the building. Timothy's daughter, Joy, now a young adult, was leading the children's program.

She welcomed us, and each team member spoke briefly to the children. After each of the team members spoke, we gave out toothbrushes and toothpaste to all the children and adult helpers.

As we were giving out the toothbrushes, I had a chance to look at the progress of the building. It had no roof yet, but there was a large tarp tied to the building to provide shade and some shelter for the children if it began to rain.

The floor was earthen, but that did not keep them from sweeping it throughout the service to be sure it was spotless for their special guests. The fact was that this children's church building was really not a building at all yet. The walls were made of hand-made red brick. The unfinished building didn't matter, because the real church was this group of precious children learning about the love of God. As I watched Joy lead these children, I wondered if she understood how important she was to the future of these boys and girls. This was a place where amid extreme poverty and hardships, they could experience love and joy at such a rich level. As I listened to each of our group share, I was struck by the impact the children and this experience was having on each one of my team members. Each year that I have taken a team, I talk about how we come to be a blessing, but we will be blessed more than we can imagine; we come to give, but we will receive so much more; we come to teach, but we are the ones who learn.

It was time for me to move into the main church service to get ready to deliver my message, so I left the group with the children.

As I began to teach, Wendy and Mike joined us in the adult service. My text for the day was from Luke 15 (perhaps my favorite chapter in the Gospels).

It is the only place where Jesus gave three parables, rapid-fire, one after the other. Remember them? The parable of the lost sheep, the lost coin, and the lost son. They all three express some common key truths – something of great value is lost, that which is lost warrants an all-out search, and when it is found, it warrants an all-out celebration. As I was telling about the lost son, I was relating to how I had been that lost son for a dark period in my life. I was sharing a portion of my own faith journey. I was explaining how I had been a cynical, proud atheist, and that I had been challenged to investigate the claims of Christ and the Bible.

I explained that after just over a year of studying and challenging, that I had come to the place where I felt I had no choice other than believing the claims and authenticity of Jesus as the Messiah. As I spoke, I had to trust that my interpreter was making this message clear.

The audience was listening with a higher than usual level of attention. But, as I was speaking, I was especially aware of one person who was listening very intently, often with tears in her eyes.

Wendy was apparently deeply impacted by what she was hearing. I would learn later that she was in the midst of making her own decision to accept Christ as her Savior. As I always do back home in our church, I gave an invitation to receive Christ. As has happened in the past, I was caught off guard by the number of people who indicated they were receiving Christ that day. I won't know this side of heaven how many of these people were genuinely putting their trust in Christ that day. I am sure some were just polite by responding to the guest preacher. Some probably didn't understand the invitation. But if it was only one it was worth more than all the treasure in the world.

I had noticed a group of young ladies just outside the church building cooking posho and matooke over an open fire.

After the service, everyone was provided a delicious meal of these items the ladies had prepared. We also had chapati (a flatbread – like a soft tortilla), binyebwa (a purple sauce made from crushed nuts), tilapia, rice, and pineapple. This would have been an enormous feast for most of the people at church that day.

After we were all stuffed, we went back to Cross City and then on an excursion by foot through the village and to the water's edge on Lake Victoria. It only takes a few seconds to realize as you look around and smell the fish-scented air, how dependent Katosi and the other little villages on the Lake are to the fishing industry. I spoke of the importance of fishing for all the countries surrounding Lake Victoria in an earlier chapter, but the sights and smells of this walk were reminders of the dependence there is on the lake. Everywhere you look you see enormous fishing nets, either spread on the ground or hanging from fences for drying and repair. Every few feet, you encounter little silver mounds of minnows. As mentioned earlier, these are used for food for both man and livestock.

ON THE EDGE OF EDEN

Nets, mounds of minnows, and the boats that catch them

The shore is lined with dozens of fishing boats that have returned from a night of fishing. It is a fairly common sight to see a group of night fishermen walking in an impromptu parade line. They are each carrying their chrome plate lanterns heading to their boats for an evening of fishing. This is just as they have done decade after decade. To the left of the beach area was the large fish market where the larger fish, the Nile perch, and tilapia are sold and shipped as described in chapter 3. These little glimpses into this aspect of Ugandan culture are enjoyable and very informative for the team. For many of these people so dependent upon the lake and its natural resources, this was where their world, their universe begins and ends. They knew very little about life outside of this area, and many of the families had been fishermen and women for several generations. They knew more about their tribal chiefs than they did about President Yoweri Museveni. The younger generation (most of the population of this village) would not have remembered the history of the atrocities of Idi Amin or any other Ugandan past for that matter. If asked about it, they would say, "What does that matter for today? This is the Ugandan way. All we need to know is how to catch fish."

Pastor Emma caught up with us and asked if I would come to preach at his church that evening. This is the same Emma that always brings his store of Ugandan gifts for us to buy, as we are getting ready to return home. Emma is an enthusiastic, joyful man who never seems to run out of energy. I said, "Emma, I didn't even know you had a church!" He then described his church, which he does in a nearby village on Sunday evenings for the local people. I was intrigued and thought if his church is as enthusiastic as he is, this could be an exciting experience. I agreed to do it if he could give me a ride. I then hurried back to my room to figure out what to say to a group of villagers that probably didn't know me and probably wouldn't understand me. I put some thoughts together and returned to the group to try to convince them that they should join me on this adventure. They were beat and I could get no takers. Later that afternoon Emma picked me up and we drove several minutes to the small village where the church was. It would really be hard to define this as a village. It was more a loose arrangement of small huts, but there were far more people gathered than I would have expected for this remote area. We entered the church to an already celebratory group of worshipers.

There was a very young primary school-aged girl with a fantastic voice and stage presence, leading worship along with some taped music and Ugandan drums. I later learned that this little girl was one of Pastor Emma's daughters. It then makes perfect sense based on his enthusiasm for life. Everything in this service was utterly Ugandan. No English was spoken at all and I wondered how in the world I would communicate with this group. It was an unusual service – the people kept going in and out additional new people kept coming in. The best way I could describe it would call it a "floating" or "plasma" service.

There was one light bulb hanging from the ceiling, and so as the evening approached, the room grew increasingly dark.

There was a man who presented a drama, actually a monologue, and a song. He was dressed as a white-bearded old man, hunched over, walking with a cane.

In was all in a Ugandan dialect that I didn't recognize or understand. The combination of the darkness, lack of understanding, and people coming and going all contributed to a bit of an uncomfortable feeling for me.

By the time it was my turn to speak, there were far fewer people there than when the service had started. They did have someone interpret for me, but I honestly can't remember what I had to say and I'm pretty sure they did not understand anything I said except that God loved them, sent His Son to die for them, and that they need to accept His gift to be sure of eternal life. The service sort of drifted to an ending, and Emma asked if I was ready to return home. We climbed back in a car, headed back to Cross City. Neither of us talked about the service, and I have often wondered if this was a typical Emma service.

After a few minutes with the team, I headed for bed.

I wasn't sure where I was going to have to travel the next morning, but I suspected that it was going to be a long, off-the-beaten-path journey...and I was right. It was in a region I did not recall traveling to on past trips.

The geography shifted from the rolling red dirt trails to roads that meandered around shallow water streams coming off of Lake Victoria. They were lined with papyrus reeds so far as you could see. Interspersed in the reeds you would see little foot trails leading off into small rice paddies. The papyrus began to give way to more upland plants and the little streams became fewer and fewer. From there, we started a steady climb into some beautiful, fertile hill country. I would not call these mountains, but they were more impressive hills than I had seen in past trips. As I rode through this beautiful land, I could understand why it is called the "Pearl of Africa." It is, as I can imagine, a broken version of the Garden of Eden. Its beauty can be breathtaking. But that beauty bears the scars of a violent past. The very roads we were driving had been lined with stacks of bodies in the mid-seventies. Bodies of mothers and fathers, brothers and sisters, innocent children, and neighbors, all to remind the people of Uganda of the diabolical nature of Idi Amin and his army. It is little wonder that this generation of Ugandans would just as soon not remember their history.

That dark time in Uganda's history is barely visible any longer, and only if you knew where to look would you find the scars left on the land from those years of terror. In a must-read book, for any who wants to know about this part of Uganda's past, in *The Teeth May Smile But The Heart Does Not Forget,* Andrew Rice states the following:

"During Amin's regime, it is estimated that between 100,000 – 300,000 Ugandans were killed, and an equal or greater number may have perished during the seven years of chaos and civil war that lasted from Amin's ouster until 1986." [16]

After nearly an entire morning of driving, we finally arrived at a large auditorium filled to overflowing with a crowd of teachers, children, administrators, pastors, and parents. The organizers from this district had clearly done a great deal of advanced preparation.

When Lawrence and I arrived, the children were performing and demonstrating their various academic and artistic skills. I am always impressed by the talent and beauty of the children singing, sometimes in English, and sometimes in one of their native dialects. When we arrived, the children that were preforming were exceptionally talented and well rehearsed. The songs were choreographed with various lead singers, speakers, and dance movements throughout. Music and dance are such a vital part of Ugandan culture and often reflect some aspect of their tribal heritage. After each group finished performing, they would go back to sitting in groups on a large red carpet in front of the room full of adults. It always amazes me that the children will perform and then sit very respectfully for hours as I teach the adults. I often wonder if this will plant the seeds in some of the children to become teachers. Or if it is so torturously boring to them that they may never want to become teachers. One of my goals as I am teaching these sessions is to provide enough illustrations and stories to stimulate encouragement and inspiration to either stay in teaching or to become teachers. Uganda is desperate for qualified teachers, especially rural regions, where adequate training, salaries, and facilities are all lacking. I am encouraged each time I hear that another of our schools has started a teacher's training facility. As I write this chapter, I have just learned that Bernard Bogere, the excellent educator, will be opening a teacher's training center. Here is his email to me, making this announcement:

Dear Tony

Thank you for this material. I have gone through, and I find it very helpful and timely because May 2020, I will be opening up a teachers' training College School operating under one of National Teachers Universities.

Lugazi Institute of Sciences and Assistive Technology is established to train teachers for Special needs education, or teachers meant to teach in Uganda schools with children with disabilities including children gifted or talented i.e. Left-Handers. This is a great opportunity to embrace Christian education. It will now be well established that we teach the same person for the 3-year certificate or 2-year diploma courses depending on one's entrance requirements. This Library materials will help a great deal.

Yours
   Bernard Bogere

This is the second teacher training facility that I know has been started since UCCS-U was established in 2011.

My day of teaching was the usual basic Education 101 material that I have described in other chapters, so there is no need for a repeat here. As is often the case, lunch was prepared at great sacrifice and served mid-afternoon. I have learned that this is partially done because it is the largest and perhaps the only meal that many of these participants will get that day. After lunch, I taught for another two or three hours and then gave away two more cows, several bikes, and some backpacks that a church in the US had given me to share. We were such a long distance from our home base and the Ugandan evening traffic so bad that it took that the ride took five or six hours. We arrived back in Katosi at Cross City at 11:00 PM. I eased into the compound quietly, expecting everyone to be asleep. But to my surprise, everyone was awake, including Timothy, Janepher, and several of his grown children. It was Timothy's birthday, and they were waiting on my return to celebrate. So, at eleven o'clock at night, we had a birthday party, with cake and all. My team had gotten together and purchased a treadmill climber for him. He got on it, and after a few minutes of coaching, got his rhythm and really seemed to enjoy this hard-to-find gift. It was after midnight before we got back to our rooms, and since the next day was our last day, we still had to throw our things in our suite cases. The return pack-up is usually much easier since so many supplies and clothes are left behind.

We were scheduled for an early departure, but I was doubtful that we would leave at the stated time (part of the Ugandan way). Everyone made it up and drifted down to the dining area, dragging their luggage across the cobblestone walkway. Pastor Emma was there to greet us with all his Ugandan wares spread across the porch.

His wife and several ladies had joined him and quickly began to show beautiful Ugandan fabric, and measuring our team for dresses and shirts. Mike had a shirt made for me, and each of the ladies ordered dresses for themselves, and Wendy ordered matching dresses for her daughters. I think Emma did very well this day selling off his Ugandan treasures. I came home with a soccer ball made of banana leaves, and a nativity set made from banana leaves, as well.

While we were enjoying Emma, his family, and all his goodies, we were also loading our luggage onto the bus.

We finally had our bags packed, made our purchases, and said our goodbyes to everyone in Katosi. We still had several things to accomplish before we boarded our plane at 11:30 that night. We had been scheduled to meet with Timothy's brother, Godfrey Kiwanda, in his government office in Kampala. As previously discussed, he is the Minister of Tourism, Antiquities, and Wildlife. His schedule is packed with appointments from early morning until evening. I knew that he was making quite a sacrifice to set aside time to meet with us. It was going to be a stretch to work our way through the gridlocked streets of Kampala, especially to the city center, even if we had left Katosi on time. As expected, we arrived hours late, but everyone seemed to take it all in stride.

We were told to go to an upscale restaurant for lunch and the Minister would meet us there. As it turned out, he was called to another meeting, and we were instructed to drive to another location where we would meet for a few moments.

We arrived at another restaurant/resort, where it was apparent that this was a common meeting area for various politicians and those wanting to lobby their positions. When we arrived, Godfrey was already in a meeting with an elegant looking professional woman, who was passionately presenting her case to him. I could not hear the conversation, but I was impressed by her zeal and his kindness as he dealt with her concerns. Everything from his body language to his speech indicated genuine concern for whatever this lady was sharing. As soon as that conversation ended, his personal military guard greeted us and escorted Timothy and me to a table where Timothy's brother and another man were engaged in conversation. Their conversation had begun as soon as his previous guest had concluded her discussion. He greeted us and quickly introduced us to a tall, white-haired man from Finland. For the first several minutes of our time together, this gentleman was part of our group. He was explaining to the Minister and to us that he and his government were committed to advocating for the children of Uganda. I am not sure what all that entails, but I was grateful to learn that this was a long-term commitment. This gentleman spent extended periods in Uganda each year. He clearly had earned respect and gained the ear of the Ugandan government. After several minutes of meeting with the Finnish representative, the conversation ended, and we all moved to another table, the rest of the team was gathered around a long table. Godfrey greeted each team member and engaged each in conversation, thanking them for their love for Uganda and their contribution to the future of the nation. He talked about his recent trip to Vietnam for a meeting with leaders from several countries to address the continued problem of smuggling ivory and the illegal exportation of animals. While Uganda has made great strides in preventing these issues directly in Uganda, one of the main smuggling highways run right through the heart of Northern Uganda.

To get a feel for the severity of the problem, take a look at the following news article from Jan 2019:

> Ugandan authorities have seized 750 pieces of ivory and thousands of pangolin scales being smuggled from neighboring South Sudan in one of the largest seizures of wildlife contraband in the East African country.
>
> The ivory and pangolin scales were discovered inside hollowed-out logs in the Ugandan capital, Kampala, authorities said on Thursday.
>
> Two Vietnamese men, suspected of smuggling, were detained.
>
> The illegal cargo was discovered after the Ugandan Revenue Authority (URA) officers scanned three six-metre containers carrying timber logs which had crossed the border from South Sudan.
>
> After growing suspicious, a team secretly tailed the cargo to a warehouse in Kampala and made the bust.
>
> "Logs were hollowed out and filled with ivory and pangolin scales then resealed with tonnes of melted wax to disguise the contraband," URA spokesman Vincent Seruma told AFP news agency.

"In a single container there were more than 700 pieces of ivory and more than 200 pangolin scales, but we expect to recover thousands of scales," he added.

The full value of the cargo has yet to be established but the agency estimated at least 325 elephants would have been killed to acquire the ivory.

Seruma said the traffickers were part of a "very dangerous racket" which takes advantage of conflicts in eastern and central Africa to poach endangered species.

The URA said it believed the ivory and pangolin scales had been packed at a smuggling centre in the Democratic Republic of the Congo.

The URA tweeted that the two men arrested will be charged with failing to declare prohibited items and concealment of goods.

"We believe they planned to bribe their way to their final destination so we are investigating the shipping agent and other contractors," the agency said.

The little-known pangolin is the world's most trafficked and poached mammal because of the demand for its meat and scales.

The scales are often used in traditional Chinese medicine and its meat is eaten in several countries in Asia and Africa.

The illegal ivory trade is the third most profitable form of trafficking after narcotics and weapons.

The seizure proves Uganda "still is a major transit point for illegal wildlife", Kristof Titeca, a Belgian researcher who recently investigated the role of individual traders in ivory trafficking, said in a Twitter post.

Traffic is driven by demand in Asia and the Middle East, where elephant tusks are used in traditional medicine and ornamentation.

Poaching has seen the elephant population fell by 110,000 over the past decade to just 415,000, according to the International Union for Conservation of Nature.[17]

As I listened to Minister of Wildlife explain the problem and some of the steps being taken, I couldn't help but wonder where this truly fell on the list of the issues the nation of Uganda was facing.

As serious as this problem is, the reality is that a rural family starving to death or a group of orphans just trying to stay alive, probably have about twenty or thirty issues that seem more pressing. AIDS, clean water, housing, the next meal, cholera, dysentery, education, child abduction and sacrifice, and several other things probably all rate at higher priority.

As a biologist, conservationist, global citizen, and Christ follower, I cannot excuse or ignore the problems that put Africa's wildlife or the environment in danger. But once again, I must default to my cry for the importance of Christian education. A population that is well educated and trained to be moral, responsible beings will become the problem solvers of the future, not problem creators.

The challenges are many, almost overwhelming at times, but we cannot grow discouraged or listen to the voices (our own or others) that would cry, "What's the use? You'll never make a difference."

I am often shocked at the indifference and willful ignorance that many Americans can demonstrate when social injustice is involved. This has been made abundantly clear on several occasions from people who engage me in conversations about the work of IACCS. One friend (who had probably had a few too many beers) said straight out, "You're nuts! I don't give a s_ _ t about the people of Uganda!" and turned and walked into his house. I stood a bit stunned, but thought, "Guess he's not going to buy a cow for us anytime soon!"

On another occasion, I was at a local restaurant having lunch with a couple of friends. A couple that attended Island Community Church on occasion entered the restaurant and sat at a table across the way. I hadn't seen them in a while, so, before I left, I walked to their table to greet them.

They had always been very warm and friendly to me. On this occasion, the husband jumped me almost from the beginning. He began to attack me for turning my attention to the needs of children in other countries while the needs in our own country were so great.

I was shocked and hurt. This couple had been in good churches for many years, but they (in fairness, the husband, not the wife) didn't seem to have a clue about the social injustice that so dominates third world and developing countries. But it was also one of those moments where the Holy Spirit seemed to take over and give the words and attitude that needed to be conveyed at the moment. I said, "Well, first the reason I go and am doing what I do is that I believe God has called me to do it and you wouldn't want me to go against what God has called me to do, would you?" I then added, "Did you know that these children are being dragged off into the jungle, being slaughtered as child sacrifices, or are starving to death because they have been abandoned? Many of their parents are dead from diseases that we barely think of in America. We have support services from our government, charities, churches, and parachurch organizations that people in third world countries could never imagine. The poorest people in America are still wealthier than 90% of the people in these poor countries. And medical care is available that the vast majority of these people will never be able to avail themselves of. If we in America don't help, who will?" And with that, I excused myself and wondered, "Wonder if he will buy a cow for a poor family here in America, probably not going to buy one for Uganda!"

One of my modern-day heroes is Gary Haugen, founder, and CEO of International Justice Mission. I talked about Gary early, but I am so impressed with the work of IJM and the heart he has for people suffering from social injustice, that I have to quote him here. In his book, *Just Courage*, (IVP) he says:

> *Western Christians simply have no idea what an utter, desperate disaster is taking place twenty-four hours a day around our world. They have no vivid picture of what life is like for hundreds of millions of people in our world who live in crushing, spiritual darkness, humiliation and despair. They don't realize that there are millions of people crying out every day to be rescued from aching, urgent hunger; from degrading and hopeless poverty; from the ravages of painful diseases; from torture, slavery, rape and abuse. The vast abundance and isolation on the Disneyland island of the world's affluent communities*

means that many Western Christians miss God's great calling to a life of heroic rescue simply because they are largely oblivious to the need. They just can't imagine that there could really be any great heroic struggle that would need their help.[18]

But there is, there is a struggle and there is a need, and we are God's plan to address them. Haugen says, "You are the light of the world (quoting Matthew 5:14-16). He then adds:

According to Jesus, we are it. You are it. The world is a dark and hurting place, and the Creator of the universe has one plan to bring light to it – and through Christ, we are that plan. Jesus is tell us that we have been rescued out of the darkness so that we can be the light to the world.

God calls us to make the transition from being those who have been rescued from the world, to those through whom God is literally rescuing the world.[19]

The day was nearly gone, we were finishing our time with Godfrey, and I realized that we were still scheduled to make a stop at the game preserve on the way to the airport. I was doubtful that this was going to happen. The conversation with Timothy's brother is always something I look forward to and feel that having his ear and voice in the Ugandan government is a good thing.

I would gladly give up the game preserve visit for the time with the Minister. We said our farewells, piled back on the bus, and started the slow, traffic-jammed route toward the airport.

As this trip ended, I was grateful for the things that had been accomplished in Uganda. But I was also incredibly thankful for the things that I saw happening in the lives and hearts of the team members. I could see God working in each of our lives and knew that not only had Uganda benefited from our visit, but that we had been changed in ways that would last a lifetime. On the flight back to Miami, Dr. Diaz sat with me and began to build a business plan to help make the clinic an on-going, sustainable clinic. Mike talked about the Shoe That Grows project for next year. Wendy spoke about what the Lord was doing in her life because of this trip. Patty was busy mentally building farms and micro industries to build sustainability among the villages she encountered. I knew that Peter was thinking of the children he loved, the cows he had helped purchase, and the feet he had washed and placed sandals on for the first time. He was probably also rejoicing in the children's church that he had been so instrumental in building. Pete was and is very humble and will never receive credit for any of his work. Usually, with a tear in his eye, he will say, "it was God, not me." For Dorothy, this trip had been an adventure; she had hugged on and shared her love for the children literally thousands of times on this trip. I wondered how this would impact her future. In mid-April, before our trip, I had performed a wedding ceremony for Dorothy and Tred Barta.

Tred was a colorful, unique individual.

He was one of the original TV adventure/nature/survival show hosts; truly an avid outdoorsman – adventurer, hunter, fisherman. He was an avid snow skier and perhaps on track to be a member of the US ski team, with a dream of the Olympics in view. Tred was also brash, loud, and self-confident. He had the mouth of a sailor (he was a sailor!) and strong opinions about most everything. But one morning, things took a drastic change for him. He woke up, and as he tried to get out of bed, he discovered that he was paralyzed from his waist down. He found that he had a tumor on his spine and that he would be paralyzed for the remainder of his life. Instead of giving up, he embraced the challenges of living the life of an adventurer in a wheelchair. His accomplishments as an outdoorsman and waterman are legendary. Many of his world records, both before and after his paralysis, still remain today. But the part that causes our paths to cross merge here.

Tred had become a Christian–still opinionated and brash, but a Christian, nonetheless. He met Dorothy, and before long, they (mainly Tred) were asking me to marry them. Tred had opinions about his theology and how God should be running things. He wanted to express those things to me to see if I might be able to influence God in some way.

Dorothy wanted to work through some of these things before saying yes to the marriage. We met on several occasions, and Tred seemed to be making satisfactory progress towards what Dorothy wanted in a husband. Eventually, they were married on Tred's charter boat in Islamorada. I knew that their marriage would be filled with challenges, but they insisted that they were ready. Not long after they had been married, Tred told me he wanted Dorothy to go to Uganda on the next trip and gave me a check to cover her expenses. Because the damage of Hurricane Irma had been so dramatic, many of the homes and resorts could not reopen and were uninhabitable.

The condo where Tred and Dorothy were living was shut down, but Tred basically refused to leave. His apartment was on an upper floor, and there was no working elevator, so Tred depended on others to help carry him up and down several flights of stairs. Dorothy went to stay with friends during this time. I think she had realized how challenging this marriage was going to be but wanted to honor her vows. I knew that for Dorothy, this was a must trip. It gave her a way to regroup and recuperate while loving on the Ugandan children. I had hoped that this would be enough of a break, and Tred's housing situation would resolve itself before we returned. Unfortunately, the housing situation got worse, and Tred ultimately moved to the Carolina coast. He, then, being the adventurer that he was, set out in his specially fitted truck and a service dog for Alaska and the Yukon; a challenging trip for anyone, let alone one in a wheelchair. Sadly, after traveling alone (except for his dog and meeting up with friends) for several months, Tred died in a car crash in the Yukon Territory. I am grateful for Tred and his decision to give his life to Christ. I am thankful that he made it possible for Dorothy to travel with us to Uganda. And I am grateful for Dorothy, her free spirit, her love for life, and the contribution she made in loving the children of Uganda.

This was a special team, and God was at work in each of their lives, and I couldn't wait to see how He would direct our futures.

Another important IACCS event that occurred was the preliminary visit to Haiti and the launch of the Haitian Association of Christian Colleges and Schools. Dr. Robert Andrews, the Vice President of the Florida Association of Christian Colleges and Schools, arranged a lunch meeting with Bill Nealey, Jr., the director of Mission to Haiti, to see if there was a relationship that could be built with our two organizations. Bill Nealey Sr. founded Mission to Haiti on January 1, 1981.

Bill Jr. runs the organization based in Miami, Florida. Bill takes teams to Haiti regularly, and has great respect among the people of Haiti.

His contact with the Christian schools would be an excellent asset for IACCS. After that first luncheon, we continued to talk and plan an organizational trip, much like the 2011 trip to Uganda. I printed the FACCS/IACCS Statement of Faith and By-Laws and sent them to Bill for translation into Creole. Mid-way through 2017, I flew to Haiti for our first look at Mission to Haiti's fantastic compound. It is an entirely self-sustaining mission with its own water system, huge power generator, dormitories for guests and visiting teams, and a large clinic. Bill had invited several pastors and school administrators to attend an introductory/organizational IACCS meeting. I handed out the materials and let them discuss the idea among themselves. Before the afternoon was over, we had elected a board and established the HACCS. The next day, we visited several schools around Port-au-Prince. We set up a larger organizational meeting at a large church facility. I believe that all of the schools in attendance joined the association that day. The potential in Haiti is just beginning to reveal itself.

The need here is every bit as great as Uganda, and the ease of getting there is a plus for visiting teams. The most significant obstacles as I see them are the political unrest and the constant effects of one natural disaster after another – earthquakes, floods, hurricanes. Year in and year out, Haiti just gets beat down and desperately needs churches all over the world to see Haiti as "one of the least of these," extending all the help that can be mustered.

Psalm 82:3,4
Defend the poor and fatherless;
Do justice to the afflicted and needy.
Deliver the poor and needy;
Free them from the hand of the wicked (NKJV)

CHAPTER 10
TRIP # 7 A VILLAGE WITH NO NAME

To love at all is to be vulnerable.
- C.S. Lewis, "The Four Loves" (1960)

"No One Ever Visits Here"

As long as I've been traveling to Uganda, I have heard conversations about a poor fishing village nearby where conditions were desperate. But each time I asked about going to the village, the topic would be quickly changed or ignored as if I had never asked the question. I was perplexed by this, but thought there must be a reason for not going to see this place. Was it dangerous? Or filled with disease? Or too far? I simply never knew or got an answer. But that was about to change. In 2018, the largest team that had joined me was assembled and ready to go for trip number 7. There was going to be ten of us making this year's journey. The team was a mix of people I had specifically targeted to go, and of individuals that others had requested be allowed to go. Six of the team members were veterans, and four were rookies. Two of the four were high school students traveling with their parents. This was my seventh trip.

Trip #7 A Village With No Name

Mike Forster (the Mayah – Ugandan pronunciation of mayor) was making his third trip. Gary Mace, our techie guy, and dive shop owner was making his second trip. Dr. Miguel Diaz was making his second trip and was bringing his teenage son, Miguel, with him. Wendy and Patty were making their second trip in a row. Two new team members were from Dade County, but had a long-standing indirect connection to me, Mike, and the community of Islamorada. Donna and Sydney Gustinger were the daughter-in-law and granddaughter of an old friend of mine. Al Gustinger had been a well-known attorney in South Florida, but my first encounter with him was not in a courtroom.

As I have mentioned, I taught marine biology to high school students for many years. One of the great things about teaching marine biology in the Florida Keys is that it is one giant science lab just waiting to be explored. It was a fairly common practice for me to pile my class on a bus and head out to one of the spots I used for field studies. One of the best places is a stretch of beach (one of the few natural beaches in the Keys) on Lower Matecumbe Key. It has been named Sea Oates Beach, because of the small dunes running next to US 1, covered with Sea Oates. The water is literally less than 30 yards from the road, so it is very easy to take a class there and do an assignment and get back on the bus in a class period. One day I was in about waist-deep water with about seven or eight students, when I heard an unfamiliar adult voice ask a question. I looked up, and there in our midst was a tall thin man that reminded me of pictures I had seen of Buffalo Bill. I invited him to join us on the exercise we were doing, which he gladly did.

When I told him I was from Island Christian School, he was quick to let me know that he was a Christian and that this was his beach and that we were welcome to use it any time. I was a bit embarrassed because I thought the beach belonged to the county. I had no idea that I had been trespassing all these years but was relieved that the owner didn't mind. That started an acquaintance that would last several decades. He would occasionally attend Island Community Church when he was in town, and we would talk a couple of times a year. Al loved to fly, fish, and to travel to the Bahamas. In 2003, Al, his son Eric, and his wife Idel and their son Eric Jr. were on the way to the Bahamas when their small plane crashed, killing all four passengers. I was asked to do a memorial service in the Keys for the entire family. The service was held at sea aboard a charter boat with dozens of other charter boats gathered around. I spoke on the ship's radio as I broadcasted the service to the people on the other vessels. So, with that as the backdrop, let me get back to Donna and Sydney. Because of Al, there was a natural connection to them, and I was anxious to have them join us when I found that they had an interest. I believe that they learned of the Uganda trips from Mike Forster. They had seen the Shoe That Grows project while visiting Mangrove Mike's Restaurant in Islamorada. Mike explained the trip, and they asked if they could join us.

The final member of the team was a very talented young lady named Allison Cipri.

I had known Allison for a few years, knew she had a very sincere heart for God and missions, and had a longing to be a part of a trip like this one. I also knew that she was an excellent photographer/videographer. I had been wanting to take a skilled photographer along who could focus just on capturing the Uganda story on film. When Allison agreed to come, I was very excited about the potential to tell the Uganda story in media form.

I really felt like this was a mature, balanced team that could accomplish a great deal in the time that we were going to have. By spreading this team out with different assignments, we had the potential to achieve more than in any other year. My time would be filled with teaching at educators' conferences each day. Also, we had a group for the medical team/clinic, a team for buying and giving away supplies, and a team for purchasing and giving of cows.

These teams would overlap and be flexible, but we were looking forward to a great trip. Allison would move between groups taking photos and videos to document the trip.

A dream team

As usual, we arrived late in the evening in Entebbe. It was now Friday, November 8, and the team had been traveling for nearly two full days by the time we got to our rooms in Katosi. I had contacted Timothy in advance to warn him that we were going to be coming with a large team. As a result, there was going to be a larger than normal amount of luggage. We had several bags of The Shoe That Grows, but we had used regular suitcases to avoid drawing attention as we cleared Customs. We had also determined that it would be better to buy several of the shoes in Mukono.

These were sturdy school uniform shoes and seemed to be favored by the proprietors of the schools. Sydney had gone to her school and conducted fundraising, and collected a variety of sports balls, including soccer balls, rugby balls, footballs, basketballs, and other general recreation balls and sporting equipment. Gary had also purchased several soccer balls and air pumps for them. All ten of us had three bags of items, most of which would be given away while on the trip. Besides, we all had our carry-on items.

The point is we almost needed a moving van just to get the luggage to our compound. In anticipation of the size, Timothy had brought the largest bus from the Winners Home.

We were pushing luggage through the windows, stacking them through the back door, and stashing them any place they would fit. We had to, just to have room on the bus for the team and the delegation of helpers that Timothy had brought with him. The bus apparently had no suspension or shock absorbers to speak of.

This would later become a bit of a source of contention with the team after several hours, days, and miles of riding on the bus. They took quite a beating on some of the treks through the rough roads/trails of the jungle.

But this night, I was grateful for the bus and especially thankful for the progress that had been made in smoothing the road from Mukono to Katosi. What had been a rutted, nearly impassable dirt trail, had become a smooth highway.

Sadly, there had been a price to pay for this progress by some of the locals who had home and businesses along the route. You will remember that I had asked Timothy the year before the road project had begun, what the large "Xs" were that were painted on all the homes and buildings along the way. He said, "They mean those buildings are going to be torn down, and the people will have to find new places to live and have their businesses." I asked if there was going to be any compensation for their displacement. I did not get an answer.

It was after 3:00 AM on the 10th by the time we got to Hotel Cross City.

We threw all the bags in one room for safekeeping and took only the essentials to crawl into bed for a rapid sleep. Apparently, right after we were settled in our rooms, we lost electric power (not that uncommon in Uganda). We then were hit with a severe thunderstorm with a deluge of rain. I guess it is not surprising, but I wasn't aware of any of this because I slept so soundly. Fortunately, I think everyone on the team had followed my advice and had slept on both stages of the flights. We were able to get up reasonably early and somewhat adjusted to the eight-hour time difference. This team was pumped, energetic, and ready to go. We gathered in the morning for breakfast, and they were already making plans for a "pump-the-balls-up party out on the lawn. But before that, most of the team was clamoring for coffee to kick start their day.

I am not a coffee drinker but have developed a real taste for Ugandan hot tea.

Timothy also knows that he can keep me full of Mountain Dew, and I can pretty much run all day!

We gathered under a large tree in the middle of the courtyard with bags and bags of deflated balls, each team member grabbed a pump, and we went to work.

It didn't take long for kids from the village to peek through the front gate and see all the balls. Of course, they began to clamor for them. We knew that giving them a ball would never work. Within seconds there would have been an uncontrollable mob outside the gate.

Fortunately, we had some smaller gifts, and Mike had his ever-ready supply of Jolly Rancher candies that he was always ready to share. At one point, one of the little guys threw a toy truck on a string over the wall, hoping it would work as a bartering tool for a soccer ball. The group was pretty moved by what we were looking at. This little truck was a clever use of a used plastic water bottle and four screw-on caps. The side of the bottle was cut open for a cabin, and bottle caps made the wheels stuck on two sticks. I honestly can't remember whether a soccer ball was tossed back over the fence in acceptance of the barter price or not. It is amazing to see how ingenious the children are in finding ways to make toys. Old tires, rims, containers, banana leaves, and vines all become treasured toys.

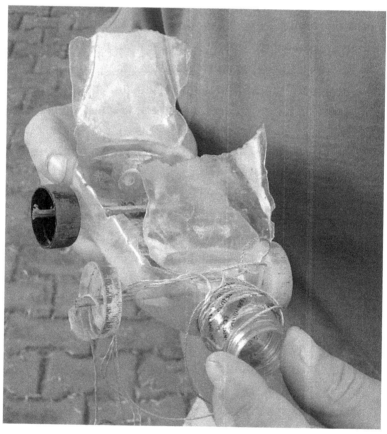

Barter price of a treasured Ugandan toy

Several of the young men inside the compound had picked up a football, and being an old coach, I couldn't resist a little coaching on how to throw, run pass routes, and catch a football. It was fun to watch these guys who had never thrown a football, learning so quickly how to throw and catch. I have often wanted to come and spend enough time to develop some sports teams in the schools. I know that Uganda has had a team from Lugazi come to America and compete in the Little League World Series in Williamsport, PA. I once asked Bernard Bogere, the UCCSU Vice President, if he knew any of the coaches. He said, "Oh, yes." And named them by name. I have not been able to meet with them yet, but hope to on a future trip.

We have started to see a few interscholastic games between our schools. Also, just before we left the States on this trip, I was introduced to a young Ugandan named Bidandi Oscar Davids. He is working hard to bring sports into the schools. My introduction came by way of an old friend named Jeff Siegel. Jeff left a successful career with Service Masters several years ago to go fulltime with a ministry he founded, known as Global Baseball. He was a successful baseball player in his own right, but that is not the only thing that identifies him. Jeff grew up in a traditional Jewish home. He embraced Judaism as his faith until he was introduced to Jesus as his Messiah. Jeff has used baseball as the vehicle to get into countries that would otherwise be closed to the Gospel. His work in Cuba has been remarkable. Also, he has been asked to be Israel's baseball coach for the Isthmian Games. He has used his skills and the Gospel message to influence countries all over the globe. At some point, Oscar had heard of Jeff and reached out to him. I somehow became aware of the relationship, and before long, was arranging a meeting with Oscar on this trip to Uganda.

When I met with him, I encouraged him to keep the relationship with Jeff and Global Baseball healthy. Hopefully, we could encourage the schools of the UCCS-U to get involved.

This has moved more slowly than I would like, but I am learning that much of what happens in Uganda happens in baby steps. While Ugandans are very generous and quick to share and meet the needs of one another, there is intense competition for every dollar because everyone's need is so great. So, sports programs are a bit further down on the priority list than dozens of other more basic needs.

Let me use this as a segue to talk about what I would call the "dark side" of the orphan crisis in Uganda and most other third world and developing countries. To do so, I will quote an article from the Guardian News, a British publication that has been around since the 1800s. It is now considered to be more liberal (to the left of the midline). Nonetheless, the article and problems that it shines its light on is something we should all be aware of as we give support to organizations. Here is what a recent article had to say:

> It only takes a few years of living in an institution for children to undergo seismic personality changes, says Pop, who started working with orphans in her native Romania two decades ago. "Nothing could prepare me for how deep the changes were to their personalities," she says. "They had no identity, no sense of who they are, and even siblings had no connection. Some children acted as if they were autistic and were touching or hitting themselves because they were never hugged, or they started self-harming. They never understood how their bodies worked." Nevertheless, in Uganda the orphanage industry is booming. The number of orphans growing up in children's homes has increased

from around 1,000 in the 1990s to 50,000 today, according to international children's charity Viva. Unlike past surges in figures in countries like Rwanda, this increase wasn't borne of genocide or war – it's in large part economic.

The financial benefits for someone who decides to run an orphanage can be considerable. People who have worked in institutions in Rwanda and Uganda say it can cost as much as £2,800 (about $3,640 in US) a year to support a child in an orphanage, and the bill is often footed by well-meaning overseas donors. Therefore, the more children drawn into the orphanage, the more money in the owners' pockets. This makes children a highly prized commodity in countries like Uganda.

Some argue that the system in Uganda amounts to child slavery. "We are seeing a disturbing trend of children being drawn into orphanages and then being deployed to help raise funds for the orphanage in one way or another, whether it's attracting sponsors and volunteers or singing and dancing for donations," says youth studies academic Kristen Cheney, the author of Crying for Our Elders: African Orphanhood in the Age of HIV and Aids.

"When orphanages are dependent on children's labour, the kids become trapped. Once they grow too old to attract donations, however, they are cast out and forced to fend for themselves in a world they do not know," she says.[20]

The truth this articles addresses reminds me of the words of Jesus when His disciples were in a debate. Remember when they wanted to know who was going to be the greatest in the Kingdom?

He said to them, "Whoever receives one little child like this in My name receives Me. "But whoever causes one of these little ones who believe in Me to sin, it would be better for him if a millstone were hung around his neck, and he were drowned in the depth of the sea. Woe to the world because of offenses! For offenses must come, but woe to that man by whom the offense comes!" (Matthew 18:5-7)

This is why it is imperative to do your homework. Know, as best as you can, which organizations in the country are legitimate and which charities you are giving money to are trustworthy. Don't be afraid to ask hard questions. I personally have a policy that says, "No accountability, no money." If there is not an accountability board and receipts can't be shown for where the money is going, then stop giving. I have also learned that there will always be some level of doubt, and every dollar will probably not be spent as we would spend it. There comes a place where we have to hand it over to the Lord and say, "Lord, I'm doing the best I can with the resources you have given me. You know the hearts of the people we are giving to, and we know they have to stand accountable to you." That's the millstone around the neck principle!

A book that I would call a must-read book for anyone who is giving to help those in need (and that should be all of us, shouldn't it?) is the book, *When Helping Hurts,* by Steve Corbett and Brian Fikkert, Moody Press, 2009. It and the study material that is available online can serve as a helpful tool in educating yourself in this arena.

Now back to the trip. After we finished filling the balls with air and playing with some of the children, Timothy took the team on a walkthrough of the village of Katosi. I loved the journal note that Allison wrote about this first daylight exposure to Uganda.

She said, *"We walked through the village it was like a scene from a movie. Children surrounded us and just seemed to multiply."*

We walked through the streets. Timothy stopped to talk to various people selling their wares along the street. He would occasionally reach into his pocket, pull out some shillings, give it to them as a gift, and then move on. I have seen Timothy do this over and over again. It is one of the things that keeps driving me back to Uganda and specifically working with Timothy. His genuine care for people is evidenced by his generosity. When we got to the end of the road, B.J. and our bus were waiting for us. Almost on cue, as we boarded the bus, the sky opened up, and it began to pour again.

The task of this bus trip was to travel to the bank in Mukono to do the currency exchange that would allow us to make the necessary purchases while on this trip. Going to the bank in Uganda is an experience in itself. As you enter, a guard is standing on the sidewalk with a rifle that looks like a WWII issue. He is in full military dress, stands or sits expressionless, and you get the idea that you don't want to do anything to tick him off. There is often a second guard on the inside of the bank with the same M.O. The bank, like most banks, looks very stately with marble columns and counters tops. The tellers are behind windows that are covered in metal bars. They are usually young men who are dressed in suits and carry themselves like they are each the bank president. They take their jobs very seriously and have been very well trained.

I always have a currency app on my phone to see if the exchange rate they are offering is in line with what it should be. One of the things that takes some getting used to is that you should have newer, clean, crisp bills. Older bills bring a lower exchange rate. The reason they have given me is that older bills are easier to counterfeit.

Once everything was squared away with the bank, the next move was to split up as a team. This would facilitate making some of the purchases necessary for this trip to be a success. We needed to buy shoes, medical supplies, bed frames and mattresses, and of course, cows. In fact, this is a good place to give a summary of our purchases for this trip.

- 15 Cows, 1 cow was pregnant
- 8 cows have birthed offspring
- 1 Cow for food
- $500 for goats
- 10 Bicycles
- $5000 in mattresses
- $5000 in beds
- $1500 for hard school shoes
- 200 pairs of the Shoe that Grows from Mike
- $1000 for insect netting
- $270 for printing
- $5,120 for accommodations, food, and transportation
- 30 soccer balls and 30 pumps
- Basketballs
- Rugby balls
- Playground balls
- Baseballs
- Footballs
- 250 John 3:16/IACCS shirts

I went with Dr. Diaz and Timothy to a shoe store in Mukono. The young man obviously knew Timothy already; I would assume from buying shoes from him in the past. Dr. Diaz was determined to get the best-negotiated price possible. After haggling over the price for several minutes, the young man agreed to sell the shoes for $15 per pair. Miguel learned that the young salesman/shop owner was a Christian, and it was as if they had established a life-long bond. Both seemed satisfied – Miguel was confident that he had gotten a reasonable price, and the owner had made a huge sale.

How could we go wrong with these shoes? After all, their brand name was *Toughees – Made Tough to Last Longer*! I love the names Ugandans use to identify their businesses; names like, *Beautiful Hair Salon* (often spelled *saloon*); or *Hotel NetWorth*; and *New Quality Cut Butchery* – with raw meat hanging all day outdoors; one of my favorites coming from the South – a chain of gas stations: *MoGas*! It is not always names that get your attention. There is a clinic along the main road just outside of Katosi that really catches your eye. There are two overweight statues (Sumo wrestler size!) out front with water continually pouring out of their mouths…like someone vomiting! That is supposed to represent someone getting well! I can think of many better ways to let clients know this is a place to come to get healthy. Forgive my moment of digressing.

Let's get back to our task of purchasing.

When it came to purchasing cows, we had learned that the price would drop a bit if you told the Ugandan negotiator that he could keep the difference between his negotiated price and the $1000 designated for the cow purchase. The money was to be used for food for the orphans or for supplies for the orphanage. We also told them that we had to approve the cow as a healthy milk cow. They also had to produce receipts for all cows.

We also had a team line up the mattresses and beds, but they could not be delivered until the last day of our trip. We had made all the necessary steps on this day to get most of the purchasing in motion.

We weren't sure what was next on the schedule.

Since this was a Saturday and a non-school day, we never quite knew what Timothy might have scheduled for our group. This Saturday, he had said we were going to a special event, but really never got around to telling us what that meant. Here is a brief journal entry as we were traveling to the "mystery event."

Journal Entry: What! Are those camels walking down the road? With riders? Yep! Camels alright, fully saddled with two riders. I asked our driver about it. He shrugged and nodded and simply said, "Yes, we have camels here." No more explanation than that. It was a first. I was used to seeing just about anything going down the road – boda boda carrying entire beds or transporting four people at a time. Boda with lumber and pieces of metal that stuck out and took up half the road. Or vans loaded with 20 or more people with dozens of chickens tied to the outside of the roof! But seeing the camels in the middle of nowhere was a bit unexpected. Now we are traveling to who knows where! I think Timothy has to attend this event and didn't know what else to do with us and probably thought we would find it interesting...whatever it is.

TRIP # 7 A VILLAGE WITH NO NAME

What! Camels on the road?

In the afternoon, we traveled to a compound in Mukono. We were escorted to a small room. There was a group of men seated around the edge of the room. They were wearing formal white *kanzu* covering, which meant this was an important event. We were given chairs and invited to watch the ceremony. We still didn't know what we were watching, but soon learned that this was the ceremonial negotiation of a bride price. This is the ritual described in chapter 7, called the *Mutwalo*. While it was a formality among Bugandans, it was still a very important part of their traditional wedding process. No English was being spoken, so it was hard to follow all that was going on. There was definitely a hierarchy and order to who was speaking and for what steps were being taken. There were 15 to 20 men sitting on very colorful handmade woven mats on the floor with their backs against the wall. At various points, women would enter the room with multiple items of food or drink that appeared to be part of the ritual. The final piece was a large goblet filled with milk. Words were spoken, and then the cup was handed to each of the men, who then took a sip and handed it to the next man in line. The final young man to drink was the groom-to-be.

It took several minutes to figure out that this was part of a wedding ritual, or to figure out who the groom was, or for that matter, who the father of the bride was. We were treated as honored guests, but were purely observers, not participants in this ceremony.

When this portion of the ceremony concluded, someone came to us and motioned for us to follow them. All ten of us were escorted to a narrow courtyard area nestled between several small rooms. It reminded me a bit of what an insula must have looked like in ancient Jewish villages.

In the Hebrew wedding, the insula, or central courtyard, was where much of the wedding would take place.

We were all seated at a long table, and mountains of food were served. This was quite a sampling of Ugandan cuisine. This was quite a treat for our rookies on the trip.

Watching them sample items with caution was fun to sit back and observe. Some of their facial expressions were priceless to see. I was reminded of my first trip and how cautious I was as I sampled the various native foods.

Priceless facial expressions.

The Enshagariz.

The Bride

Once we had all had our fill, we were escorted to another courtyard. This was obviously the place where the main festivities were going to take place.

There were elaborate white tents and canopies set up with pink, red, purple, and blue ribbons and banners decorating them. The ground was covered with mats. On top of the mats was what must be Ugandan confetti. It looked like it could have been paper run through a shredder. We as a team were seated off to the side under one of the tents. We had only been seated a few minutes when music began to play and a procession of young ladies, called the *Enshagariz*, dressed in brightly printed *gomsei*, began to dance their way into the center of the crowd. And a young man wearing the ceremonial *kanzu*, covered with a bright blue sports jacket, danced and led the procession of young ladies. The best way to describe what was taking place was somewhere between a parade and a dance. Seated in two special seats were the bride's parents, and much of the ceremony was in front of them. This is the part of the pre-wedding festivities known as the *Kwanjula*. The final girl to enter was obviously the bride-to-be. I can't imagine the Queen of Sheba being any more elaborately adorned than she.

After several songs, some directed to the bride, others directed to the families, several gifts were offered to the bride and her family. The ceremony lasted for several hours and was still going, but we had another stop to make.

We all boarded the bus and were off to the Collene Hotel for dinner and a UCCS-U board meeting and dinner. Bernard Bogere, Lawrence, and his wife were already there, waiting for us. We introduced the group and then had dinner together. We had an informal discussion about UCCS-U and IACCS, but I would be hard-pressed to call this a formal board meeting. I think both Bernard and Lawrence were hoping for a bit more structure, but at least we got to cover some important ground while we met.

It was after 11:00 pm by the time we got back to Cross City Hotel, I excused myself from the group to be sure my message for the next morning was prepared. I knew what I wanted to convey at the morning service. Still, I always want to be sure by looking over my notes. I wanted to make certain that I was stating everything in ways that my interpreter could easily communicate it to the Ugandan congregation. Even though most of the people in the church would understand English, our American accents made it difficult for them. It was interesting to hear them tell us that we had funny accents when we were feeling the same way about their English.

In any case, I hoped to communicate the following principles:

- The challenge of Scripture to be bold and courageous for Christ.

- As a church, we are to be on offense rather than defense. I talked about how Jesus said, "The gates of hell will not prevail against the church." The Church is to be charging the gates of hell!
- We cannot be lone ranger Christians (try to communicate that to a Ugandan!)
- The Bible says 365 times "Fear Not," one for every day of the year.
- The Bible teaches in John 16:33, "In this world you will have trouble. But take heart! I have overcome the world."
- As the Church, be the hope and future for Uganda and an example of the Church to the rest of the world.

I felt like I was ready to communicate what God had given me, so off to sleep I went.

The next morning the team was up early and very eager to get to the church. The main excitement was because they wanted to see the children, interact with them, and see the progress on the children's church. When we did the climb up the hill to the church, I noticed that everyone's pace quickened the closer we got to the children's church. I recorded these notes in my journal about the children's church:

Dr. Diaz had sent money to finish the roof, so he was very pleased to see the roof completed. Gary Mace was thrilled to see that the building had been completed to the level it was (He had not been to the site since it was just a bare cleared piece of land). *When we first started the project, there was a jungle.*

We ("We," meaning Pastor Kakooza and his work crew) had to level the ground, dig the foundation, buy the initial lumber and posts to get the project going. The children's church now has a level, dirt floor, walls, and a roof.

The windows are there as openings with no bars or glass, and the doors are just openings. The children's church is being led by Joy, Timothy and Janepher's oldest daughter.

I got to go in for a few minutes to interact with the children before being ushered into the main church service. Our two teenagers (Sydney and Miguel Jr.) quickly bonded with the children, as Alison recorded in her journal, *"Jr. and Sydney each had a special moment as children said to them, 'I'm going to miss you.'"*

The church was packed with people! Many of the older children from Winners Home had been brought in. There also seemed to be a larger adult crowd than in some years in the past. I looked out at the group, and in an instant, felt the Lord prodding me to change my message. I was still able to cover the points I had outlined the night before, but the following notes are written directly from my journal that I wrote that evening:

Preached on Luke 15 (yes, the same passage from the year before, but with a new twist) – justice, mercy, grace (I wrote the words big enough for everyone to see, on three large pieces of paper). Mike, Allison, Wendy, and Gary were in the main service, while Miguel, Miguel Jr., Sydney, and Donna were with the children.

In the adult service, there were many familiar faces. They brought in many children from Winner's Home, which really filled the service.

As I preached on the lost sheep, the lost coin and the lost son, I played the video of the song Never Ending Reckless Love of God, by Cory Asbury.

(I guess the official name of the song is Reckless Love.

Remember how the chorus goes?

*Oh, the overwhelming, never-ending, reckless love of God
Oh, it chases me down, fights 'til I'm found, leaves the ninety-nine
I couldn't earn it, and I don't deserve it, still, You give Yourself away
Oh, the overwhelming, never-ending, reckless love of God)*

I talked about how God would go after that one lost sheep.

I talked about the celebration, the party, when that which was lost was found.

After the clip ended and I had told the story of the lost sheep, I went to the lost coin, and finally the lost son.

I talked about how the lost son, when he had come to his senses, knew he deserved justice, but he hoped he might get a little mercy from his father if he went home, confessed his wrong, and begged to be taken on as a hired hand.

But what he got was way more, a billion times more than that. He got grace. I explained how his dad had thrown his arms around him and welcomed him back as his son. I acted it out and related the story in such a way that

Trip # 7 A Village With No Name

I wanted people to see themselves as that son receiving God's underserved grace.

As I told these stories and related them to justice, mercy, and grace, I couldn't help but to long for the day when _____ (the name of a friend, that I so long to see come to Christ) finally makes a decision for Christ. What a celebration that will be!

Later in the trip, I had the opportunity to tell _____ (that person) what a good friend they were. I wanted them to know Christ because I want our friendship to last for eternity.

As I copied these words from my journal, my eyes filled with tears as I recalled this friend and this message.

After the service ended and we had lunch, we got to go on one of the most impacting excursions I have been on since traveling to Uganda. Once again, here are my notes from my journal:

Sunday afternoon, we walked to the fishing village near Katosi. These are the poorest people I have seen since beginning my visits to Uganda.

It was approaching evening, and the fishermen were heading out to Lake Victoria. These were traditional wooden Ugandan fishing vessels, with old Yamaha outboard motors, nets, and lanterns.

Many of the fishermen wore orange lifejackets because they can't swim.

There is a strange rock formation that resembles volcanic pumice (this area covers the entire ground area where the village is located. It is a fairly flat smooth surface, which allows the nets to spread out easily and the huts to be built on a stable foundation). Several square game boards have been carved in the rock, and the people of the village play some type of game with them.

Large frames standing on legs about four feet tall have been built, and stand in various locations on the rock. The table-like structures are covered with a fine-meshed screen where the minnows dry and are separated from sand and debris. Those on the drying tables are used to feed humans. The minnows on the ground and piled on the nets are used for animals.

A lady asked if she could show us her home. She took us into a mud hut that was perhaps 15ft x 15ft at the most. The roof was made of sticks tied together as a frame, covered by old clear plastic visqueen. She asked that I pray for her home and family because two of the children were very ill. We invited her to send the one child to see Dr. Diaz at the clinic the next day, and he was able to give the other some treatment on the spot to help him.

I could barely pray for this family because I was getting so overwhelmed with emotion.

Several of the team members were wiping away tears and sniffling. I am sure we were all thinking the same thing: "What must it be like to try to raise a family in this level of poverty and need." It is almost unfathomable to think about. Most of us sit in the comfort of our homes with clean water, plenty of food, and medical treatment readily at hand.

Here, none of that is true. Will my baby die tomorrow because of something as simple as impure water? Or will they be attacked by some bacteria, parasite, or virus, which could be easily treated if a doctor were just more available (If they had the money for the doctor or the medicine)?

When I'm neck-deep in helping people amid this level of poverty, I don't really care much about those who may be saying they are poor because they want to be poor. Or they are poor because they can raise more money by remaining poor (except for groups like the village where everyone remains drunk all the time and won't work or the orphanages that exploit their children). I know there are times that this is true, but not in places like this. I think, most of the time, people who say these things are just ignorant to the need or just want to keep their money in their pocket for themselves. If I kept money to myself, I think I would be guilty of violating the principle of Hebrews 13:1-3: *"Keep on loving one another as brothers and sisters. Do not forget to show hospitality to strangers, for by so doing some people have shown hospitality to angels without knowing it. Continue to remember those in prison as if you were together with them in prison, and those who are mistreated as if you yourselves were suffering."*

Please pray for my home and children. A place to call home

While there (at the fishing village), *a man was introduced as the pastor/chief of the village. After talking, we walked through the village with him. He then asked if I would go into his church and pray for it, his congregation, and him* (Let me pause my journal for a moment and describe the church. It was a rectangular building about 30ft wide and 50ft long. Almost anywhere in America, this building would have been mistaken for a barn for livestock. The sides were made of wood slats with light shining between them. There were no doors or windows, and the floor was a dirt floor. There was one small light bulb hanging from the ceiling attached to an extension that ran out through an opening to a generator. The pews were actually homemade benches that were only about a foot above the floor. There were probably enough benches to seat a couple dozen people. While this was Spartan construction to this pastor and the people of this village, it was a source of pride and stability. It was a great reminder to me that the Church is not the building or the furnishing. It is made up of the body of believers that come together in the name of God. I felt extremely honored to lift this place, the pastor, and the congregation up in prayer.

I thought to myself, "I probably should be asking this pastor to come pray for our church!" What a vital lifeline this church was to this community).

As we walked casually back along a beautiful trail that ran along a hill that overlooked the lake, Janepher talked about several plants that had medical value. She described how they had been used for generations to treat various diseases.

We stopped on a high point on the hill overlooking Katosi, the little fishing village, and Lake Victoria. We paused, talking about what we had just seen and how we might be able to help long term. We snapped several photos of the group that would be one of my favorite pictures of the team.

The team after visiting the fishing village

The walk to the fishing village had more implications and impact on this trip (and on future trips) than I could have ever anticipated. I did not know how the journey to the village had come about. I had known about the village since my first year in 2011 and had wanted to visit, but for some reason, had never been able to get anyone to take me there. So, when the team, led by Janepher, started walking there, I was surprised and excited about the opportunity. I was under the impression that Timothy or Janepher had suggested that we go for the visit. Another event that had occurred that would have a future impact was that Dr. Diaz and Donna had talked with the pastor of the village while we were there, and had asked him what might help them be more self-sustaining as a village. He had said that if they could start a piggy farm, the village could sell the pigs and have a source of food. Dr. Diaz told them that if they would build the place to put them and the feed troughs that he would make sure that they got the pigs.

I was excited about the idea and hoped they would follow through on their end of the project. The good news was that by the time we had landed in Miami at the end of the trip, they had downloaded pictures of the piggy farm being completed. They had cleared a plot of land, built pins, feed troughs, and shelter that would accommodate several pigs. Dr. Diaz immediately followed up on his promise and sent the money for the pigs.

They quickly acted and bought a small herd of pigs.

At the time, all this seemed right. However, I found out later that this had created some tension. It would be easier to write this chapter and ignore the tension. But this tension addresses a reality of life in Uganda and the constant competition for dollars to support the endless list of needs that each ministry and community faces. I am still on the uphill side of this learning curve and don't have neat and clean answers to address this problem. Let me see if I can explain the problem to the best of my understanding and attempt to address the motivations involved. Remember that I have spent a good bit of time talking about how generous and sharing the people of Uganda are. That is absolutely true, but they are also extremely territorial and protective of their funding sources, and in most cases, rightly so. Let me try to explain. To Timothy, I represent through IACCS and Island Community Church, one of his ministry funding sources. He wants to see Winners Home and his other ministries' needs met. He also wants to see the schools and orphanages that are members of UCCS-U have their needs met. But he expects something in return from the ministries in UCCS-U. He expects them to be involved and engaged in the association. If they are not, they fall lower on his charitable list. There are also times when I think his lenses get blurred. For example, on this trip, he expressed the need for mattresses and beds for dormitories. I recognized that he was talking about a need for Winners Home. I made sure that all the money that I designated for this need came from money raised through the church or others in the community, not specifically for or from IACCS dollars. Some of those in UCCS-U don't always understand that. I must do a better job communicating to them that this is not IACCS money and not money earmarked for UCCS-U. I also began to emphasize that the primary purpose of IACCS is to assist in the unification and instruction. We are here to help UCCS-U and the schools improve, not finance them. In other words, to remind the schools of what we stated at the formation of the UCCS-U. I have begun to remind them that the cows and other gifts are just that, they are gifts, and not to be expected as an obligation from IACCS.

I have found that at almost every conference or teaching session I do, there will be one or two (sometimes more) individuals that will come up and express their need. I can usually spot them now; they try to pull me aside and speak in low tones, like they don't want anyone to know they are asking for funds. When I get back to my home in Florida, I can count on receiving more than my share of emails that begin something like this, "My Dear Poppa, this, is your beloved son…"

I usually do not respond when the emails start that way because most of the time, it is a subtle way of asking for me to meet some need (or want). Here is a usual shopping list: computers, bricks and mortar for buildings, library books, money for school fees for children, money for medical bills, money to attend seminary… the list is pretty endless. I have met some of these needs with personal funds and funds that others have given me, but I explain to them that I cannot use IACCS money to fund individual needs. I am increasingly making sure Timothy and the UCCS-U board understands this as well. Timothy and I have had several long, difficult conversations about this.

It wasn't until the 2019 trip that I began to discover the mystery behind the reluctance to go to the fishing village, that it was

Trip # 7 A Village With No Name

someone in our group that had initiated the request to go to the village. When we had returned from the fishing village, the team was excitedly telling Timothy about the piggy farm. I had noticed that even though polite, his facial expression did not share the same enthusiasm. As the 2018 trip was coming to an end, he pulled me aside at the Entebbe airport and ask me to sit and have a conversation with him. He started by telling me that he felt like we had dishonored him and gone behind his back to go to the fishing village. I assured him that was not our intention and that I was not sure who had initiated the visit and had assumed that he had sent us there.

I then asked why in the world, he would object to us going and helping these poor people. He tried to explain that he didn't object to the help, but there was a process and order to be followed. He seemed to be trying to express that we needed to keep him in the loop. He felt that he has a better understanding of what the priority of needs are and what groups were more deserving of assistance.

He then said, "Some areas remain poor because they choose to live that way." I still don't understand this fully, but I am beginning to see, as the article I shared earlier, states that some groups and organizations remain poor because it brings in more money, and in some cases, have lifestyles that lead to squandering the aid they receive. The villages that stay in a drunken fog because of their native brew are an example of this. You already read my rant earlier on both sides of this issue. On the one side, it is an excuse not to give. On the other, it is a legitimate problem.

I told Timothy that the money that had been given for the piggy farm had been private money, that the people had a right to spend it as they desired, but that I would try to keep him in the loop in the future. That seemed to help, but I know there will be additional conversations about this. I am currently working with the UCCS-U Board of Directors to set up procedures to make sure that all gifts that we give away will be done at the approval of the board.

When we got back from our walk to the village, we got to eat our first "normal" Ugandan meal together back at Cross City.

I love this time because it is so relaxed and casual. I get to watch the group and see how their hearts are being moved. Listening to their impressions of the adventure so far brings pure joy. I always like to tell the new members to look at the kitchen where their meals are being prepared. It is fun to watch their expressions. The doorway to the kitchen is an opening with an old sheet hanging as the door, the kitchen itself is very narrow, probably not more than 8-feet wide. There is no stove, no refrigerator, no dishwasher, or running water. The food is cooked in large pots and skillets over an open fire in the center of the kitchen. It looks every bit like a fire pit you might see at a campsite. There is a large sink where dishes are placed. Water has to be brought in by buckets to wash the dishes. In many of the upscale Ugandan homes, this is still the typical kitchen area configuration. In some cases, the kitchen will actually be in a separate small building right next to the main house.

As we ate the evening meal, I loved hearing the stories and experiences of the team. At one point, I asked Timothy to share his testimony with the group. I wanted the team to be aware of how God had worked in his life (see his testimony in chapter 2, Trip #1).

Monday morning, November 12, was to be a great day of the team buying and giving away several items. We knew that we had at least two cows and five bikes to give away. We made a quick visit to Winners Home so that those who had never seen the Rick Strong Playground, or all the facilities, could get a look and interact with some of the children. The children were making full use of every playground structure available to them…no, that's an understatement! They were piled on every piece of equipment to two or three times what the reasonable limit should be. I took a picture of a seated merry-go-round that had seats for eight children, and there were double that many piled on. A bench-style swing set that should have held six small children had a dozen medium-sized kids on it. I remember thinking, "this playground equipment doesn't stand a chance, but they are sure enjoying it while it holds up." I was right. On this year's trip (2019), the playground equipment had all been removed and was lying in a pile by the main office building. I asked Timothy what had happened, and he told me that there had just been too much use. All the kids coming in from the village and from the orphans had worn it out.

I said, "You know that is unacceptable. We must get the Rick Strong Playground functional again. I am going to leave you with the money to make the necessary repairs. Please get it fixed."

From Winners Home, we moved on to begin our day visiting orphanages and giving away several items. Our first stop was to give away a very special cow. This cow even had a name. She was MoMaMo. Obviously, there has to be a story behind this name. One of the joys of being a teacher and school administrator is that you have a long history with former students. If you live in the same community for many years, you end up doing life together. Many years ago, a young lady named Marlen Martinez attended our Christian school, graduating in 1981. She went on to become a dynamic mom, who is deeply involved as a volunteer in our community. You will also recall that in chapter 1, I wrote about working as a teacher's aide in 1967-1968. One of my students was a young man named Mark. So, there are lots of years of connection here; Marlen and Mark got married several years ago and have raised a family in the Keys. We would see each other from time to time in the community, and one of their daughters works out at the gym where I do. One day, as we were working out, she came over and began to ask about Uganda and the cows. I was happy to tell her about it and asked why she had asked. I had not realized that she was Mark and Marlen's daughter until she explained that her mom (Marlen) wanted to buy a cow and name it after her three daughters. So that is how MoMaMo came to be because her daughters are Monica, Mallory, and Molly. They decided that the first two letters of each of their names would make a perfect name for a Ugandan milk cow. I had told their story to the team and asked Donna if she would do the honors of giving away this year's first cow. She said, "Absolutely!" We had to rehearse the name several times to get the Ugandan children to remember and say it. One of the remarkable things about this gift is the level of sacrifice that I know the Meeks family made to give a thousand dollars for this cow. To me, this was comparable to the widow in Luke 21 because it represented a sacrificial gift from the heart.

This year, when we went back to Uganda, we paid MoMaMo a visit. The children are still calling her by name, and she is producing a steady supply of milk for them.

MoMaMo, along with toothbrushes and toothpaste for the entire school, was given away reasonably early in the morning, and we still had many visits to make. We would travel through the North Buganda Providence, Mukono, Igana, Kumi, Nairika. We made a quick lunch stop at Javas, rapidly becoming an oasis for the team.

The route was a large rectangular weave through small villages and jungle that was going to cover many miles in South and South-central Uganda. As we traveled, we stopped at orphanage after orphanage. Each stop involved the children putting on some type of performance. Then we would give away toothbrushes and toothpaste, athletic balls, shoes, bicycles, and two more cows. Our first stop after lunch was a very memorable one. When we arrived, the children and adults were lined up outside the buildings and came running to greet us, even before we got out of our bus. They were all carrying limbs with large, bright green leaves. They were waving them wildly in celebration of our arrival, and one older girl was singing, dancing, and hugging everyone in our group. All the children were dressed in bright orange uniforms with white collars. The combination of the green leaves and orange uniforms was a beautiful sight. They seated us as guests of honor and then put on a full performance of dancing, singing, and speeches. When their program was over, we went outside where Dr. Diaz and his son gave them a cow, and the celebration got even bigger!

We then drove for hours through very rough jungle roads to our last stop. Our last set of bicycles was given away in complete darkness at Wisdom Junior School in Nairika. It was between 7:30 and 8:00PM, and yet there were children of all ages everywhere. It was darker than dark as we approached the school, but in the distance, as we were approaching, you could hear cheering and singing coming from the children. They were so anxious to see and be seen by visitors that I think they would have stayed up all night had that been required. I took a picture of their sign outside their main building that gave their name, and then gave their motto and their mission. Motto: Try our best; Mission: To produce God-fearing citizens.

For my own peace of mind and to help our drivers find directions, one of the things I've started doing is to use Google Maps or Waze on my phone to track where we are going. Here is a rundown of this trip for the team this day: Katosi to Igana, just over two hours; from Igana to Kumi, about two and a half hours; from Kumi to Nairika, two and a half hours; and Nairika back to Katosi, another three hours. In addition to these stops, while the team was giving away the gifts, I was being driven to other locations to meet and encourage schools and orphanages in other remote areas. Reminder, this is Uganda; these are not paved roads, let alone interstate freeways.

It is rugged, exhausting travel, but it is worth every mile to see the joy of the people we are visiting. This was just day one of the visits and giveaways, what was the rest of the week going to be like?

Tuesday, the 13th, was the day set aside for another of the big Children's Day. The sky opened up, and we had a downpour in the early morning; just to add to an already challenging task of pulling off this event. We wondered if the day would have to be canceled. Not only was this going to be hard on the tents, sound system, and just about every other aspect of the event site, it was going to be very difficult for those traveling through muddy roads to get here. It is usual for these events to start late to mid-morning to give all the schools time to get to the event. This is an enormous sacrifice for many of the schools. Some must travel for hours to get to the event location and often have to work out transportation through some pretty crazy and exotic means. For some, it even means walking a great distance.

It shows how highly valued these events are to everyone. The option of canceling the event because of weather was really not something that could be considered.

All the schools began to arrive, and the competitions began after several introductions and speeches. The panel of judges is very serious (and pretty stern!) about the competitions.

The performances and competitions were very much like in past years, singing in large groups along with dance, dramas, recitations, Bible drills, and preaching (by the children). These are wonderful and have obviously been well-rehearsed, but I begin to feel a prodding to have a conversation with the UCCS-U leadership about expanding the competitions to include other academic areas.

We had talked about this in the past. Still, it seemed that I wasn't communicating or casting that vision well enough. Or, perhaps they just weren't interested in making the changes. Maybe, they just need a model to show them how it was done. For many years the Florida Association of Christian Colleges and Schools and several of the national Christian school associations have conducted excellent academic competitions.

These have been conducted at several levels: local, regional, state, and national competitions. The events have included art displays, science fairs, essay competitions, debate, math drills, brain bowls, Sword drills, and others.

When I returned to Florida, I took each of the FACCS competition manuals. I rewrote them to fit a model that I think would work in Uganda and other countries. I then sent copies to the UCCS-U Board, and it is my hope that these will eventually be used to expand an already enjoyable event. My vision for this would be to have regional or district competitions, and have the finalist participate in the finals at Children's Day, which would be a national event.

Like many of the initiatives and projects that IACCS is trying to move forward, this takes longer than would be hoped for. It often feels like you have made the proverbial three steps forward, two steps back. It is again a reminder that when you are just trying to keep several thousand children alive, things like where to get food, providing adequate medical care, and maintaining safe and healthy accommodations win the priority battle.

The competitions continued until just after 3:00 PM. The team was split up and given a position at one of three serving stations.

Like previous years, we were going to be feeding everyone at the event. I would guess that there were two thousand in attendance. As we began to serve, I noticed large chunks of beef in the stew that we were spreading over the rice, matoke, and posho. I asked one of our team members where the beef had come from. I was holding my breath because I was afraid the answer was going to be that they decided to butcher one of our milk cows. I was relieved and humbled when I was told that the team had all chipped in their own money. They had bought the beef just for this event. Feeding this many people meant that it probably took a whole cow! Eating this late in the afternoon is a good way for the children to be sure to get one large, substantial meal. Even in traditional, intact Ugandan families, only two meals are served, a lunch and a dinner. Breakfast is often a cup of tea or a bowl of porridge.

Because Winners Home, where this year's Children's Day was being held, is right on the shores of Lake Victoria, children from all over the village can walk in. When there is food to be had, you can be sure the children will come. I had been serving for quite a while when I noticed children that were not wearing school uniforms coming, getting in line for food.

I also saw various school staff try to prevent them from getting food. After the children from the orphanages and schools had all been fed, there was still plenty leftover. Without having to say a word, I noticed all of our team piling food on the plates of the children who had straggled in.

I love Alison's account from her journal:

It was time to feed the 2,000 children!

We had three stations, each filled with rice, beans, and meat (this meat was provided by our team); it was a $600-$700 dollar cow that we bought on Monday.

The endless lines of children filled the stations for 1-2 hours (we couldn't serve fast enough!)

Near the end, we did start to run out of meat – then the beans – soon we were just serving rice and gravy (but the children seemed thankful…and hungry).

As the competition continued, we were invited to eat lunch – the same as what we served. It actually wasn't bad (lots of salt).

After the children, teachers, and other guests had been fed, we were escorted to a classroom that was set up with our meal. We ate the same food the children ate. A special guest joined us for lunch.

It was a member of the Ugandan government. His full name was Johnson Muyanja Ssenyonga. He has served as the People's Mayor of Mukono and is a member of the Parliament. His degree is in education from Makerere University, and holds a master's degree in human resource management in education from Uganda Christian University, in Mukono. We had the honor of spending an extended period of time together. He spent a good deal of time talking with me about IACCS and the work being done in Uganda.

He expressed his gratitude and encouraged me to continue to press for improving the quality of our schools. He also acknowledged the vital role these schools were playing in providing education for children who would otherwise not get an education. I personally believe that every opportunity we have to build relationships with those representing the government in the countries we are serving, the children and the association benefit. This is especially true when they are also of like faith and understand the importance of Christian education.

When we had finished eating and meeting, we returned to the courtyard for the conclusion of the competition and the presentation of the awards. It was AFTER 6:00 pm when the contests ended; the awards were given out somewhat hastily because many of the children had so far to travel. But we weren't through. We still had all the items we had brought to give to the groups before they headed back to their home districts.

Before we finish Children's Day, I have to mention two children from Winners Home that have captured the hearts of at least a couple of the returning team members.

One is a little guy I call the Artful Dodger, as in the character in the Charles Dickens' book, *Oliver*. Not because he is dishonest or conniving in any way, but more because he has a streetwise, whimsical wit about him that makes him irresistible. For the last two or three years, when we arrive at Winners Home, I can be sure that one of the first guys to coming running to me will be this young guy.

Honestly, I am not even sure he is one of the children from Winners, but somehow, he has a way of knowing when I am coming, and will be first on the spot when I arrive. He usually is close by throughout the entire time we are at the school. I have often told my wife that if I ever stowaway a child and bring him home, it will be this young man. Actually, I would never do that to him, because I'm afraid I would ruin who this incredible young Uganda man is to become.

The second little guy is the special buddy to Mike Forster. Mike (the Mayah) has a special heart for children who might be considered "special needs." I have talked about this little guy earlier and his angelic singing voice. But Mike has taken such special notice of this young man that it is worthy of mentioning again. The little guy is small in stature and seems to be suffering from his spinal disease, but is loved and cared for at Winners, and is huge in his personality. He seems little fazed by his condition, but it does limit some of the physical things he can do. Mike makes it a point each year to seek his special buddy out and to give him some kind of special gift. This young man is one of the painful reminders of the difference between Ugandan children and children growing up where medical treatment and care is readily available. He will probably live out his childhood at Winners, and then, as an adult, be left to fend for himself in a pretty tough existence.

The next day, Nov 14, a Wednesday, was another big travel day for the entire team. I was heading off to the central region, where I would conduct another educators' convention, teaching both administrators and teachers. The conference was in Kibogha, about a 4-hour drive from Katosi. I guess there had been some talk and concern for my wellbeing because of the amount of time I was having to spend traveling out to these locations and then teaching for so many hours. I had expressed that I didn't mind and felt like it was the best way to accomplish what we were trying to do in providing teaching to the greatest number of people. There was just no way that they could all travel to Kampala or Mukono without unrealistic sacrifice. I think because of these conversations and her desire to see what took place at these conferences, Wendy volunteered to go with me. I was grateful for the help and the company. Traveling that many hours allows you to get to know someone so much better.

It was after noon by the time we arrived. Out of necessity, this conference turned into what I had envisioned. I would come in and teach and try to challenge, encourage, and inspire the staff, and leave much of the teaching to those from that district. This event also had some of the elements of a Children's Day, with performances and competitions among schools. While I was teaching, Wendy served as a judge for the competitions. One of the things that really stuck as a lasting image was a little guy who genetically had albinism and Down's Syndrome, as well. He obviously got your attention, but the thing that was so memorable was the way the children so diligently looked after this child. Almost all

Ugandan children are hard-wired to be caregivers, whether it be for younger children or children with special needs.

Giving of a bike and care of a very special child

One of the joys Wendy and I got to share at this location was the giving of several bicycles to some very, very appreciative lead teachers.

As we were finishing our time giving away the bikes, we received a call from Timothy giving us instruction. We needed to go to another very remote location somewhere even deeper into the jungle. The team would meet us there to give away shoes to an orphanage isolated from anyone. I was a little concerned because this was going to press us into some pretty tough, remote terrain that would be very challenging for the rest of the team in the larger bus. I had already heard some grumblings from the group about too many hours spent on the bus. That said, at times, they had been lost as they were trying to find some of the remote orphanages. They had voiced that they were spending so much time riding and trying to find their way that they weren't getting to help at the orphanages. If they got lost in daylight, what was it going to be like when it was pitch-black? We proceeded despite those concerns. Dr. Diaz and I began to text back and forth about Sasquatch sightings as we were getting so deep into the jungle.

Miguel – Sasquatch sighting!

Tony – Sasquatch family road crossing

By the time we made it to the location, it was so dark that the only light we had was from our phones and the headlights from the vehicle. It was impossible to tell anything about the orphanage. We saw one small building, but could really tell nothing about it. We were standing just outside our van trying to meet and converse with a bunch of children and their teacher. Even that was difficult because we couldn't see them well and they spoke no English. Somewhere in these awkward moments, we got another call from Timothy and the group that they were not going to make it. The bus couldn't handle the off-road requirements, and it was just too far. Yikes! We had a problem! We were surrounded by kids and adults, it the dark of the night, expecting shoes from us and we had nothing! The shoes were on the bus with the team. We didn't even have Jolly Rancher to give them…and we couldn't communicate with them other than through Lawrence. He and Timothy talked, and I guess he explained to them that they weren't going to get shoes that night, but that they would be sent later.

I know he, nor we, were happy with this situation, but there was nothing else to be done. After bidding farewell, we began to weave our way back out toward a location on a main road where we would meet the rest of the team. Wendy and I had a successful day at the conference/Children's Day. I could tell that the rest of the group was tired and frustrated with the distance they had traveled. They had not been successful in giving away all of the shoes and other items they had planned for the day. I talked with Timothy and got assurance from him that he would make sure the shoes got to the children. Thank goodness for a Javas in Jinja where we could grab a late dinner, take the edge off of the tension, and head back to Katosi for a late night turn-in.

The next morning (Thursday, Nov. 15) was going to be every bit as busy. I was scheduled to spend all day teaching in the region of Luwero. Usually, this trip would be about a three-hour journey, but when the rain comes, it can take much longer. The rains had come! Despite that, Lawrence felt that it would be best to take an off-the-main-road shortcut that would save some time. It wasn't long before we were slipping and sliding our way down a very rough dirt road through the jungle. I don't know whether it was because of the adventure the night before or in anticipation of the road conditions we were going to encounter today, but Lawrence had commandeered a 4-wheel drive vehicle. It was a good thing because we would still be stuck in the jungle somewhere. There was one area where it so was slick that even with 4-wheel drive, we began to slide sideways toward the ditch. We actually slid into the ditch but were able to pull ourselves out. We were inching forward, but it was very slow going. We had to stop more than once because entire herds of cattle were using this narrow road as their trail to get wherever they were going. To add to the problem, we could see a large dump truck just ahead of us. Without warning, the truck dump began to lift in the air. Thick, wet, red clay began to pour out directly in front of us. I looked at Lawrence with a "What are we going to do?" look. As the truck emptied and pulled away, we could see that there was a narrowest of roadway left uncovered. It was really just a path half on the edge of the road and the other half in the ditch.

I was sure we were going to be stuck or crashed in the ditch, missing the conference entirely. We inched our way along the edge of the road. Lawrence questioned how far the main road was that we were supposed to intersect. He had apparently never seen Waze or Google Maps used. I pulled mine up and said about two miles. He looked at me like I was some kind of prophet and said, "How do you know that?" He knew I had not been this way before and did not know my way around Uganda that well.

I showed him how to use the app, put it on his phone, and launched him on a whole new world of navigation.

As we traveled along our route, I noticed something that I wrote about in an earlier chapter but had never witnessed it firsthand. Every so often, we would drive past a plot of land or a house with a sign painted on it that would read, "This plot not for sale," or "This house not for sale." I asked Lawrence about it, and he explained that this was an example of someone's property that another person was trying to wrestle away or take from a vulnerable individual. Unfortunately, gullible Westerners often fall victim to schemes where a property has been snatched from a widow or some other vulnerable individual. It is then sold to unsuspecting people, thinking they are getting a great bargain. In some cases, they even believe they have done a humanitarian act by taking the property off their hands.

There are, of course, laws on the books to prevent this crime. Still, it is difficult to have the manpower to provide enforcement in remote areas. Plus, there is always the issue of corrupt authorities who have been paid to look the other way. Sometimes they have even been known to participate in the takeover.

I couldn't help but think about our rookies on this trip and what their interpretation of Uganda must be. We arrived in Entebbe in the dark; drove to Katosi in the dark (we passed through Kampala and Mukono, but you couldn't see the city because it was dark). We walked through the village of Katosi, hiked to the unnamed fishing village, had the jungle adventure last evening, and more of the same today. It would be like being dropped off in the middle of *Okefenokee Swamp* and thinking that this must be what all of America looks like. Indeed, there is plenty of jungle with huts and native villages throughout the country, but there are also modern, thriving city centers that are making tremendous strides to lead Uganda out of the "developing country" status.

Remarkably, we made it to the school where the conference was being held without being too late. I had seven workshops to cover with this group.

The list below gives the workshop titles:

Workshop Sessions: *(2 ISP each)–list titles)*
___1. *Philosophy of Christian Education*
___2. *Core Values of a Christian School*
___3. *The Important Things a Teacher Must Know*
___4. *What Makes a Good Teacher?*
___5. *Tips on How Our Schools Can Make a Difference in Our Localities*
___6. *Evangelical Approach to Christian Education*
___7. *Open Forum Topics*

I had solicited help prior to my arrival by sending the following letter to all of our UCCS-U schools:

My Dear Brothers and Sisters of the UCCSU:

Greetings from the United States. In November I will be returning to Uganda with another team to be with you. Many of you have been in my teaching sessions for several years now and have received the study sheets. I do not want to repeat or be redundant it the material I present. For that reason, I am asking you to help me determine how to be the best help to you.

Here are some questions for you to respond to:

• What topics for discussions or teachings would benefit your school the most?

• What do you perceive as the greatest educational need in your school?

• Would it be beneficial to help you develop your school mission and/or vision statements?

• Would you be benefited by working on steps that are necessary to lead your school toward accreditation?

• Would it be beneficial to assist you in developing five and ten-year plans for your school? In other words, where would you like your school to be in five or ten years?

If you have other topics, I would like you to share them with me.

Thank you and God bless you. I am anxious to be with you once again.

Sincerely in Christ,
Tony Hammon, President
International Association of Christian Colleges and Schools
Email: hammon@bellsouth.net

Timothy had sent me an email as a result of this letter, giving me the suggestions for workshops he felt that the members of UCCS-U wanted and needed.

You may have noticed that in the workshop session list that the following *(2 ISP each)–list titles)* was shown. I had set up a program for Ugandan teachers and administrators to be able to get credit for continuing education by attending the Educators' Convention each year. I did this for two reasons. One, I recognize the importance of continuing education, and second, I knew that ISPs would provide an incentive for schools to really make an effort to attend the conventions. Appendix #2 shows a sample of the form used.

I have made these forms available for the last two years and hope that they will become a regular part of the UCCS-U's membership requirements.

We were able to get through all of the workshops and have some very healthy educational Q&A time, as well as useful input from this audience. It always makes for a good teaching session when there is exciting audience participation. When we broke for lunch, we went outside and were eating under the shade of a beautiful hammock of native trees. I had invited anyone who wanted to come and ask questions while I ate lunch to come join me.

I usually eat a very light lunch while I'm doing the workshops. I like to use that time to do some informal teaching with anyone who wants it. As I was finishing lunch, a young male teacher introduced himself. I invited him to sit for a while, and he began to jump right into a series of great questions. He was a high school science teacher with a desire to continue his education, to become a school administrator and pastor. He was very proud of his science lab and showed me several pictures of his classroom. Most of his questions centered around class control and lesson plan development. We spent several minutes together, and then it was time to resume our workshops. I invited him to stay in touch, which he has done; and this year, I got to spend time with him again. He thanked me and told me how much what I had shared with him had helped him be a better teacher.

When the last session ended, we were able to give away two cows to two different orphanages that had attended the convention. It is always exciting to watch the process as they have adopted various ways of selecting who shall receive the cows. At this location, it is clear that their method is done through sort of a drawing.

A name is finally selected, and the recipient is clearly surprised by the gift. There is always a great celebration, and often, many tears of joy.

As we were getting ready to leave, a young woman approached us, introduced herself, and gave us a business card. She had been appointed to be an educational representative for Ugandan education for this district.

She was very excited about what we were doing to improve educational quality for her district. She then asked something very unexpected of us. She introduced us to her mother, who had joined her for the conference, and then asked if we would give her a ride to her home. She wanted to provide us with some special gifts and introduce us to the rest of her family.

Trip # 7 A Village With No Name

It was getting late, but how do you say no to such kindness? We all piled in Lawrence's vehicle and were off through some back roads through the jungle.

In a few miles, we came to a clearing where there was a charming home, and a more substantial structure, which she explained was the church her husband pastored. When we walked into the church, there were several small groups spread out throughout the room, engaged in organized Bible study. Her husband got up from one of the groups and introduced himself to us, and then asked us to pray for the church and their ministry there. After that, he went right back to the Bible study with his group. We walked over to the house where the lady went inside for a few moments and came back with some beautiful handmade quilts or bedspreads.

They clearly meant more as a gift in the Ugandan culture than I fully understood, but I could tell that they were treasured by Lawrence. I am not sure if she intended for me to have one of them or not, but after we drove away, I told Lawrence that I thought he should keep them both. So began the long drive back to Katosi. Fortunately, Lawrence stayed on the main roadway back to Mukono.

While I had been away teaching, the team had been split up to accomplish several things. Dr. Diaz, Donna, Sydney, and Miguel Jr. had gone with Dr. Shammah into Kampala to buy medical supplies for the clinic. Dr. Shammah is a young doctor who has made tremendous personal sacrifice to make regular visits to the clinic in Katosi to serve the people there.

He also looked after several of the people from the fishing village where we had put the piggy farm. Plus, he had been instrumental in the oversight of that project. He and Dr. Diaz have established an ongoing relationship.

The people of Katosi and the smaller fishing village will benefit tremendously from their shared efforts.

The clinic team had gotten a firsthand look at how clinic work is not for the squeamish. Children came in with various kinds of infections and sores on their feet from no shoes. There were numbers of people with various upper respiratory issues. One man came in with a condition that made me realize that it was important to not just have any high school student work in the clinic. Fortunately, both Sydney and Mike were there working with their parents. Dr. Diaz shared his diagnosis with me. I was a bit shocked, but then realized how much sense it made in these remote villages. The man had been diagnosed with gonorrhea. As tragic as this diagnosis was, the tragedy was that he had only been married a few days. This was another reminder of the importance of the role that Western medical teams, clinics, and the church play in changing some of the tribal views and practices on sexual behavior.

In the meantime, the rest of the team, Gary, Alison, Mike, Patty, and Wendy, were with Timothy visiting more orphanages, giving away cows and other items, and finalizing the arrangements for the beds and mattresses to be delivered the next day. Alison was getting some great photos and videos at each of the stops she was making.

She had exactly done what I had hoped she would do and had really captured some great images of Ugandan life.

As usual, the team made it back to Katosi long before I did, and scolded me a bit for doing a repeat of the long, late trips.

I expressed that there is just no other way to accomplish what we are trying to do right now.

One additional happening this day was that I got to reunite with Joshua Mugole. At the same time, I was at the last conference, I had gotten reports from both Timothy and Lawrence that he had some illness and that he was not doing well at all. His diagnosis had been vague, something to do with his liver. He lived so far away from any really substantial hospital that it was not easy to even get the right diagnosis, let alone proper treatment. While we were at this conference site, Joshua had gotten a driver to bring him over so he could see me. I was shocked when I saw him because he had lost so much weight and looked very frail. He had his paperwork from the hospital that he had been to. It had a diagnosis, so I asked if I could take it and share it with Dr. Diaz. He readily agreed, so I took a copy with me. He told me that he had not been able to work for about six months and that his doctor told him that he would not be able to work for six more months.

His children could not go to school because the family could not pay the school fees, and he could not return for treatment because he had no money for the hospital. I obviously could not stand to let that go unresolved. When I got back to Katosi that evening, I shared the report with Dr. Diaz. He looked it over and said it was probably a misdiagnosis (he has found that many of the diagnoses are not accurate.) When I got back to Florida, Colleen and I put together what money we could, and a friend for the church agreed to cover his children's school fees. He was able to go back to the hospital, get a more accurate diagnosis, and begin treatments.

On Friday, November 16, we had come to our last full day of teaching, visiting schools, and giving away the final items we had planned to give.

John Caldwell, maker of a line of shirts known as H-Blue-O, and member of Island Community Church, approached me a few months before this trip. He asked if I would be interested in taking along some of his shirts. My response was, "Of course, we would love to take them." He designed the shirts with the IACCS logo on them and filling up the entire front of the shirt was the whole of John 3:16. The shirts came in a rainbow of bright colors that I knew would go over big in Uganda. John has given several hundred of these shirts.

This first year, I had the largest of my suitcases jammed full of the shirts and had planned to give them to some of the kids. I wasn't sure how that was going to work, because we didn't have nearly enough for the thousands of children we would encounter. The problem had taken care of itself because when we arrived, and I showed the shirts to Timothy, it became clear that these were all adult sizes. So, we decided that we would give everyone who attended the Christian Educators' Convention a shirt. We didn't give the shirts out until the end of the workshops on the day. It was a good thing, because when I started trying to hand them out in what I thought was a match for the size of the person lined up in front of me, I almost had a riot on my hands. Everyone wanted a small shirt! If I gave them a blue, they wanted red, or yellow, or brown, or... I finally just handed them all out to the group and said you figure it out, and if you can't, then go without.

As usually happened, they suddenly figured it out, and everyone seemed happy. At the end of the day, we took a group photo with them all wearing their John 3:16/IACCS shirts. I didn't see anyone without a shirt, so I guess it worked out.

To get to this conference, I had ridden a bus with a group of teachers and William, the administrator of Winner's school. As we were traveling to the meeting, I sat with William and got to ask him several questions about things I had seen but did not fully understand yet. One was the tower-like structures I had seen several times on this trip. These towers came in various sizes and types, but they were all handmade structures that stood fifteen to twenty feet in the air. They were primarily constructed of bamboo poles and had what looked like a little thatched-roofed lookout tower on the top. Some are covered with a fiber covering with tribal designs on them; others are open all the way until you get to the roof at the top. I was told that they meant the "King was here." I asked if they were talking about the President. They explained that there is the President of the country and that there are Kings for each tribal region. One of the men told me that the King was held in higher esteem than the government officials.

The other thing that I observed and felt like I needed further explanation for was a witch doctor's compound right on the main drive coming into Katosi. I had asked Timothy what it was, and his reply was, "That's the witch doctor." No expression, no concern, just "The witch doctor." I had responded with, "What? Why is that guy still here? Why haven't you led him to Christ or had him thrown in jail!" I was assuming he was a full-fledged, card-carrying child abductor that I had heard Bob Goff talk about.

Timothy calmly responded, "He is not our enemy." I was not so calm, so I almost yelled, "What, he is against everything you stand for. You need to go after that guy!" Timothy just smiled and said, "That's the way Americans think." That was the end of the conversation, but I still wasn't satisfied and wanted to go with Bible in hand and knock on the guy's door. I need a lot more explanation on this one. So, on this bus ride to the conference I asked about it as we drove by his compound. The response I got this time was no more satisfying than the one from Timothy. I guess the closest comparison I can make would be the way the American Church sort of ignores the fortunetellers that pop up in almost every community. They are there. We know they are not right, but we don't get too amped up about them.

The King was here.

The resident witch doctor!

When we arrived at the conference center, I was still mumbling under my breath about the witch doctor. I was no more satisfied with the answer I had gotten.

But it was time to go teach.

For the rest of the team, the day had started with them going to Winners Home. The 300 new beds and mattresses had been offloaded from a large truck, and they were there to celebrate and oversee. They were all lined up in the center courtyard, and the kids had surrounded them with singing and celebrating. The words Alison wrote in her journal captured the importance of these beds and mattresses:

We were given a tour of the girls' dormitory. The feeling I got in there was overwhelming. The beds they were using to sleep on were horrible, torn, some had no sheets, the frames were all rusted out.

We were given a tour of the new dormitory, which overlooked the lake, cool breeze, clean, but not complete.

The beds they were sleeping on were horrible!

The new beds are here!

Patty did three one-hour purity classes with groups of older children. When she returned from the classes, the girls had given her necklaces they had made from paper, rolled tightly into brightly colored beads. That launched Patty on a whole new ongoing ministry of having the girls make the beads. She has sent to America where she had a group of volunteers who make them into necklaces and bracelets, which are sold in shops here in America. The money is used to buy more beds for the orphanages. She called the program, "Beads for Beds."

The team, minus me (I was off teaching in Mukono), made several school/orphanage visits throughout the day. At each stop, all of the teams were giving out the diverse array of sports balls and pumps that were remaining after the Children's Day. We had given away all of the Shoe That Grows sandals, and so now we were ready to give away the school uniform shoes. These were the "Toughees" that Timothy had wanted us to buy for school children and that Dr. Diaz had negotiated for the price. At one of the stops with just the right number of children, the team gave away all of the shoes. Gary, Mike, Wendy, and Alison went with Timothy to give two more cows away. These were given to two different orphanages. By the time the cows were given, and there were the usual celebration and time spent with the children, it was approaching evening. Mike had a very special place in his heart for a home that cared just for babies and wanted to stop to buy food and supplies for them.

After buying several fifty-pound bags of rice, flour, sugar, grain, toothbrushes and toothpaste, children's small recreational balls, and a special treat of ice cream, we traveled back to this extraordinary place filled with babies. The greatest treat of this part of the trip was watching the joy it brought to Mike as he interacted with the children and the staff. I have visited this site at least two other times in past years. You may recall I had mentioned a conversation about putting a garden in to provide food for not only this orphanage, but for other orphanages as well.

It was completely dark by the time we made it the babies' home, but I had noticed as we pulled in that there appeared to be a pretty healthy garden growing. After we had finished unloading all the supplies and everyone was playing with the babies, I decided I would slip out to see the garden. It was called The Flatlands Garden and looked like it was well on the way to providing a regular supply of fresh vegetables for this and other orphanages.

We left the babies and headed back to Katosi. As we sat around the dining area, I enjoyed just sitting and listening to each of the team members trade stories, talk about what moved them, laugh, and shed tears of joy. This had been a great trip with a great team. We had to get back to our rooms because we had to pack and decide what we would leave behind and what we would take back with us.

The next morning was Saturday, November 17; a day of mixed emotions. We were sad because we had to leave people we had grown to love, and joyful because we would be home with family and friends by Sunday afternoon. We all got our luggage together and met down by the dining area.

Pastor Emma, with his family, was there to greet us with his traveling Ugandan tourist store. I have purchased several small items over the years, like the bracelet I wear with UGANDA written with thread in the national colors. I also have a treasured soccer ball made of banana leaves and vine. I usually stand back and let the team members pick out the things they want to take back to remember their trip. However, this morning Emma had brought a nativity scene made of banana leaves and sticks. I asked him how much he wanted for it. If I remember correctly, he said 15,000 shillings. I shook my head no and said I wouldn't do that. He was shocked, thinking he had already given me a bargain price.

15,000 shillings amounts to just over $4.00 US. I smiled and said I have to provide you with $20.00 for it. That was almost 74,000 Ugandan shillings. In rural areas, that could be as much as a week's salary. I would guess Emma made several months of salary that morning from the team! Around 11:00am, it was time to start the journey to the airport in Entebbe. Our flight was not until after 11:00pm. But we had several stops to make. We were going to Winners Home to say goodbye to our friends there, and to load onto the bigger bus. While we were at Winners, I noticed that Wendy had gone to the water pump and filled a

2-liter Mountain Dew bottle with water that was indirectly from Lake Victoria.

She told me that she and Miguel Jr. had talked and that when they got back, they wanted to be baptized. If nothing else had happened on this trip, that one decision would have made it all worth it. Wendy had gone from being a seeker, but now she was a growing follower of Jesus!

We boarded the bus, intending to stop at a game preserve, but we had made a colossal miscalculation. There was a very special event taking place this Saturday afternoon. As we drove toward Kampala, I began to notice cars and buses and boda boda, all flying national flags and banners as if they were driving to a Super Bowl. I asked Timothy what was going on at about the same time he was remembering that this was the day that the Ugandan national soccer team was playing a championship game!

We came to the place where the traffic was completely gridlocked. Even being stuck in a traffic jam in Kampala can be a learning experience. As we were stopped, I saw a full-grown fellow running and dancing on the sidewalk in a chicken costume. He wasn't selling anything or appeared to have a particular agenda. The crazy thing was that nobody seemed even to notice him or pay special attention to him. Maybe he just enjoyed dressing up like a chicken! As soon as your vehicle stops, vendors from all directions descend on you, selling everything imaginable, from the famous chicken-on-a-stick, sodas, watches, shoes, toilet paper, backpacks, magazines; you name it, it's for sale. You can see why Customs was so nervous about us bringing so many of the Shoe-That-Grows into the country. They had to assume that they were going to end up being one of the sale items. Stay stuck in traffic long enough and you will be able to hear an entire sermon from the "street preachers" who walk down the middle of the road with their Bibles open or held over their heads, preaching from the top of lungs with all their might. These "street preachers" as they are called, are young and old, male, and female.

Street preachers in America are often viewed as folks who have been off their meds a bit too long. But in Uganda, they are a part of the everyday life of most communities. Sometimes their messages are crystal clear and spot-on, proclaiming the Good News of Jesus, and at other times they are more screwed up than you can imagine. But somehow, God takes it all and uses it for His glory. I have encountered dozens of men and women who have told me that they were first introduced to Jesus from a street preacher.

You keep your windows up, as mentioned earlier, to avoid snatch-and-grab. That then makes sitting in traffic that much more enjoyable – no A/C, and temperatures that probably climb to a 100-degrees in the vehicle! After a while, you're so hot that you just leave your windows open as if to say take what you want, it's too hot to care! As we finally began to move again, I looked out the windshield of the bus to see a sight that only could be seen in Uganda! Going down the main highway was a boda boda carrying a full bed frame. I couldn't help to chuckle at the thought of trying to get away with such a thing in America.

Trip # 7 A Village With No Name

All in a day's commute!

It was a good thing we had allowed so much time to get to the airport! By the time we got through traffic, about the only thing we had time to do was stop at Javas for dinner.

We finally made it to Entebbe airport and headed for what has become an end-of-trip tradition. After clearing Customs, we all headed for the KLM lounge. For $40 of the best-spent dollars you have ever experienced, you can get a full-fledged shower, food, and very comfortable couches to get ready for your two days of flying home.

After nearly two weeks of hot, dusty, sometimes no showers, longer than long days, and exotic foods, this is just what the doctor ordered! But this trip had one more twist to it. Gary grabbed a chicken salad or tuna salad sandwich from what looked like a little refrigerated serving window. None of us thought about it or noticed it, but the serving area was not refrigerated.

Within minutes Gary was sick from a raging case of food poisoning. It was a good thing Dr. Diaz was along and had some meds that he could give Gary.

He was still so sick all the way home that he could barely walk. In fact, when we got to his home in Florida, he was so weak that I had to carry his luggage upstairs for him, since he could almost not make it up the stairs by himself.

He will probably never eat anything again from that lounge!

Before we wrap up this chapter, I must mention two other things that happened in 2018.

The first is to mention an amazing woman and ministry in Uganda. Her name is Katherine Hines, and her ministry is Hines Ugandan Ministries. Katherine is an American who has given most of her adult life to caring and living in Uganda. She left a successful career in 1994 to devote her life to the children (and adults) of Uganda. Katherine has a beautiful school, clinic, and runs an AWANA Club. She has written a book, **They Call Me Momma Katherine.** In it, she tells her story and gives a very good look into what it is like to minister in Uganda.

We have been corresponding over the last several years, and I look forward to the day when we can work together to assist Uganda and its vulnerable children.

The second person is Hugh Pilcher from Great Britain. I was introduced to Hugh by one of our teachers, Hedy Menendez, a converted Jewish girl who has become a vibrant testimony for her Messiah. Here is the first introductory email I received from Hugh:

Subject: Introduction to Jesus Loves the Little Children Organization

Dear Pastor Tony Hammon,

Hi, Hedy encouraged me to get in touch with as you know so I will tell you a little bit about this ministry to children.

In 2009, I started helping vulnerable children in the Kigumba area with a club for children hanging around the streets and a sponsorship programs for 21 Primary School children. At that time, I was working for another church organization and altogether I have been in East Africa for over 11 years working with development projects.

In 2016, we were registered with the Ugandan government as a foreign NGO and we now have two main programs for Schools and for severely disabled children. We are sponsoring 40 children mainly to Primary School who would otherwise be missing out on school due to poverty reasons. Each month we bring them all together for the 'Jesus Club' where we share Jesus with them and encourage their social skills with games, Bible stories, singing, and a cooked meal, etc.

School is so important for young children for several reasons and we also want each child to know Jesus as their own personal savior.

With the children with special needs we have a fortnightly club with different activities, including basic physiotherapy. We have helped children with aids, such as wheelchairs and sent some for treatment. The parents/guardians really appreciate all we do and say they have never seen anything like this! We make the children very welcome, pray for them, and God's presence is with us when we meet.

God is the director of all we do, and it is His initiative and plans we are following. He is using me to help most vulnerable children, and I have an assistant and several volunteers. We depend on God and without asking for money last year people donated £10,000! Praise God!

I am glad to share what God is doing here through me and others and of His desire to help little children.

God bless you,
Hugh Pilcher, International Coordinator

Since this initial email of introduction, Hugh and I have corresponded regularly, and IACCS has been able to purchase goats for a number of his families. We have purchased the goats because Hugh does not feel that they are in a place where adequate care can be given to cows.

As IACCS continues to expand in Uganda, it is my prayer that these and other ministries will lead us further and further into the country to benefit as many schools and orphanages as possible.

CHAPTER 11
TRIP #8 – DROPPING LIKE FLIES

"If I find in myself desires which nothing in this world can satisfy, the only logical explanation is that I was made for another world." - C.S. Lewis, "Mere Christianity"

A Year of Changes

If this seems like a strange chapter title, hang in there, and I think it will make sense.

Let's first talk about the changes.

Not long after I had taken the position of IACCS President, I began to get a much broader view of Christian education. It was a view on a global scale. It was a deeper sense of the great need for the advancement of Christian education throughout the world. At the same time, I began to sense that God wanted me to build an effective succession plan for the future of the church I had pastored for thirty years.

There are ample studies out there about the aging of both congregations and pastors all over America. When I was a young man and began to pastor, the congregation was young as well; as I aged, the flock aged as well. I have seen far too many churches age with their pastor and eventually fade away when their pastor ages. I did not want to see that happen to ICC.

I began to pray and ask God to help me with this process. I was to turn 70 in September of 2018, and after praying, speaking with our elders, and my family, we picked that as the date that I would step aside as senior pastor. A young man, Trevor Mann, had grown up in our church and had been in our school from 2-year old preschool until his high school graduation, had returned to work as our youth leader, and then as the worship leader. Trevor had been working as a youth leader at another church that was about 25 miles away from our church. This is a good church and one that I would consider a sister church of like faith. I was happy for him and happy that God was blessing his youth ministry. We had a dynamic youth ministry as well, led by Lisa Porter, another of our graduates. I had felt for some time that Lisa was one of the most gifted leaders I had ever known, and that God had great plans for her. It was pretty clear that being a youth leader was only a stepping-stone to her future ministry. It wasn't long before she got a call from a large academy in Huston, Texas, to come as the chaplain and mentor to a school full of young ladies. She accepted the position. We tried to replace Lisa, but that was a massive challenge because she had been such an influential leader. At that time, someone suggested that I contact Trevor and see if he would be interested in the position. I said, "No, I would never do that. I would not want to hire someone away from a sister church so close by."

With that, we went on looking for another person to hire. A few months after that conversation, Trevor's mother came for a visit. I commented to her about the talk about him coming as a youth leader and what I had said in response. With that, she said, "I wish you had." She was saying she wished we would have made the offer.

Trip #8 – Dropping Like Flies

I asked why.

She said he is feeling like God is calling him into some other ministry and is not planning to stay there. His position was only part-time at the church, and he was hoping for some full-time ministry opportunity. I didn't say anything but just filed it away mentally. Several weeks went by, perhaps even months. We were nearing the end of our school year with all the usual festivities of graduations, awards, parties, and banquets. Trevor's daughter, Lacy, was in sixth grade at the time, and was about to participate in a sixth-grade graduation/banquet ceremony. I had been asked to help with a slide presentation that evening. I had to run to another building to find a piece of equipment for the presentation.

As I pulled into the parking lot after getting the stuff, I saw Trevor just getting out of his car. I did not plan to say anything to him. But this is as close as I ever get to hearing God's audible voice. I got the clear prodding: "Go tell Trevor you are interested in talking to him about becoming the youth leader." I didn't want to do it, but when I got out of my car, we greeted one another, and I said, "Trevor, I hope you're not offended by what I'm about to say, and I'm only going to say it once and never bring it up again. If you are ever looking for another ministry opportunity and are not involved with (name of other church), I would be interested in talking to you about being our youth leader." I have to be honest and say I don't think I was in control of this situation at all. God seemed to have my tongue and my brain in those moments, because it seemed as if He said, "I want you to pass the mantle to Trevor one day." I certainly didn't say that to Trevor or to the church, but I also never forgot it. Trevor's response was a bit of a surprise. He said, "Really! That's interesting, we probably should talk." If I remember correctly, he called me later that night and twice the next day. I repeated my concern about the church where he was serving, and he said that he would speak to his pastor/boss because he was planning to leave no matter what. I told him that I would leave that conversation with him.

One of the requirements that I have always held in high regard was for our leaders to finish their college degrees. Trevor had gotten involved in ministry and had never finished college. I told him that he would need to get that completed while he was with us. He got enrolled almost immediately and was very faithful in completing his degree. After completing his degree, we encouraged him to begin work on his ordination process, which he did and completed in 2017. Trevor officially came on board as a youth pastor in 2011. Between then and September of 2018, he began to take on more responsibilities, while I worked with our elder board on a succession plan.

In 2017, I began to talk publicly about the succession and to deliver sermons where I talked about it. I never lost the sense that God was raising Trevor up to be the next pastor of our church, but I also did not feel that I should force or dictate the selection of the next pastor for ICC. I had a sense that if God wanted Trevor to be the next pastor, it would happen.

The church called Trevor as the third pastor in the history of Island Community Church with well over a 90% vote in early 2018.

While I was aware of my sense of leading to begin the succession plan, I was not fully aware of the transition that was taking place in my heart. As I began to see, the desperate need is among ministries for Christian education, both in America and other countries. I had seen firsthand the difficulty meeting the needs of the children. I began to undergo a heart change toward God's call on my life. I sensed He was calling me to a heightened role I was to play through IACCS. So, on September 16 of 2018, the church held a retirement bash for Colleen and me, and I officially stepped down as senior pastor of ICC. I was not sure what would happen next, but I knew that my sense was to invest more time in IACCS. This represents the first change.

This year's trip was the first post-retirement trip to Uganda. I had made another trip to Haiti to see how the association was developing there.

The second significant change was that, while the Florida Keys was slowly recovering from Hurricane Irma, families were still struggling, and the infrastructure of the Keys was strained. United Way had done a study known as The ALICE Study. ALICE is an acronym for Asset Limited, Income Constrained, Employed. That basically is a measure of the people living in a community that live above the U.S. poverty level, but earn less than the cost of living level for the county they live in. That means that they are not earning enough just to meet basic needs like food and shelter. After Hurricane Irma, that number rose to 48% for our county. The study further showed that 54% of Florida Keys families with children are considered ALICE or living below the federal poverty line.[21]

Why mention this here? Basically, for this reason: if basic needs cannot be met because income levels are too low, most families will not be able to put their children in private schools of any kind.

The elder board, financial advisory board, and school board met several months after Hurricane Irma as enrollment dropped. We could see the financial strain this was going to put on the church. We determined to give it a year and see if enrollment would increase or if the funds could be raised to make up the deficit.

As the 2018 school year began, we had made no gains in enrollment, and the ALICE numbers had not significantly improved. Our boards met, and there was a unanimous consensus that we were not going to be able to keep the school open beyond the end of the school year. We made the announcement to our parents, and they begged us to give an extension of the decision to see if the deficit could be made up. However, at the end of that extension, our enrollment was less than half the minimum number required. So, at the end of 2018-2019, our school was forced to close. I tried to propose every imaginable school model. I even asked our elders to give it another two weeks so that we could fast and pray that God might provide us with a way to keep the school open. In the end, I had to agree that the school had run its season. We had to wait and see as God moves in a different direction. This has been and still is one of the hardest lessons I have had to learn. However, I do believe that God is still sovereign, and as Scripture says, *"will exchange beauty for ashes"* (Isaiah 61:3 NKJV). Once again, my focus was sharpened toward IACCS and the struggle almost every school is facing. Schools in rural America and all across the globe find it difficult to keep the balance of what parents can afford and pay a proper wage to teachers.

It is a constant reminder to me of the struggle that day in and day out ministries in third world countries face just trying to keep their doors open.

The third change actually involves two changes in Uganda. They both involved deep loss. In August, we received word that Bogere Kijje, our faithful driver, had passed away. Almost every mile of every trip since 2011, driving our groups had been driven by this quiet, humble man. I knew him only as B.J. (I guess from "Kijje" sounding like B.J. to me.), but I had grown very fond of him and was deeply saddened by his passing. But his passing showed another incredible, compassionate side of Timothy. B.J. had a grown son, and when we arrived in Uganda in November, we had a new driver.

As we were loading our luggage on the bus, I thought, my goodness, this young man looks a lot like a younger version of B.

J. I soon learned that was because he was his son. But the thing that puts a lump in my throat (even as I write these words) is that Timothy is looking after him as a father! He is making sure his needs are met.

The second loss represented even deeper roots to Timothy. His father passed away on September 4. This was a hard loss for Timothy, and it impacted him deeply. I reached out to him as soon as I knew of his loss, but it was very difficult from a continent away. When we arrived, we expressed our sorrow to Timothy and his family. Almost immediately upon arrival in Uganda, I noticed a deeper tenderness in Timothy's spirit, which probably reflects the spiritual impact the losses have had on him.

The last change is, in a way, a segue between the changes to the "dropping like flies" theme. As you've already seen, hurricanes are a big part of our July through September lives in the Keys. 2019 was no exception. Hurricane Dorian came blasting through the Atlantic and was heading straight for us.

When it got to the Bahamas, it looked like it slammed on its brakes. Dorian churned, ripped, and tore Abaco and Grand Bahama Island with Category 5 winds for a total of 22 hours. Many of the small towns on Abaco were utterly destroyed.

Early reports are that up to fifty lives are believed to have been lost. But that number was hard to determine because everyone was displaced.

Had they escaped to Nassau, or have they washed away, never to be seen again? Before it left Abaco, Dorian had been reduced to a Category 4 hurricane, and suddenly it took a right turn veering away from Florida. So, what does that have to do with our trip to Uganda?

For starters, Mike (the Mayah), who indeed was now the Mayor of Islamorada, had reached out to help the people of Hope

Town and others on Abaco. As always, he was pouring every ounce of energy and resources into helping in every way he could. Somehow, he had met a family who had lost everything.

They had no home and nowhere to go.

There was a grandmother, a dad, a mom, and two sons. They became Mike's personal project, and because they were Mike's project, they partially became our church and my project. The husband/father was responsible for the lighthouse in Hope Town, and so he remained behind with the oldest son to try to restore their home and tend the lighthouse. This lighthouse is one of only three manually operated lighthouses in the world. It is an essential navigational link for those sailing this region of the Bahamas. The grandmother, mom, and young son came to stay in a home that we had on our church property that had come available as a result of the school closing. Mike was fully funding this family and took them on as his own. He purchased a car for them (I became the Drivers Ed instructor to get them use to driving on the opposite side of the road). Mike led a campaign to get clothes, toys, food, everything that they needed to feel at home. In addition, Mike had reached his term limit as a village council member and had just launched a campaign to run for a county commission seat. As a result of all of these events, Mike felt it necessary to drop out of this year's trip.

A few weeks after Mike began to talk about not being able to go, Gary, had a stroke.

Fortunately, he was airlifted to Miami and was given the proper treatment (recombinant tissue plasminogen activator [tPA] or alteplase) to reverse the effects of the stroke.

However, none of us felt it safe for him to travel to Uganda. Gary has become somewhat of a poster child for the importance of recognizing the symptoms of a stroke and getting proper immediate medical treatment. A video of Gary giving his testimony about his recovery was made by the hospital. In the video, Gary gives credit to the entire medical team, the treatment, and most importantly, to his God. That team and medical treatment would not have been available in Uganda. Ironically, we got a first-hand view of this when we arrived in Entebbe. After expressing our sorrow to Timothy for the loss of his father and B.J. I asked how each had passed away. Both had passed because of a stroke. Both might still be alive with proper diagnosis and treatment. As far as I have been able to determine, the medical treatment that Gary received does not exist or is very rare in hospitals throughout Uganda.

Dr. Diaz had told me early on that he was not going to be able to go because he and his wife were expecting a baby right at the time the trip was planned. Peter had also let me know that he could not go this year.

When the dust all settled and it came time for me to finalize everyone for this trip, I was the only guy left from previous trips. To find a guy willing to go at the last minute was not possible. I did a Facebook post around that time, teasing my guys for all having to bail on this year's trip. The title of the post? DROPPING LIKE FLIES!

When going to Uganda, several requirements can't happen overnight. First, you have to get permission to enter Uganda by obtaining a visa from the Ugandan Embassy in Washington D.C. That in itself takes several days. Then there are a series of immunizations along with a yellow card showing that all shots have been obtained. If you arrive and they don't see the correct vaccines, or there is something awry, you stand the risk of being turned away at the airport.

In some years, we have been required to have an invitation letter from a host before our visa is processed. Additionally, your passport must be in order and not about to expire.

There is just no way to do a last-minute add-on for the trip. So, the team this year was going to be a GIRL POWER team (you will see where this name came from a little later in the chapter). Donna and Sydney had worked all year doing fundraisers. Plus, they had been collecting items for the children. Wendy was now my veteran, making this her third trip, and a newcomer named Melania Kaulb. I had officiated her wedding to her husband Skip, a few years ago, and am good friends with her in-laws. She had expressed an interest months earlier, and so I gave her the information, and in no time, she was handing me a check for her airfare. Melania had been born in Romania and could relate well to the children living in poverty. She was able to share her story several times on this trip to encourage the children of Uganda.

Our 2019 journey began on Monday, November 4, flying from Miami International Airport. As usual, we landed the following morning in Amsterdam. We had about a three-hour layover before we boarded another plane headed for Entebbe, Uganda. At the end of the trip, we had our usual agonizing one-hour layover stop in Kigali, Rwanda. It is so painful because you are just a few miles from your final destination.

We finally made it to Entebbe late on Tuesday, the 5th. It was late, but we cleared Customs very quickly and met Sammy, Timothy's son, and his crew to take us to Katosi and Hotel Cross City. It was a sad moment because B.J. was not there to greet us.

I did not notice at that time how much our new driver resembled a young B.J. The next day when I was in less of a fog and could see him clearly, it became apparent that he was his son, and it was some time later in the trip that I learned how Timothy was looking after him. We did not see Timothy that evening because he was leading a pastors' conference, along with four guests from Finland. As usual, it was a very short night; 3:00 AM to bed and then up by mid-morning to get things off and running. When we arrived at our usual morning breakfast area, Pastor Timothy, Janepher, and their granddaughter, Eliana, were there, as well as the four guests from Finland.

These four were all engaged in various kinds of ministries, one was a pastor, and another a teacher. A husband and wife team both spoke at various times throughout the week, but I am not sure what their official roles were in Finland. I do know that they were faithful servants of the Lord. We had a quick breakfast, and it was off to do a conference, but this time it was a pastors' conference in Mukono. On the way, while riding in the van, we pumped up soccer balls because the ladies were going to visit another school to greet children and give them some gifts.

I taught at the conference and spent some time in a Q&A for pastors. It was interesting to field their questions. Some were the same issues that any pastor in America might face. Then there were a whole variety of topics that would make our problems pale in comparison.

Problems like the lack of instruction in the Bible or pastoral training, church members dying of AIDS. Or, how about problems like children dying of childhood diseases that would be curable in other parts of the world? Then there's the issue of children being abducted, others being abandoned. Add to that the constant concern for where their next meal would come.

These and a host of other issues represent the daily struggles of Ugandan pastors. Another problem that is now centuries old, that Timothy mentioned almost in passing, is the treatment of a militant Islamic group, which has burned churches and killed hundreds. One year, just before I left Florida, someone handed me an article about a pastor who had been murdered because his church was too close to a Mosque. I didn't share that article with my wife. The conflict between Christians and Muslims is nothing new to this region of Africa. Islam was first introduced to Uganda in the early 1800s by Sudanese soldiers led by Emin Pasha, and the arrival of traders from the East African coast.[21]

The most militant Muslim group is the Tabligh, pronounced *Cablick*. They are a strict sect that have their origin in India. They primarily operate under the name, "Allied Democratic Forces" (ADF) or the "Uganda Muslim Liberation Army" (UMLA).

Here are some examples of reports of their activities:

- On the morning of Sunday, August 14, 2016, armed assailants raided Rwambongo District in the city of Beni, in North Kivu province of the Democratic Republic of Congo (DRC) near the Uganda border. On that occasion, more than fifty people were killed, and an unknown number left with injuries, according to a United Nations report.

    After their establishment, the ADF had come into the spotlight for a number of violent incidents, including their attack on a technical Institute in Kabarole District (western Uganda), in which fifty students were burnt in their dormitories and 150 were abducted. Since then, the group has persisted in carrying out numerous attacks that target both the army and civilians. The group has also been linked to a number of terror attacks in Kampala and to numerous assassinations of Muslim scholars opposed to their ideology, including a Shia leader in 2015. According to a report released by the Bureau of Democracy, Human Rights and Labor of the US Department of State, a total of twelve prominent Muslim scholars have been killed in Uganda in the past four years by the ADF.[22]

Most of their activity centers on the belief that the current government is restricting Muslims from holding political offices, and their belief that the country should adopt sharia law. Generally speaking, the Christian and Muslim population function in harmony with some of the Christian schools having Muslim children who attend.

I mention all of this simply because I want to express how different and how challenging being a pastor in Uganda can be. Imagine what it was like for some of these pastors during Idi Amin's terror! Most were just children then, but some remember deeply and painfully. As I think about their lives and ministry, I am humbled by their faithfulness and their deep dependence and faith in God. I think the most important thing I can bring to them is just solid Bible training and healthy church practices.

The next morning, Thursday, November 7, the team was up early because Donna and Sydney had arranged a visit to Cross City from a friend that we had met the previous year. You may recall Xavier. He was a wildlife safari guide that had also been diagnosed as having a stroke. He had been a very healthy young man when we met him the year before, but this year as he walked into our breakfast/meeting area at Cross City, he was gaunt and was clearly suffering from paralysis on one side of his body. His speech was affected and so it was even difficult to communicate with him. It was extremely painful to watch and listen as he talked about his struggles, his lack of funds to get medical treatment, and his inability to even get an accurate diagnosis. Several times during the conversation he had to stop because he couldn't hold the tears back. He talked about how difficult it was to be a good father and husband, and how he was making every effort to keep his business alive. He had a driver who now had to accompany him everywhere he goes. As usually happens, the driver sat patiently in the safari van while Xavier sat and talked with us. He told us that he had been told he needed stem cell therapy but could not get it in Uganda. After a brief visit, it was time for him to return home. Donna walked him to his van, gave him a suitcase full of supplies and handed him an envelope with a check in it. I never asked Donna or Sydney how much the check was for, but I am sure it was a generous gift. After Xavier left, we were in contact with Dr. Diaz, who believed that his diagnosis was not correct. In a follow-up doctor's visit in Kampala, we heard that he indeed had been misdiagnosed and that he apparently was suffering from some other neurological disorder as well, that had led to his paralysis. Last time I heard anything about his condition, he was trying acupuncture with some Asian specialists. The treatments seem to be helping and he is reported to be at about 60% of his function prior to the stroke. A sad side note to this, which leads into the discussion, which is about to follow, is that his wife believed that his condition was a curse or some form of witchcraft. Instead of remaining by his side and providing much need support, she took their baby and left. No medicine, unsure diagnosis, lack of medical service, witch doctors, all compound the health issues that the people of Uganda face. In addition to this, there are the compounding problems of lax regulations, not nearly enough enforcement, centuries old superstitions, and some very unscrupulous people.

There are reports regularly coming out about people using toxic chemicals as self-proclaimed curing proprieties for everything, from cancer or malaria to HIV/AIDS. For example, a faith-based group in the US and Great Britain have been offering up a drink of mix, made of sodium chlorite and citric acid. The two chemicals when mixed, produce chlorine dioxide, a powerful bleach used in the textile industry.

As many as 50,000 Ugandans, including infants as young as 14 months old, were given this mix to drink. In another instance, a young well-intending American girl got deeper and deeper into caring for malnourished children of Kampala. Over time, she allowed Ugandans to believe that she was a medical doctor or trained medical professional performing procedures that should have only been done by properly trained medical personnel. Then there are the witch doctors offering up just about any concoction imaginable to cure diseases. That's not to say that there are not some natural chemicals found in the incredible biodiversity of Uganda that can cure diseases. You will hear about examples of some of these later in the chapter. But the witch doctors are doing some terribly evil things in Uganda. In an online article, *Uganda Where Dead Children's Bodies Are Big Business*, written by Sofi Lundin for the Norwegian Refugee Council, there are chilling accounts of how the witch doctors are still abducting, mutilating and killing children. Much of the article is just more graphic than I want to print here, but I would urge those who are serious about addressing this problem and want to learn more to read the article and prepare to be heartbroken. Here are just a few quotes from the article:

- UGANDA/Buikwe: In the Buikwe district in southern Uganda, at least one child is killed each week. A belief prevails that blood and body parts of children can create wealth and cure illness, and the bodies of dead children have become big business.
- These are some of the stories I have been told when meeting the locals in Buikwe district, 45 kilometres east of the capital Kampala. Here, superstition and poverty have created a market where witch doctors and their agents have become rich because of people's beliefs that blood

and body parts from children create wealth, cure disease, and ward off evil spirits (I won't report the graphic stories here).

- This practice, which is widespread throughout the country, kills hundreds of children each year. The first reported child sacrifice in Buikwe took place in 1998. Since then, child sacrifice has become more common. According to a report by the Ugandan police, 729 children nationwide were registered abducted in 2013. The number is most likely higher. Today, on average, one child a week is abducted and killed in Buikwe, the area known to be the child sacrifice district of the country.
- I meet Obed Byamugisha (30) in Lugazi, in the heart of the Buikwe district. Supported by the international children's charity World Vision, Byamugisha has travelled from village to village in the last two years, looking for ways, together with the local people, to stop child sacrifice. Over the next few days I traveled with Byamugisha on his motorbike to meet the families of children that have been killed, surviving children, and a witch doctor that describes how the holy spirits inform how the children are to be killed. We drive on muddy roads, through lush forest passageways and into villages with poor infrastructure, few schools, inadequate healthcare and lack of water, making an uncertain tomorrow. People's lives here are highly influenced by superstition. Every third household has their own place of sacrifice, where traditional healers and witch doctors promise good health and wealth to their customers.

In a small village, behind a house between some trees, Jimmy Yinda lies buried. The grandmother, who looks well over 70, but in reality, is merely 56, is lying on all fours on the grave of her grandchild who never reached the age of two before he was brutally murdered. The father, the uncle, and the siblings who played with Jimmy on the day he vanished are out of words. They are still in shock over what happened and live in fear over losing more family members. After Jimmy's murder, two people were arrested, but corrupt authorities and lack of evidence soon let them back in the village again.

- Edward (who still may be a practicing witch doctor) says that he now cooperates with Obed Byamugisha and World Vision. He is a so-called "change agent," a person who was formerly a witch doctor, but now works to apprehend those who conduct child sacrifices. In the last year, Edward has witness 12 killings in the area.
- "It is a difficult and dangerous job. Witch doctors and agents have a lot of money. They are powerful people and I have been threatened several times. Anybody who tries to take their livelihoods from them lives dangerously. A poor man will never win a battle for justice in Uganda. The ones who win here are the ones who have money, regardless if he kills children or not," he says. Byamugisha says that Edward and others who used to be witch doctors are important allies in the battle to end child sacrifices.
- "The challenge lies in that it is not easy to know who to trust. We are often threatened. Many meet us at the door with a knife. But we certainly need to involve the witch doctors. They are the ones closest to the locals and they know the practice best. Without them, we have no chance of success," says Byamugisha, and gets back on his motorbike.

On the way back, he points between the trees. This is where the witch doctors operate in hiding. Being a witch doctor is illegal in Uganda, meaning many hide behind certificates that say they are traditional healers. Others move so they can maintain anonymity. This is why there are no accurate numbers of witch doctors, but according to World Vision and other organizations there are several hundred in the Buikwe district alone.[23]

I feel like the issue of witch doctors, superstitious medical practice, misdiagnosis, and lack of adequate medical care is such a crucial issue that it is worth pausing to discuss and highlight. But now, let's get back to our trip.

About midmorning, we went over to Winners Home to see the fire damage. The fire occurred on a Sunday morning when there weren't many people around and church services were taking place. There were two separate buildings where the fire had occurred. In the main building where the central office was located, the fire had completely destroyed the room where there were several computers (called the computer lab) and the library. Across the drive, there was another separate room that had burned that was adjoining a classroom wing. I asked Timothy what he thought happened since there were two separate fires. He said that it was still being investigated, but thought it was done on purpose. It is hard to say what happened because of all the hundreds of children that live in the dorms. Additionally, there are bare wires (insulated, but no male or female plugs) that run from whatever they are running electrically. The exposed ends are jammed into a wall outlet or receptacle of an electric generator. Why there aren't more fires and electrocutions baffles me. I was able to give Timothy some of the IACCS money that had been generated from our church and my generous Rotary Club friend. I was able to do that without using IACCS money that had been raised for the other orphanages and cows.

There was a major setback that I briefly mentioned in an earlier chapter. When we arrived on the property, the first thing that got my attention was not the burned rooms; it was a pile of playground equipment that had been the Rick Strong Playground. It was a complete wreck!

The playground had been moved from the spacious open field location down by Lake Victoria, where Timothy had so proudly placed it, to this pile of twisted metal by the office building. As described earlier, Timothy explained that too many kids from the village had used it because there was no adequate fencing. My response was polite but curt. I said, "You know that is unacceptable. It needs to be fixed before we return. Mike will be heartbroken to learn this!"

That was all that was said about the playground or the fire, but I left the money he said it would take to restore the playground.

As we walked the grounds, I did what I always enjoy doing, I stopped and watched two or three teachers teaching their classes. I took a video just so I could be reminded of what a good job these teachers do with such limited resources and so many students. I commented to the person walking with me, "Despite the fire, there is still good teaching going on." As I often do, though, I go back and watch the video, and there is always one concern I have. It is this: most of the teaching is depending on memorization of rote answers. One of the things that I am trying to emphasize in the workshops is helping teachers learn how to create high-order thinking. Designing questions and exercises that lead to children becoming problem solvers and thinkers.

We walked down the steep hill that dives from the upper buildings toward Lake Victoria. I glanced at the water system that had been installed, the water stations that exist all across the grounds, and the still beautiful Wilsie House. It made me reflect on how grateful I was for IACCS and the opportunities we have had to minister in Uganda. How amazing it is to think of Timothy and Janepher taking a few children until God prodded and provided for them to provide for nearly a thousand children through Community Concern Ministries. What a quantum leap, from crocs grabbing children gathering water at the lake, to a pure water system to keep them safe.

As we walked past the building and out into the field, I saw a group of men building a large stage for Children's Day. Tomorrow there would be children everywhere, and schools would be gathering and performing. Amid the loss that Timothy had experienced in recent months, he still was looking into the future. He said, "Come, I want to show where we want to put the chicken farm." There has been conversation almost every year about three projects: a large garden, a chicken farm, and fencing around the property. Each year, I feel like he is lobbying for us to make those projects happen. We have helped, but still recognize the obligation to benefit all of the IACCS schools in Uganda and elsewhere.

I am not sure why, perhaps it was the temperature or the direction of the wind or something else, but there was a steady stream of beautiful birds flying about.

Not all the same kind, but an array of colors and sizes: blue, green,and yellow. It was a reminder of just how wild and beautiful Uganda can be. As we walked up a little rise to get a full few of where the chicken coop would be built, there was a young man that was making brick from scratch. We asked Timothy about it and he said that he was making brick for the orphanage to finish the fence, and for the repairs on the burned building. The whole process takes a matter of minutes.

The young man scoops wet mud/clay in his hands and throws it down into a wood-frame with two rectangular spaces. The frame is on a table just large enough to hold it about waist high. The mix is then patted down, getting it smooth, and removing air bubbles. He then uses his hands to scrape off the excess, and tosses it back in the mud pile. Once he has the mud looking like firm usable bricks, he turns the frame on its side and carries it to a place on the ground covered with a burlap-like tarp. When he pulls the cover back, rows of brick that he is allowing the sun to cure are exposed. He turns the frame over, and two perfectly formed blocks are added to the rows. The bricks are once again covered with the tarp, and the process begins all over again. The process was fascinating, and one could not help but think about the potential for cottage industries of brick-making being done throughout the country.

As we walked down toward the open field, I had to pause and chuckle, because there in front of us were two of the biggest turkeys I have ever seen; one, a big Tom, and the other, his plump mate. Since it was November, I had to comment, "Timothy, it's a good thing these turkeys are here in Uganda. If they were in the good old USA, they would be on somebody's Thanksgiving dinner plate! Last year, the surprise animal was the camel; this year it's the turkey.

We made our climb back up the hill. As we did, there was a class of young children sitting under the shade of an enormous, stately acacia tree that dominates the center courtyard of the campus. As we got near, a few of the children stood, and they all began to cheer and wave. The beauty of these children and of their little place of rest under the tree made it possible to forget for a moment the struggles these children face day-to-day just to survive. The joy they have comes from an inner peace that is not based on how many toys they have (they have none), or what video game has just come out, or whether they have the latest fashion to wear. It is gratefulness for being alive and even if, but for a few moments, knowing that someone from the outside cares and loves them. And, that's what keeps drawing me back to Uganda!

We made our way back up the hill to prepare to go to the next orphanage. We paused for a bathroom break in the only bathroom on the campus that was made for visitors. As we were taking that break, I decided to go sneak a look at the clinic once again. Little had happened, and that was disappointing. From the clinic, it is only a few steps back to the main gate of Winners Home. Just next to the gate entrance is the water tank and pump station that had been installed on our second trip. Lined up outside the fence in front of the water tank were dozens of the familiar yellow five-gallon water jugs where villagers were drawing water. Two pipes were purposely put there for them to have a safe, constant water supply.

What a great reminder of how our work in Uganda goes – some things are working great (water system), some things have progressed little (clinic), and some things have lost ground (Rick Strong Playground). I have to remind myself not to get discouraged, to focus on moving the ball down the field, correcting the things that can be fixed, and repairing what is broken.

The morning had quickly slipped away, and we still had many miles to travel. Our first stop was familiar to those of us who had been part of the 2018 team. We had returned to visit the orphanage where MoMaMo, the cow, is in the rural countryside outside Mukono. When we realized that this was where she was, we asked if we could see her and take some pictures, so that we could take them back to Marlene and her family. We walked a short distance and very excited to see that MoMaMo was very healthy and producing milk for the babies. After a few photos, we were invited into a large room where many of the school parents had been invited to celebrate with us. The children were extremely talented and well coached in their singing and presentations they did for us. During a break in the children's performances, Timothy called Sydney up, honored her, telling about her hard work and love for the children of Uganda. He then had her give several soccer balls to the children representing their school. The administrators also paid special honor to Timothy as president of UCCS-U. They awarded him with a certificate of appreciation.

We then took a route that I had not traveled before. Donna, Sydney, and Wendy were very quick to tell me that they distinctly remembered this path from the year before. This had been an excursion the team had been on while I was elsewhere doing a conference. It didn't take long for me to realize why they remembered this area so vividly. We drove for miles through sugar cane fields just off of Lake Victoria. The odor of fermenting and rotting sugar cane filled the cabin of our van. After many miles, the smell was sickening. That's why the ladies remembered this location, and I won't soon forget it either. We arrived at an orphanage somewhere between Mukono and Jinja. I was scheduled to speak at a pastors' conference there at 4:00, and it was 3:45 when we arrived. No time really to refresh, just walk in, greet the pastors, and start. It was good to see Bernard Bogere, along with several other familiar pastoral faces from past years. I spoke to the pastors for one session. The goal was to encourage them with the importance of their role to communities and the importance of a clear, bold proclamation of the Gospel.

As we took a break between speakers, a group of children sang some beautiful traditional hymns as only these beautiful children can do. As they were singing, I had an opportunity to read some posters, handmade by the children of this orphanage. Each poster was hanging on the walls of the classroom, proudly conveying somber messages. At first glance, they appeared to be pictures of houses, soccer balls, basketballs, or scenes you would expect children to draw of their world, but then you read the messages:

Poster 1: Choose to Delay Sex
Poster 2: Aids kills
Poster 3: Abstain from Sex – this one included a special note: Primary six as my fellow class we should abstain from sex at this early age – May God Bless You,
Poster 4: Avoid Early Marriage Please

What! These are primary six children (sixth grade; twelve or thirteen years old)! How sad that children's innocence can be ripped away at such an early age.

After I had finished speaking, we had the opportunity to go outside to speak and greet a large group of children of all ages sitting on the ground. We gave away some gifts and spoke words of encouragement to them. I couldn't help but notice a young boy sitting directly in front of me who was clinging tenaciously to a homemade soccer ball. He had torn ragged cloths with no shoes on scraped and scarred feet. Visible were several sores on his face, and he did not look very healthy; again, a painful reminder of the lack of adequate medical care and proper hygiene in many of these remote areas. That's not intended to reflect disparagingly on this orphanage or the care that they are giving to the children. It is intended to magnify the enormity and complexity of the problems they face.

It was now late afternoon, and we had to begin the long drive back to Katosi to prepare for the Children's Day the next morning.

I failed to mention that in the morning, this day had also been our largest purchasing day. We had purchased ten cows, some more *Toughee* school shoes, mattresses, and half a cow for Children's Day.

On Friday, November 8, the team was awake early; I believe because we were anxious for the Children's Day, and because we had a huge number of soccer balls that had to be pumped up to be given away. When I came out of my room, the ladies were all sitting on the floor, air pumps in hand, with soccer balls surrounding them and filling the hallway. It actually didn't take long with everyone pitching in, and the balls were all put back in bags to take over to the event.

Girl Power pumping soccer balls.

Honoring Timothy's father

As we were walking down to breakfast, I greeted the young man that is sort of the gatekeeper/guard at the Hotel Cross City. He sleeps/lives in a tiny room that doubles as the guardhouse just inside the front gate. It is probably not more than seven feet wide and eight feet long.

When someone arrives at the compound up the little dirt trail (it would be unfair to call it a road), they stop outside the big metal gate and honk their horn. He then looks to see who it is that wants in and opens the gate. This young man has been living in that room since I started coming in 2011, and Timothy seems to take care of him completely. I had to pause and take a photo of him this morning because of the shirt he was wearing. It had a picture of Timothy's dad printed on it. His English is not good enough for him to explain why he was wearing it. He clearly felt a family tie to Timothy's family. Each year, I try to give him some extra gift of clothing or insect netting or just money.

The Children's Day was in full swing when we arrived. There were hundreds of teachers, administrators, parents and children, children, and more children. The same format that had been followed in the past was taking place as each school made their presentations. At a break, an adult team was introduced as New Hope Ministry. A very knowledgeable lady, who appeared to be the founder of this ministry, spoke. I was excited about the things she had to say and that they were full-time in Uganda.

She spoke with great passion about the importance of Christ in education. She said, "Where there is no Christ, there is no education." She then talked about the importance of Christian education being holistic in its approach, addressing the affective, cognitive, and psychomotor needs of each child. She then challenged the teachers to tackle the difficult problem of how to teach the Bible while using the state-mandated secular curriculum. She told how her ministry was providing the training and materials necessary to make that possible for teachers in Christian schools. She called out some of the teachers from classrooms she had recently visited. She said, "Some teachers didn't have Christ in the classroom! I could tell from things on walls. There was no Biblical integration. You need our training!" I had to agree with her. She went on to say, "We want to see transformation in this country. And when you teach the teacher, then the teacher will teach the children from a biblical perspective. In the end, you won't have corruption in our country. And in the end, you won't have violence. In the end, we will have a different country. In the end, we will have a generation that glorifies God."

It was now time for us to take our place at one of four feeding stations. We (the team of five) all went to one station, and our new friends from Finland were assigned to another station. As usual, when you look at the endless line of children, you wonder how there could possibly be enough food for them all. But there always is.

Remember also that these huge meals are being cooked over open fires in giant cauldrons. Ash from the fire, the occasional insect that gets fried as it flies over, all become part of the mix.

Children's Day Competition

Trip #8 – Dropping Like Flies

New Hope Ministries

The Team feeding the children

Let the feeding begin

I was relieved to see that our cow had made it into the stew. It was the usual mix of vegetables, beans, rice, and beef. It looked and tasted very much like beef stew would taste here in the States. At one point, as I was scooping rice onto plate after plate, dumping more rice from the big serving pots, I noticed that I was standing about an inch taller than usual. I looked at my feet covered in rice. I was standing tall on rice that had caked on the bottom of my shoes.

Once we finished serving, we were invited to eat our lunch. I noticed that there were adults who had not gotten food, so I loaded my plate with food and carried it over to a group of teachers sitting under a tent. I placed it before them and walked away. I did not want them to have an opportunity to refuse it. I think our entire team did the same with their meals. One of the assignments that Mike had given me was to find his little friend. I had not seen him and was growing concerned that something might have happened to him.

I showed his picture to the administrator at Winners, and he told me he was somewhere on campus and doing fine. I caught a brief glimpse of him sucking on a popsicle that had been part of the special treat for Children's Day. I snapped a quick photo of him, but he was on the move, so I didn't get to greet him just yet. As we were finishing up serving the children, he came up to me, and I was able to snap a photo of the two of us to send to Mike. We spent a few seconds in conversation, and then he was off to play with his friends.

After the meal, we all gathered out in the field where we gave seven cows to seven different ministries. We went cow to cow to cow with a mob of screaming, cheering children at each of the stations. One of the five of our team would be handed a rope that was attached to a tree with a cow on the other end. A few words would be spoken, there would be more cheering, and dancing, and the cow would be handed over to the proud new owner.

Once the cows had been given away, we gathered back in front of the stage. Sydney was called forward to begin to award the mountain of soccer balls that we had to give away.

I had noticed a peculiar absence all day at the gathering. Bernard Bogere had been at the two pastors' conferences, but he, nor Lugazi School, were at the Children's Day. He is an integral part of UCCS-U and is vice president of the association, so this concerned me. I asked Timothy about it. At first, he said he didn't know, but would give him a call.

Later, he told me that he had said he had a wedding to attend. I was not satisfied with that answer, and so asked some of the other leaders. They indicated that it was a soft protest about the way the competitions were going, how the awards were being managed, and no formal board meeting. I tried to get the board meeting set up several times, but something always prevented it from happening. I am still not sure what happened. We have corresponded since returning to the States and all seems to be going well for now, but I think this will be a hot topic for next year's trip. I keep reminding the UCCS-U board and schools that this is their association. If they want it to be healthy, it is going to be up to them to preserve. They need to organize it in such a way as not to depend on me coming once a year for two weeks to make their association successful. I also reminded them that the primary purpose of IACCS was not to give cows or gifts to them, but educate and guide them through school improvement, not financial support.

There has always been a conversation with some of the Ugandan leadership with what they call "twinning." As best I have been able to discern, it would be what we might call adopting a school. I have found that as these schools look at American Christian schools, they get an erroneous idea. They perceive them as incredibly wealthy and could easily take on the support of a Ugandan school. I have explained on more occasions than I can count that this is not the case and that most schools struggle just to meet the needs of their own schools. I have also explained that lack of accountability and follow-through has created a degree of distrust among some donors. This is especially true with the "adopt a child" programs. I think there will always be a need for these conversations as we move forward with the work of IACCS, and each year, we get a little better in presenting our work and purpose.

On Saturday the 9th, I was scheduled to do a teachers' convention in Luwero, a solid 2-1/2 to 3-hour drive from Katosi. This was the same place where the young, enthusiastic science teacher had joined me at lunch and asked great question after great question about teaching, class control, grading, and just about everything else you can think of from a young man desiring to be a great teacher.

When we arrived, we were greeted by the school administrator, who was very anxious to show us the school more thoroughly than the year before. He was very proud of his school and what they were accomplishing. He should have been. This is a remote school that really has a desire to improve each year. He showed me several classrooms and introduced me to several of the resident students on campus. He then took us into the library. As is the case with most of the schools that I've visited, this was not a library, this was a room with a lot of books stacked and piled on shelves. The librarian expressed her frustration about how she could not organize the books and how children took books when she was not there and then never returned them. I asked her if she knew about the Dewey Decimal System. She said she had never heard of it.

I spent several minutes explaining the basics of the Dewey Decimal System. I pulled up an excellent online resource for her to get some tools to get her started in organizing in proper categories and using a card catalog system. I then explained what an accession book was and how to set it up to keep track of the resources she had. I did not bother to tell her about the online services or the programs that she could buy to do most of the work electronically. Technology and reliability are just not there yet in rural Uganda. Next, we went to the computer lab. There was more equipment in this lab than in many.

Sadly, though, it looked like people from other countries had packaged up old computers and sent them to Uganda without regard for their level of obsolescence. Most would have lacked the memory or speed to be very useful for much beyond learning how to use a keyboard. The school is doing a good job with what they have. They just need so much more. I am currently considering shifting from buying as many cows to buying computers. I am attempting to strike a reasonable financial agreement with an in-country computer company that will either lease or sell computers to us.

The next stop on our school tour was to the spot I had looked forward to seeing since talking with the young science teacher and seeing his pictures from the previous year. It was the science lab. The lab was a multipurpose facility used for all science disciplines. Behind chain-link fencing were shelves storing miscellaneous lab equipment. The area contained a few science models, microscopes, some glassware, a few chemicals, and various lab equipment that had probably been donated over time. There was a human skeleton model standing in one corner of the room. Along the front of the room were several cages with guinea pigs and other small lab animals. The lab tables were handmade but adequate for their purpose. It was not a lab that would meet any of the standards required for American school labs, but it was the best lab (in fact, the only lab) I had seen in Uganda. One of my projects between now and the next trip is to modify and make available a set of lab standards that will be adequate for use in Uganda.

Our next stop was to an impressive little pavilion that housed a unique water system providing clean drinkable water for the entire school. It was produced by a group known as, *Impact Water* (impactwater.co). They are providing water systems in Uganda, Kenya, and Nigeria. On their website, they give the following statistics: 6,419,250 = Number of students with safe drinking water; 15,850 = Number of schools installed to date; 732,458 tons of CO_2 diverted. It is our hope to be a cooperative relationship with Impact Water and other water groups, like 4Water, to meet the clean water needs of the schools in Uganda.

We were very late getting into the conference, and Lawrence kept urging us to hurry. I knew we were late, but the tour was well worth it, and I gained a wealth of information to help other schools along the way. Besides, the host administrator was the one giving the tour, so I assumed that we were pretty safe.

When we entered the conference area, words were being shared by some of the Luweero District leaders. From the very beginning, it was apparent that there was a deep sense of purpose and desire for this district to succeed and help their schools become the best possible.

They were taking their role and the UCCS-U very seriously. They had prepared a formal report, which they submitted to me. Throughout the report, they were incredibly gracious to the UCCS-U leadership and to me as president of IACCS. They reported that the "UCCS-U in Luweero began around the middle of 2018 when it was introduced by Bishop Kakooza and his team. This is now our second convention here in Luweero and at the same place." They then reported their achievements as follows:

- We have maintained UCCS-U in Luweero through today
- Our cow project is doing well. One cow produced a female calf about 4 months ago and the other is pregnant.
- We started on self-school inspection (I am assuming they are talking about a self-study model that I left with them the previous year), which we shall complete soon when the academic year begins.
- We have attended some of the meeting at the national level.

Then they listed several challenges:

- The moral for the union is still wanting.
- Organizing the convention and the Children's Day in term 3 when the national examinations are going on at P.7, S.4 and S.6 is not easy (I told them at the end of this report that this was my fault because I did not know the dates for the national exams and would try to adjust our schedule to avoid this in the future).

- We still need more and more motivation.

Lastly, they listed two expectations:

- We still expect more members to join our union.
- We have high expectations for our international and national presidents, especially on this day.

It was encouraging to see these men and women taking a proactive role in the leadership of the association.

After the report, I was introduced and began my teaching sessions. One of the first things that I did after thanking everyone and encouraging them to keep up the good work was to keep leading as they are. I wanted to do a quick survey with them before I forgot.

I asked how many of their schools used the Dewey Decimal System? No hands went up. I asked how many knew what the Dewey Decimal System was? No hands. That was the motivation to send the information on setting up the Dewey Decimal System back to them as soon as I returned to the States. Hopefully by now, those that I sent it to have disseminated to the schools in the association.

I then began the teaching sessions.

There were seven sessions in all, so I had my work cut out for me if we were going to cover all the topics. This year's workshop titles were:

- Qualities of an Excellent Teacher
- Core Values of a Christian School
- Building Strong Christ-Centered Curriculum
- Building Effective Curriculum With Dynamic Lesson Plans
- Tests and Measurements
- Creating Thinkers, Not Parrots
- The School Improvement Process

I want to include the outline from session one here and then talk about something very special that happened after this session. Here is the outline:

Qualities of An Excellent Teacher

1. An excellent teacher sees their profession as a calling, not just a job or vocation.
2. An excellent teacher lives a life that is above reproach.
3. An excellent teacher loves their children and seeks to inspire them to be all that God made them to be.
4. An excellent teacher works with all their might to be prepared each day.
5. An excellent teacher is always learning and growing.
6. An excellent teacher views himself or herself as a mentor.
7. An excellent teacher seeks ways to meet the needs of each individual child.
8. An excellent teacher acts professionally at all times.
9. An excellent teacher is prepared.
10. An excellent teacher has good routines for every second of the day; from the first second of the day, for transitions throughout the day, and the last second of the day.
11. An excellent teacher has fair, consistent, reasonable classroom rules.
12. An excellent teacher uses more positive reinforcement than negative consequences.
13. An excellent teacher continually looks for opportunities to praise individual students.

Obviously, I believe that each one of these points is important, but it seems that every time I do this workshop, I seem to hone in on a couple of points. The first is viewing teaching as a calling. I always say teaching is not just a job; it is a high calling because you are shaping the minds of the next generation. I then challenge them to see their students, even the most challenging ones, as God sees them. I usually tell the story of the late Dr. Howard Hendricks, beloved professor at Dallas Theological Seminary. On numerous occasions, Dr. Hendricks has told the story of what a terror he was in early elementary school. He had earned a reputation, which the teacher gladly passed on to the next teacher who was going to be having him in her class.

But he tells how all that changed in one moment when a teacher in his middle elementary years said to him, "So you're little Howie Hendricks. I've heard a lot about you, Howie, and I don't believe a word of it! We are going to have a great year together." He says that moment changed his life. Somebody believed in him. His teacher saw him as God saw him.

At the end of that session, I opened it up for comments and questions. After a couple of teachers had asked questions, a lady stood and said something along these lines, "I want you to know that you changed my life. Last year, you taught us to see our children as Jesus sees them; to love them, to love them as Jesus loves them; to pray for each of my students. I did not love my children as I should. I began to pray for my children. I now love my children. You have made me a better teacher." When I got through wiping my tears away, I thanked her and told her that she had just made my trip. I said if nothing else happened on this trip, she had made it all worth it.

I found myself teaching with new enthusiasm and energy after that. It is incredible what words of encouragement can do to change a life. They can lift a spirit–and it seems to work in all directions, the student, the teacher, and even the workshop leader.

You have made me a better teacher

A joyful cow winner

Every session was full of participation and interaction with the audience. It really felt like great learning was taking place and that the schools would be better because of this day. As I spoke, I made the Continuing Education Certificates available to the schools. Hopefully, the schools will see the value of establishing this program for their schools.

We really didn't even take time to break for lunch but had a late meal after wrapping up session six. I knew there was not enough time to launch into the workshop on *Developing a School Improvement Plan,* and we had discussed this topic briefly the year before. As we ate, we had a group discussion about guiding a school improvement plan. I believe that the Luweero District could be the first to really drive this plan forward.

After we ate, the leadership of the district got together and developed some type of drawing and game to determine who would receive the cow. I have absolutely no idea how they made the final determination or how the game was played. Still, I was thrilled that they developed what seemed to be a very fair plan that everyone was satisfied with. In the end, a very excited female lead teacher/administrator won the cow. Lawrence and I said our farewells to everyone, I had a brief conversation with the young science teacher again, and we headed out on the long drive back. I still had a few minutes of preparation for Sunday morning and another session in the afternoon for the pastors' conference.

Sunday morning, we followed what has become a pretty regular routine at this point–Breakfast – Children's Church – main service – lunch – afternoon activity. When we arrived at the children's church, we were amazed to see the building nearly finished. It was fully plastered with a large plastered cross filling up the exterior front wall, and the entire facility was nearing completion. More progress has been made here than on almost any of the other projects. The only thing that I saw remaining to be done was completing the floor. The five of us, with Timothy, stood on the newly constructed porch/overhang that surrounded the entrance and side of the children's church and shot a video back to our church in Florida. Wendy was going to be leading the main part of the children's program, and Melania was able to share her testimony about growing up poor in Romania, receiving Christ, and how that had changed her life. Both ladies have commented on how this one event caused tremendous personal spiritual growth. I did not know much about Melania's story before this trip but thought about what a perfect fit for these children. As for Wendy, the growth was so heartwarming.

After greeting the children, I walked over to the main church to greet the people and get ready to speak. I was surprised to see a whole new church configuration. Everything had been rotated 90^0 so that everyone was much closer to the stage. The flooring had been completed, and there was new lighting and ceiling fans. All in all, it gave the church a much more established look that should only strengthen the future of the ministry.

As usual, the worship team was already leading in lively worship as we entered the service. There were several things on this morning's service schedule. I was already thinking about how to keep my message short and simple and still give a clear Gospel. The worship team finished leading us, and then two young men looking to be in their late teens came up, and music began to play.

These were two gifted street dancers that did a presentation for the whole church. I learned later that these young men were part of a dance troop that Donna and Sydney had arranged to have dance costumes made for them while in Florida, and had brought them to give to the team. There will be a sad side note to this part of the story a little later in the chapter.

Our friends from Finland were also sharing briefly in the service, so I decided to do something a little different and a little shorter. I used the theme of adoption. The selected passage was Galatians 4:4-5, *"But when the set time had fully come, God sent his Son, born of a woman, born under the law, to redeem those under the law, that we might receive adoption to sonship."* I told how I, like many of the people, especially the younger ones, had been adopted. Here is how I told the rest of my story. When I was five years old, I was taken/snatched by my biological mother to Galveston, Texas, for what was supposed to be a short trip. The short trip turned into weeks of pure physical torture. I described how her drunken alcoholic boyfriend would pull his huge cowboy belt off, double it up, and flip it over so that the hook on the back of the buckle would be exposed. He would then beat his son, and when he was through with him would turn and beat me. Once I was staring at him as he beat his son, knowing that I was next. He looked at me, swore, and said, "What are you looking at you little _____?" I didn't dare answer, but I remember to this day what I was thinking. It was "I am trying to remember your face, and when I'm grown, I will find you and kill you!" To show how gracious God is, I can't even begin to remember what this man looked like.

The beating continued day in and day out, usually on the back, buttocks, and back of the legs. I don't recall ever changing clothes the entire time I was there. One night, the other boy and I had been sent to bed in a small top bunk we shared in a tiny room just off the living room where a drunken party was in constant progress. We were starving (probably quite literally) when someone staggered into our bedroom and gave us a metal bowl of scalding hot soup along with two semi-clean spoons. Because the ceiling was so low, we couldn't move around very well or sit up completely.

As we were trying to get in a position to eat the soup one of us spilled the entire boiling stew all over the bed and ourselves. We were so hungry that we were using our hands and the spoons to try to eat as much as we could before it soaked through the sheets. As we were doing that, there was a knock on the front door. No one answered the door, so the knock came louder this time, and then again, even more emphatic.

Finally, someone staggered to the door and opened it. I peeked out through our slightly cracked door and couldn't believe my eyes. There stood my grandmother, the one who had raised me since birth. She had borrowed the money to buy a bus ticket and travel from Boggy Depot, Oklahoma, all the way to Galveston, Texas. When I saw her at that door, I scrambled down from the bunk and dashed into her arms. She held me tight, soup and all. And I'll never forget what she did next. She lifted off my grimy, soup-soaked shirt and ran her hands across my back as if feeling the pain of the abuser's belt buckle on her own back. She looked at the marks on my body. Then she turned, looked the man and my mother in the eyes and said, "You'll never touch this boy again!" She took my hand, and we walked out into the night. From there, we traveled back to our farm in Oklahoma.

I remember my grandparents sitting around the kitchen table, talking in hushed tones. Was I going to be okay? What if my mother tried to take me again? I heard the word adoption.

They came to me, gathered me in their arms, and explained what adoption meant. Then they asked me if they could adopt me.

It didn't matter to me. My grandparents were the only real parents I had ever known.

Legal papers were filed, and it was time to go before a judge. The only one in our county was bedridden, but he agreed to meet with us.

He called me over, and standing by his bedside, he asked, "Do you want your grandparents to be your legal parents?" You know that if they become your parents, your mother will not be able to snatch you away? Is that what you want?"

I said, "Yes, sir, I do," He replied, "Then you are now officially Tony Hammon." I had parents who loved me and would protect me.

The church had gotten very quiet as I told my story. I was sure there were dozens of people in the audience who could tell even worse stories than mine. But I also knew they could relate – especially to the concept of adoption.

I kept looking over at our friends from Finland, especially the one who was a teacher. He cried almost all the way through my story and was deeply moved by it. After I told the story, I made the application to the Galatians 4 passage, describing how we were adopted as sons and daughters of God because of what Jesus did for us, and how that bond could never be broken. No one could snatch us away from the adopted relationship we have with Him.

Near the end of the service, all of the children from the children's church came in and went to the platform to lead us in several songs. I noticed that they were all wearing or holding crosses that had been made for them by Donna and Sydney. After we dismissed the service, it was pure joy watching how the children flocked to each of the team members. They just love to love and be loved. As I was leaving, one of the little guys that is just dripping with leadership potential asked me where Mike was. I thought he was asking about Mike the Mayah, but Wendy quickly told me that he was asking about Mike Jr., Dr. Diaz's son, who had been there the year before.

I asked if he wanted to send him a message. He said, "Yes." I took my phone out, recorded his message, and sent it to Mike. Here is his message:

"Mike, we miss you so much. Next time, please come. We miss you so much. Bye bye, God bless you."

After we finally rounded up all the five of us, the four from Finland, Timothy, Janepher, and his son, we recognized that we needed a couple of vehicles to get everyone back to Cross City. We finally got it worked out, and all settled in for lunch. Before I began to eat, a pastor that was staying at Cross City reminded me that he had wanted me to meet a lady who was working as an evangelist for World Evangelism Team. We were introduced, and when I heard her name, I realized that she had been emailing me throughout the year. Her name was Mary Beatrice Namaganda. She had traveled eight hours to meet with me for about 30 minutes. I did not have much to off her in the way of help. She asked for advice about a couple of organizational things, and I think my responses were helpful. I remembered that I had brought several Bibles with me and was looking for the best place to give them. I felt this was probably the best place I could possibly give them. I invited her to come to the dining room to have lunch with us.

When she finished lunch, she said she had to leave, went out to catch a boda boda to ride another 8 hours back to her home. We have corresponded several times since returning to the US. She clearly wants someone to give her ministry advice and to bounce ideas off of.

It was now time for the Finnish team and I to go back to the pastors' conference. The four ladies in my team declined and said they were ready to get a good night's sleep.

I have learned that one of the key requirements for maintaining your cool in Uganda is extreme flexibility. I was scheduled to speak in Iganga. That was close to Jinja, which is close to where the Source of the Nile is located.

I asked Timothy if we could take the ladies there while I was doing the workshops. He said he was not sure and that we would have to see how the schedule was going. This was Monday, November 11, and we only had this day and two more to accomplish all of our tasks. We stopped at Javas to meet up with Lawrence. I assumed that I was going to go off with him to the conference. Then Timothy was either going to take the ladies to the Nile or to another orphanage. They talked for a few minutes, and then Timothy gave the familiar "We go" order, which meant that we were ready to do something.

Instead of going with Lawrence, who was off to complete some other task, I piled back in the van with the team.

Before I could figure out what we were doing, we were at the Source of the Nile. Timothy had just felt like we needed some recreational time and knew that I had not been able to do anything but teach at conferences for at least the last four years.

As we walked down a steep roadway down to the waters of the Nile, we walked past numerous vendors trying to convince us that we needed to buy their treasures. There were fabrics, pieces of art, carvings, games, musical instruments, hats, all with Ugandan symbols on them. Some beautiful others are typical tourist trinkets. As we got to the edge of the point where the Nile and Lake Victoria are joined, we walked out on some large pieces of granite. I kicked into biology mode for a few minutes because there were several brightly colored, diverse insects, especially dragonflies.

There were purple and green species that were so brilliant that they were almost fluorescent. As we were taking photos of the river and the diverse biota, I heard an unfamiliar voice speaking to the ladies. I looked up, and a young mid-eastern man was offering to take pictures of all of us. My first reaction was that he had a hustle on and was going to want money for taking photos or was going to take off with our camera equipment. But I couldn't have been more wrong. He was just a genuinely nice guy looking to be helpful and friendly.

As he was taking pictures and talking with us, two other guys walked up, and introduced themselves. They were a trio of father and sons. We soon discovered that they were from Pakistan and had recently come to Uganda to open a restaurant in Kampala. We learned that they had a chain of eateries known as BaBa's and had quite an online and YouTube presence. As we were walking up to an area where there are a number of the river fishing/tour boats, they asked us if we would like to join them on the boat that they were going to rent. We decided to join them. It was quite a trip.

The two sons were busy filming video for their YouTube channel, and I was fascinated by the variety of wildlife and foliage. Our young guide was very knowledgeable about the wildlife and story of the Nile and its relationship to Lake Victoria. At one point, he looked at Timothy and asked in Lugandan, "Did anyone ever tell you that you look like the Minister of Tourism?" Timothy laughed and told me what he said. I responded to the guide, "That's because he is his brother." The guide didn't believe it at first, but when we convinced him it was so, he felt like he was guiding a celebrity. We traveled up into Lake Victoria and stopped and stood on a pile of rocks were the Nile bubbles up out of the Lake. When we got back, we were taking a group photo, and someone from my group asked if they wanted to take a group photo in front of the bust of Gandhi. The father very sternly said, "No! We don't do Gandhi." It had not crossed my mind that some Pakistanis might not agree with Gandhi, but there are at least three.

I had to marvel at this day. Here were four girls and an American pastor, a Ugandan pastor, and three Pakistanis in a small boat having a great time without regard to nationality or ideology. After the boat ride, we exchanged emails, and they told us to watch for their video called *Documentary Nile River Lake Victoria Trip*

Uganda (turn the volume down and enjoy a tour of the river and the lake).

We were finished with our tour of the Nile and time with new Afghani friends, and it was time for me to get back to work. It was now time to conduct the Christian Educators' Convention in Iganga, for the Jinja District. UCCS-U has divided the country up into districts with district representatives for each region. This was a great idea and provided better representation and prevented schools from having to travel so far for events. I had to try to cover the same materials as in the previous conference but only had half as much time. We had given away a cow at this site; I was able to find the cow as I was walking to the outhouse. She was in good shape and had been producing milk for the orphanage. The ladies were here to give away soccer balls and toothbrushes and to join us for lunch. Just before lunch was served, the man that I have called Arsenio (because he looks like Arsenio Hall) sought me out. We have become friends, and he has interpreted for me on several occasions.

He was anxious to tell me that he had started a high school this year and that the enrollment was already over 300 students. He told me about a history teacher who was working for him that he was anxious for me to meet. This young man was a Muslim, and Arsenio wanted me to explain the Gospel to him.

I pressed him a bit that he should be the one to do it, but I got the idea that he wanted me to show him how. I pulled the young guy aside, and with Arsenio watching, began to explain God's love for him and how Jesus had paid the penalty for all his sin. He said he was almost ready to make a decision to receive Jesus. Still, it was a hard decision because of the shunning he would receive from his family and community. I was confident that he was going to make a decision while we were talking. At just the wrong time, someone came and interrupted the conversation and said, "Come, we must eat."

I replied, "No, please, I must finish this conversation." Unfortunately, he had me by the arm and was escorting me into another room for the meal. I tried to get the young man and Arsenio to follow us and join me in the meal. But I had the sense that there is some hierarchal structure that would have been violated by them joining us. I grabbed Arsenio later on and told him to please be sure that he and the teacher join me the next day in Mukono.

As we began to eat, I could tell that the ladies were a little nervous about what we were being served.

I did not want to offend our hosts, so I told them just to take a small amount of food and move it around on their plate. One of the ladies objected, saying she didn't want any to go to waste. I assured her that it would not go to waste, that someone would eat it. That seemed to solve the problem and avoid any offense. After we finished lunch, Joshua, the one who calls me his son and was experiencing such severe health problems, met me outside the conference area. He couldn't stop hugging and thanking me. He looked like he was about 90% recovered from his illness. His wife was there, and we were reintroduced. She thanked me over and over for the children's school fees. I reminded her that this was a gift from one of our church families, not from me. I then gave him some personal money I had brought with me and had said, "Lord if I see Joshua this year, I will give him money for his children's school fees again" (Remember from before that I told him not to tell anyone). I didn't want to start getting constant appeals for school fees from a host of others. While I was conducting the workshop session in the afternoon, the ladies visited a school in Kamuli District, not far from where I was teaching. This was a very resource-poor school. The buildings were all wood slatted or made of mud and sticks. The ladies were able to give away several soccer balls and spend the afternoon playing with the children. I did not get to visit this school. But after seeing the photos that the ladies shared, I determined that this needed to be one of the schools that we gave attention to in the future. UCCS-U has divided the country up into districts with district representatives for each region. This region's representative was a head teacher/administrator, appropriately named Moses, he was young, bright, and ready to see the UCCS-U flourish. I left him with the particular challenge of taking the competition manuals I had sent and use them to develop regional competitions.

After the last session, we all gathered for photos in front of the school. We were also going to give out the John 3:16 shirts to all of the delegates. I just got out of the way and let Timothy deal with the color/size jostling.

I had learned from last year that this could turn into a bit of a challenge. Timothy was like a scolding parent dealing with children who were being selfish. In the end, everyone seemed to have a shirt and was content. I also had been giving out copies of the Jesus film on DVD at each of the conferences.

A pastor friend of mine in Florida had given me 500 copies, and at this conference, I gave the last one away.

That was the good news. The bad news was that some of the delegates who wanted a copy did not get one, and I still had another day of Christian Educators' Conference to conduct in Mukono. That was going to be the largest of all conferences, so it probably was just as well that I had run entirely out.

After we had given out the shirts, the DVDs, and said our goodbyes, we headed back toward Katosi. It was late afternoon and I was enjoying the rolling hills and the glimpses we were getting of Lake Victoria, the low sun casting colors that made the area even more beautiful. I was shocked back into the reality that I was in Uganda. Despite the occasional glimpses of stunning beauty, there are sometimes gruesome reminders of the struggle for survival these people face each day. As we drove by the village of

Trip #8 – Dropping Like Flies

Mayuge, several mud buildings that look like every other building appeared along the dirt road. But these were different. Outside each building there were a number of coffins. I counted nearly thirty as we drove by. Some still being cut from rough lumber, others ornately finished and brightly varnished.

Bright white varnish finish seemed to be the premier coffin of choice if you had the shillings, but if not, there were the simple pine boxes. As chilling as that was, what put a lump in my throat was the fact that interspersed among the large adult coffins were any number of tiny coffins for babies and small children.

As beautiful as the trip to the Source of the Nile was, this drive-by here at Mayuge was a real jolt back to reality. It was a welcome break when we came to Unja, and made a dinner stop at Javas, before the long drive home. Stopping at Javas anywhere around the Jinja region is always interesting because you see more mzungus, NGO workers, and volunteers here than any other place. We picked a spot on an outdoor patio in the cool of the evening and truly enjoyed just sharing and relaxing. I kept watching a table close to us where there were four or five mzungus. They seemed to be fun-loving folks and were really enjoying themselves. Overhearing an occasional comment that made me think they were probably Christians and that they must be teachers, I couldn't resist getting up, going over, and engaging them in conversations. I gave them an IACCS business card and introduced myself.

They introduced themselves and their various roles as staff at Amazina School, a classical Christian education school that has a staff of about 150 individuals, a mix of Ugandans and Americans.

They are a nonprofit and try to raise enough support to avoid having to charge high school fees. I was intrigued enough to ask if I could visit with them next year when we are there. They graciously extended an invitation. I wondered if we might see Sydney at a place like this at some point in the not too distant future.

Tuesday, November 12, was the last of the workdays, and the largest of the conferences was scheduled for Mukono. The location was the same place where several of the conferences had been held in the past. It was the site where the UCCS-U had been launched. It also was the site where the newsfeed had been filmed in our second or third year. The name of the large auditorium was the Blessed Christian Church. A new young pastor and his wife, Samuel and Anne Kawumi, had been called. India had been their choice or leading for seminary, and they had been well trained to lead this ministry. They were homeschooling 6 of their own children and are starting a Christian school in 2020. It didn't take long in the workshop session to realize that this was an enthusiastic, well-trained group of educators. They were fully engaged in all of the questions and answers and participated openly in the conversations. Sitting directly in front of me was an elegant, professional female educator who was quick to respond when I would throw a question out regularly. At one point, when we had taken a break, she came forward and gave me three books on Christian education and Christian curriculum.

They had been written and produced for application in Ugandan education. I have been trying to encourage books being written by Uganda educators and have talked about it every year since coming to Uganda.

Another participant sitting off to my left was a girl that took extensive notes and seemed to be trying to write every point down. I later learned that she was the wife of the pastor. When I got back to Florida, I had the following email waiting:

Good evening Tony Hammon,

I'm Mrs. Anne Kawumi. I attended the Christian Educators' Convention that was held yesterday at Blessed Christian

Church (I homeschool our 6 children but planning to open up and enroll other children starting next year).

I gained a lot from the talk. Particularly touched by the point that we are equipping saints for the work of the ministry.

God Bless you as you further his work and I'll be blessed if you could share your teaching insights and experience. I'm passionate about the body of Christ discipling the nations through the education system without putting the burden on seminaries and theological institutions.

Kind regards.
　　Anne

Since that initial email, I have corresponded several times with her, as well as her husband. I recently sent them a copy of the proposed IACCS International Accreditation Manual.

While we were doing the conference in Mukono, the ladies, Sammy, and Janepher went to tour the garden that Timothy had been dreamed of and finally had functioning well. There is already an abundant crop of pineapple, bananas, and a variety of their common vegetables. While touring the garden, they got to know Sammy a lot better. He opened up about what it was like growing up in Katosi, being so poor, not having shoes most of the time, and how he just got used to sores on his feet all the time. He talked about how he almost felt guilty now that he was grown, wore shoes, and didn't have sore feet. He spoke about the new business he was starting, running safaris. He knows his country well, with excellent knowledge of the geography and flora and fauna of Uganda. He is a handsome, personable young man that should do well dealing with the tourists that will come his way. He also knows that he will be involved at some level in his father's ministry as his father ages and passes the baton to the next generation.

While they were exploring the garden, it began to rain. Since none of the ladies had rain gear, Sammy acted quickly by making umbrellas from elephant ear plant leaves.

Sammy on safari

When it rains, improvise.

After the garden tour, Sammy also took the ladies to another poor fishing village. They told me about it and said it looked like another place for a piggy farm; another project for another year.

It was the end of a very full day, and now it was time to get back to Cross City and pack. Before going back to my room, I had gone down to the dining area to grab a Mountain Dew and spend a few minutes talking with Timothy. After we finished talking, I walked back to my room. When I entered the hallway where our rooms were, I saw one of the sights that always warms my heart. Sydney was sitting on the floor, surrounded by several Ugandan children; one of them was the young man who had sent the video message to Mike on Sunday. They were playing and talking and laughing, and Sydney was giving her stuff to them as gifts. She was going home things-light but relationship-heavy. What impact, what will Sydney do in the future; such a heart for justice, and for helping children.

The last day was Wednesday, November 13. We knew this was going to be a busy day. We were all filled with a mix of emotions – the joy of returning to our families, but sorrow that we were having to leave the people we loved here with so much yet that needs to be done. Timothy had scheduled a meeting with his brother, Godfrey Kiwanda, the one who is the Minister of Tourism, Antiquities, and Wildlife. We were to meet and then he was going to give us a personal behind-the-scenes tour of the wildlife preserve/rehab zoo, on the way to Entebbe. I was pretty excited about this because we had been trying to make this happen for the last three years. Our timing had never allowed for it, primarily because of traffic in Kampala. This year it looked like we might make it. The morning was spent saying sad goodbyes, shopping at Pastor Emma's traveling Ugandan shop (which he always spreads out on the porch of the dining area), and playing with Timothy and Janepher's granddaughter, Eliana. I knew this morning would be particularly tough for Sydney, because this was her last year of high school, and would be in college next year. So, this could be her final year of making this trip with us. She had grown very close to Eliana, who seemed to be her constant companion when we were anywhere around Cross City. This morning, they sat on the front steps blowing bubbles and giggling with each other. While I was videoing the two of them playing, Timothy gave Eliana a little sucker that we had brought with us to give away. I hadn't noticed, but several little faces were peering through an opening in the front gate. Instead of just eating the sucker, Eliana took another sucker and walked to the gate and shared it with a little hand sticking through the opening, she walked back, got another from her grandpa, and did it again, and again; another of those lessons on sharing that seems to be taught to these children at such an early age.

Trip #8 – Dropping Like Flies

It was time for us to leave Katosi if we had a hope of meeting with Timothy's brother and making it to the wildlife center. So, we said our goodbyes and the five of us, along with Timothy, Sammy, and BJ's son, piled in the van and headed toward the heart of Kampala, where Godfrey's government office was located. As usual, we hit Kampala and hit traffic, nonmoving traffic. The time we were supposed to meet Godfrey slipped right on by as we sat unable to move in the gridlock of traffic. There was no apparent reason for the heavy traffic other than this is just the norm in the nation's capital. We finally made it to the downtown area where the central government offices are located. The security of government buildings is very tight. You have to do just about everything short of giving blood to clear security. But we finally made our way up to Godfrey's office. We were escorted into a conference room with beautiful pictures of Ugandan nature. That prompted Sammy to talk about his dreams for his safari business. He told about a region of the country that is so mountainous (where the gorillas are) that there is always snow on their peaks. I told him I wanted to come and teach him how to ski on them, and that he could then run unique safaris that took people snow skiing in Uganda! Actually, even if I hadn't been just kidding, that would probably never happen because on the Ruwenzori Mountains, glaciers are rapidly disappearing. This range straddles the border of Uganda and the Democratic Republic of the Congo and reaches heights of 16,761 feet.

But it is estimated that by the 2030s the glaciers will be gone.

After about thirty minutes, Godfrey's assistant came and escorted us to his office. This was an amazing experience because his office was filled with photos and displays of Ugandan history, wildlife, and culture.

When we entered the room, he greeted us as if we were old friends that he had not seen in years. He laughed and said to me, you look like you have gotten younger since I last saw you. I made some comment about him sounding like a politician. We hugged and laughed together. He then took us on a verbal tour of some of the things on display in his office. He took a plaque off the wall of the Crested Crane, the national bird. He was describing it, and as he finished, he handed it to me and said I want you to have this as my gift to you. I am looking at it hanging on my wall above where I am typing right now. It brings back fond memories. After he made the presentation to me, he turned to Sydney and called her up. She was presented with one of the handmade mats that the school children make. Timothy had told his brother of the countless hours she and her mom and given this year to raising funds and making things to bring for the children.

This was the perfect gift for her.

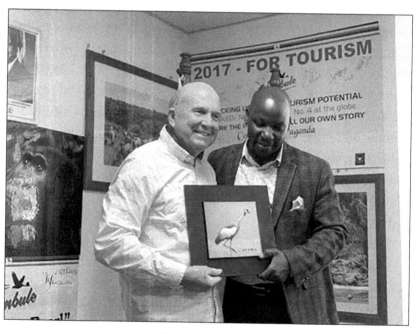

A treasured gift

A gift to Sydney from school children

Wendy had a gift for Godfrey as well. She had a political campaign from Mike, the Mayah, who was now running for county commission. Godfrey gave him a message of encouragement, wishing him success in his campaign.

Melania was snapping pictures throughout this entire exchange and commented that this was all just amazing to her.

She thoroughly enjoyed this morning. This by far was the greatest amount of time we had ever been able to spend with Godfrey, and was probably important for what needs to be done in the future. Before we left, Timothy prayed for his brother and our safe return to America. It was now time for us to go to the wildlife zoo. Godfrey told us that he was going to be unable to join us because he had several meetings scheduled for the afternoon. I am sure the fact that we had been so late in our arrival had made it extremely difficult for him to schedule anything more with us. We drove on out of Kampala and were entering Entebbe, just about ten minutes from the airport, when we arrived at the Uganda Wildlife Education Centre known as the UWEC. On their website, they state that the UWEC was established in 1952 as a center for wild animals that were found as causalities. In 1956, an animal orphanage was created, and in 1962 the National Zoo was established. Since that time, it has become a highly recognized and respect center for rescuing and rehabilitating animals from the wild and attempting to breed endangered species in captivity to be released into the wild.

When we arrived, it was clear that they had been expecting us, but regretfully had to tell us that the behind-the-scenes/feeding tour was not possible for this time of the day. They said because it would not be safe. When I hear the terms "wild animals and "would not be safe," I pay particular attention! We were grateful that they were not running the risk of putting us on anyone's dinner menu. We were given a very delightful, knowledgeable female guide that was assigned to take us around and answer any questions we might have. I may have driven the rest of the group a little crazy because my biology background kicked in, and I had a thousand questions to ask her. Our first stop was in the education center where there was an impressive display of animal skeletons, pelts, and an array of trapping devices that had been confiscated from poachers.

We saw elephant skulls, one old and one young. The guide let us feel the teeth to see how the old elephant's teeth were worn down, which ultimately would lead to starvation. We saw rhino skulls and learned that when the rhino horn is cut off, it will regrow in about three years, but the tusk of elephants will not.

I will stop here because it would be easy to meander into a lengthy biology dissertation.

One of the things that amazed me was the garden area where all the plants and been labeled and their various uses for medicine described. For example, the Velvet Combretum can be used for cough expectorant, leprosy, and stomachache. Bothriocline tomentosa is used for abdominal pain, stop vomiting, cough, after birth pain and ruptures, and diarrhea. Astrolochia serperantaria is used for what else – snake bite. Do any of them work? I have no idea, but somewhere along the line, they have gained the reputation as working.

The animal diversity was remarkable. Seeing lions as close as we did was almost like encountering them in the wild. The "Girl Power" theme came from me when I saw a sign they had by where the lions were roaming about. It said, "The lionesses do almost all of the hunting (and in Big yellow letters); GIRL POWER!" I thought that was appropriate since the team had been all girls this year. I have done a couple of talks since getting home, and I've always had a slide in my presentation of that sign and say, "The girls did all the work this year while I laid around camp!" It brings a chuckle, but no one believes it.

We took the entire afternoon, and I know I could have spent another week there, but it was time to grab some dinner and head to the airport.

You can guess where we stopped for dinner: Javas! But this was a special stop. I saw a side of Timothy that I had never seen before. There was a tenderness and vulnerability that I had not seen before. I alluded to it earlier and suggested that perhaps it was because of his dad and B.J.'s passing. As we were eating, Donna began to tell him about the boys from the dance troop, the uniforms they had made for them, and the story one of the young men had been spinning as he texted with Sydney. He had told her that after their performance on Sunday, his house had burned down and he needed money. Timothy did not believe that to be the case and knew that he would have known about it had it happened. We also had something happen earlier in the trip that I have not written about yet that affected this moment. On the second day after our arrival, when we usually go to the bank to make our currency exchange, Wendy called me to her room. I could tell that something terrible must be wrong. She was shaking, and tears came streaming down her cheeks as she described how a large sum of money was missing. She knew where she had put it, and now it was missing. We have never locked our rooms while in Katosi because everyone has been so trustworthy, but there had clearly been a theft. I took it to Timothy, and he was deeply troubled by it. We had evidence pointing to an individual but could not prove it and felt we needed to leave it with Timothy. He had commented on this incident several times during our trip, and I knew that he was worried and saddened by it. These two incidents were hugely troubling to Timothy, and he began to tear up and said it hurt him that people would try to take advantage of guests like that. I had never seen that level of concern from him before. That led to a lengthy conversation about all the calls and appeals we get from people when we get back to our homes in America. He was not aware that this was going on to the extent that it was or that it was happening from the people that we described. He said he would try to address that from his end and that we should not respond to any of those requests.

It was time for some good news.

I noticed that Wendy was telling Timothy about when she and Mike Jr. had been baptized after returning last year.

I tuned into the conversation just when Wendy was saying to Timothy, "Oh, you didn't know that?" She was talking about the fact that she had not been a Christian when she came to Uganda the first year (two years earlier).

I noticed that Sammy began to film her telling her story:

"I really didn't know Tony that well. But knew that it had affected Mike's life greatly. And so, I wanted to come for the experience of it. I think I was already thirsting for that.

As I look back now, I know that He (the Lord) was making a way for me and opening my eyes little by little.

But it was after experiencing your family, your people, and the children. And really getting to know Tony and learning to know more just about Jesus as opposed to my idea of religion I had before, but it was a couple of weeks after we got home that I accepted Jesus." Wendy went on to describe how she had taken the water from the well at Children's Home in a Mountain Dew Bottle, and in January, she and Mike Jr. had been baptized.

I just sat and smiled and thanked God for allowing me to see this moment and allowing me to be a part of Wendy's spiritual journey.

It was now time to begin the process of clearing Customs and getting settled in for our long flight back to Florida. I love the fact that we don't leave until nearly midnight each year. After a good shower and clean clothes in the KLM lounge, you are ready for a good night's sleep when you buckle in.

On Thursday morning, at the end of our first leg of our flight, while we were at the airport in Schiphol, Amsterdam, I checked my email to make sure flights and all were still on schedule, and our transportation was set when we arrived back in Miami. Thankfully all was in order. But there was another email that got my attention. Two days earlier, Lawrence had asked me to pray for the son of one of the elders in his church, who had a full vat of boiling food spill all over him. He had been burned from head to toe. Lawrence had sent me some pictures of the young man.

They were horribly sad. The first picture of the little guy showed him before bandages, and in the remaining images, he was bandaged like a mummy. It didn't look very good, but I would have guessed he would recover. That was not the case. The message this morning read, "The boy has gone to be with the Lord." What a reminder of the reality of how harsh life can be in third world and developing countries. Here we were in one of the most amazing, state-of-the-art airports in the world, on the way home to more luxury than many of the people in these countries could imagine. It drove back the urgency of the job that I believe God has called me to.

Because we gained so much time on our return flight, we landed in Miami by mid-afternoon. It was great to be home, but the group was already talking about next year's trip and things that we needed to do.

Chapter 12

Some of Us Someday Are Going to Come to Life

"Crying is all right in its way while it lasts. But you have to stop sooner or later, and then you still have to decide what to do." - C. S. Lewis, "The Silver Chair" (1953)

Together, we have traveled on the journeys this book has led us. I have been intentional about weaving themes and lessons about God, Uganda -the nation, Uganda – the people, Uganda – the culture, the work of the International Association of Christian Colleges and Schools (IACCS), and the importance of Christian education into each chapter. As has been stated or eluded to often, Jesus Christ and His message is the hope of the world. As He uses and empowers His Church and the ministries that are birthed through His Church, it, they, are the hope of the world! The message, the euangelion, the Good News, the Gospel of Jesus' redeeming work, is the only hope for a broken world. And educating future generations in that Good News and the principles for living and managing this world with His future kingdom in view is not an optional endeavor that we may or may not choose to pursue. It is a mandate! Check out these passages from the Word of God:

In Psalm 68:6,7, we get the following set of marching orders, "…He commanded our fathers to teach to their children, so the next generation would know them, even the children yet to be born, and they in turn would tell their children. Then they would put their trust in God and would not forget his deeds but would keep his commands."

> Deuteronomy 6:5-9, "*Love the Lord your God with all your heart, with all your soul, and with all your strength. Take to heart these words that I give you today. Repeat them to your children. Talk about them when you're at home or away, when you lie down or get up. Write them down, and tie them around your wrist, and wear them as headbands as a reminder. Write them on the doorframes of your houses and on your gates.*"

> 1 Timothy 4:10-11, "*This is why we work hard and continue to struggle, for our hope is in the living God, who is the Savior of all people and particularly of all believers. Teach these things and insist that everyone learn them.*"

And then we have the very words of Jesus in Matthew 19:14, "*Let the children come to me. Don't stop them! For the Kingdom of heaven belongs to those who are like these children.*"

To neglect Christian education anywhere in the world is to deny children, the very thing that Jesus calls us to. There is a plaque floating around these days that says, "If we don't teach our children to follow Christ, the world will teach them not to." I believe that the greatest thinkers and problem solvers should rise up from a citizenry that is centered in Christ.

That won't happen by accident or through osmosis. We must be intentional about establishing Christ and greatness of God as the foundation for all education. Is not all truth God's truth? If the answer is "yes," as I believe it is, then that foundation should drive us to ask hard questions. It should motivate us to consider and solve the most complex problems. Whether they are in the field of science, art, engineering, or any other task that a person may face.

One of the authors I enjoy reading is Philip Yancey. He has challenged my thinking for several decades now. He has quoted C.S. Lewis often in his writing, and you can see how this man's spiritual journey and writing have helped shape Yancey. One of my favorite quotes Yancey attributes to Lewis is, *"We writers are not nouns. We are mere adjectives pointing to the great Noun of truth."* I would have to expand that to say of any of us trying to live our lives for Christ – We Christ followers are not nouns. We are mere adjectives pointing to the great God of the universe. We are to be the transmitters, first and foremost of His unending, unconditional love.

May I echo the words of the song, *The Proof of Your Love*, by For King and Country:

So let my life be the proof,
The proof of Your love
Let my love look like You and what You're made of
How You lived, how You died
Love is sacrifice
Oh, let my life be the proof,
The proof of Your love

The C.S. Lewis quote that introduced this chapter said, *"Crying is all right in its way while it lasts. But you have to stop sooner or later, and then you still have to decide what to do."* We can and should cry for the hurting, abused, oppressed people of the world. We can't just shake our head or click our tongue and say, "Oh, that's awful!" There comes a time when each of us have to decide what to do. May God give each of us a "Popeye Moment": "I can't stands it; I just can't stands it no more!"

Were you puzzled by this chapter's title? It is from another C.S. Lewis quote. I'll let that quote close this journey. Someday, some of us are going to respond to the fire in our belly placed there by God, and *we are going to come to life.*

Oh, and when we do, what a ride it will be!

May the proof of God's love be reflected through me and the work that is being accomplished through the International Association of Christian Colleges and Schools.

"And that is precisely what Christianity is about. This world is a great sculptor's shop. We are the statues and there is a rumour going round the shop that some of us are some day going to come to life." -CS Lewis

Bibliography

1) Article written for WLRN, **50 Years Ago, Miami-Dade County Played Key Role In Nation's First Statewide Teacher Strike** By JESSICA BAKEMAN • MAY 30, 2018 PG 7

2) Stearns, Richard **"The Hole in Our Gospel Special Edition."** iBooks. https://itunes.apple.com/us/book/the-hole-in-our-gospel-special-edition pg 16

3) Stearns, Richard **"The Hole in Our Gospel Special Edition."** **iBooks.** pg 17

4) Hines, Katherine *They Call Me Momma Katherine: How One Woman's Brokenness Became Hope for Uganda's Children*, Aneko Press (June1,2016) pg 19

5) **SITUATION ANALYSIS OF CHILDREN IN UGANDA – 2019, UNICEF, https://www.unicef.org/uganda/media/5181** pg 62

6) https://www.smithsonianmag.com/history/uganda-the-horror-85439313/#04Q1mrqKPtveCgT.99, Feb 2005 pg 63

7) Museveni, Janet Kataaha **My Life's Journey,** Fountain Publishers, Kampala, Uganda 2011pg 91

8) Ibid. pg 91

9) **Christianity Today, July 19, 2006** pg 94

10) **Beliefs about people with albinism in Uganda: A qualitative study using the Common-Sense Model,** Caroline Bradbury-Jones, Peter Ogik,, Jane Betts, Julie Taylor, Published: October 12, 2018, https://doi.org/10.1371/journal.pone.0205774 pg 119

11) **Data as reported by UN.org** pg 137

12) **Data quoted from e-africa.org** pg 140

13) WorldBank.org, **Educating Girls: A Way of Ending Child Marriage and Teenage Pregnancy, Dec. 2017,** 1818 H Street, NW Washington, DC 20433 USA (202) 473-1000 pg 176

14) **Country Reports on Human Rights Practices for 2018** United States Department of State • Bureau of Democracy, Human Rights and Labor pp 177-181

15) **Bulamu Healthcare,** 1933 Waverley St., Palo Alto, CA 94301 Online article 2019 pg 188

16) Rice, Andrew **The Teeth May Smile But the Heart Does Not Forget,** PICADOR, New York, New York 2009 pg 196

17) **2020 Al Jazeera Media Network** pg 200

18) Haugan, Gary A. **Just Courage, God's Great Expedition for the Restless Christian,** Intervarsity Press, IVP Books, Downers Groove, Illinois. Pp 31,32 pg 202

19) **Ibid** pg. 30,31 pg 202

20) **2020 Guardian News** and media pg 212

21) **2020 United Way of Florida** pg 252

22) **Uganda's Militant Islamic Movement ADF: A Historical Analysis**, Abdulhakim A. Nsobya University of Cape Town December 2016 © 2008-2020 ResearchGate pg 257

23) Lund, sofi, *Uganda Where Dead Children's Bodies Are Big Business,* Norwegian Refugee Council, Nov. 17,2016 (NRC. no) pg 260

Union of Christian Colleges and Schools -Uganda (UCCS-U) Statement of Faith

- We believe that whatever the Bible says is true–which means that we believe in the inspiration of both the Old and New Testaments.
- We believe that man was created by the direct act of God and in the image of God.
- We believe that Adam and Eve in yielding to the temptation of Satan became fallen creatures.
- We believe in the incarnation, the Virgin Birth, and the Deity of our Lord Savior Jesus Christ.
- We believe in His vicarious and substitutional Atonement for the sins of mankind by the shedding of His blood on the Cross.
- We believe in the resurrection of His body from the tomb, His ascension to Heaven, and that He is now our Advocate.
- We believe that He is personally coming again.
- We believe in His power to save men from sin.
- We believe in the necessity of the New Birth, and that this New Birth is through the regeneration by the Holy Spirit.

- We believe that salvation is by grace through faith in the atoning blood of our Lord and Savior Jesus Christ.
- We believe that this creed is a sufficient basis for Christian fellowship and that all born again men and women who sincerely accept this creed can, and should, live together in peace and that it is their Christian duty to promote harmony among the members of the Body of Christ, and also to work together to get the Gospel to as many people as possible in the shortest time possible.

2018 UCCSU/IACCS Christian Educators' Convention Professional Development Certificate

The Union of Christian Colleges and Schools – Uganda and the International Associations of Christian Colleges and Schools Award to

Name

the below listed In-service Points (ISPs) for each workshop/session attended at the 2018 UCCSU/IACCS Christian Educators' Convention held in Katosi, Kiboga, Luweero, and Mukono, November 13-16, 2018.

I verify that I attended the following Workshops at the UCCSU/IACCS Christian Educators' Convention.

Workshop Sessions: *(2 ISP each)–list titles)*

   ___1. <u>Philosophy of Christian Education</u>
   ___2. <u>Core Values of a Christian School</u>
   ___3. <u>The Important Thinks a Teacher Must Know</u>
   ___4. <u>What Makes a Good Teacher?</u>
   ___5. <u>Tips on How Our Schools Can Make a Difference in Our Localities</u>
   ___6. <u>Evangelical Approach to Christian Education</u>
   ___7. <u>Open Forum Topics</u>

Total ISPs earned: _____ *(not to exceed 14)*

Teacher's Signature

For UCCS-U/IACCS Administrators and Teachers, please present this certificate to your school Administrator to be signed and placed into the Master In-service file on your behalf.

3/25

1/25